JOURNAL FOR THE STUDY OF THE OLD TESTAMENT
SUPPLEMENT SERIES
171

Editors
David J.A. Clines
Philip R. Davies

Executive Editor
John Jarick

Editorial Board
Richard J. Coggins, Alan Cooper, Tamara C. Eskenazi,
J. Cheryl Exum, Robert P. Gordon, Norman K. Gottwald,
Andrew D.H. Mayes, Carol Meyers, Patrick D. Miller

JSOT Press
Sheffield

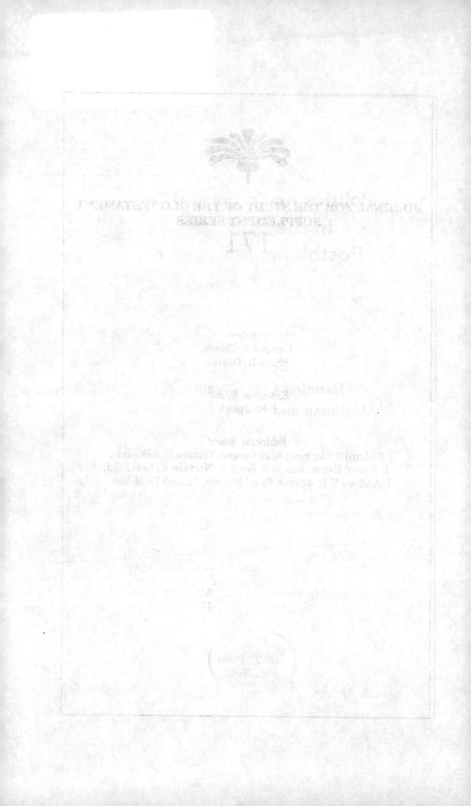

Politics and Theopolitics in the Bible and Postbiblical Literature

Edited by
**Henning Graf Reventlow,
Yair Hoffman and Benjamin Uffenheimer**

Journal for the Study of the Old Testament
Supplement Series 171

Published by JSOT Press
JSOT Press is an imprint of
Sheffield Academic Press Ltd
343 Fulwood Road
Sheffield S10 3BP
England

Typeset by Sheffield Academic Press
and
Printed on acid-free paper in Great Britain
by Bookcraft
Midsomer Norton, Somerset

British Library Cataloguing in Publication Data

A catalogue record for this book is available
from the British Library

ISBN 1-85075-461-6

CONTENTS

EDITORS' PREFACE

This is the third volume to be published containing papers read at meetings between the Department of Bible of Tel Aviv University and the Faculty of Protestant Theology of the University of Bochum. We are grateful to Sheffield Academic Press for including these volumes in the JSOT Supplement Series. With the first symposium, held in Tel Aviv in December 1985, a new kind of dialogue was introduced between biblical and postbiblical scholars, belonging to two different traditions—Jewish and Christian—while being both anchored in the one Bible. The strictly scholarly character of the papers presented was guaranteed from the beginning, as these conferences were initiated and held under the auspices of the above-mentioned universities. But another result of this ongoing dialogue is the growing friendship between scholars belonging to two nations divided by the tragic events of the preceding generation.

The general topic we chose for this conference, 'Politics and Theopolitics in the Bible and Postbiblical Literature', was intended to leave room for contributions on a wider range of biblical and post-biblical studies, thus showing the deep impact of the biblical heritage on the life and thought of both communities. All these contributions are grouped in one way or another around the catchwords *politics* and *theopolitics*, thereby expressing the firm persuasion of both communities that human politics throughout the ages have been influenced and even dictated by the deep belief in the all-embracing rule and providence of God. Our experience shows that a scholarly open-minded dialogue about the differences between the Jewish and Christian traditions and about the features peculiar to each does away with age-old prejudices and prepares the way for a better mutual understanding. We are thankful for these discussions and hope that we will be able to continue our dialogue. The next meeting, scheduled for 1994 in Bochum, will focus on 'Eschatology in the Bible and in Postbiblical Tradition'.

We would like to express our gratitude to the Evangelical Church of Westphalia for making possible the journey of the participants from Bochum. They are grateful for the hospitality received from their colleagues of Tel Aviv University.

Tel Aviv
Bochum

Henning Graf Reventlow
Yair Hoffman
Benjamin Uffenheimer

ABBREVIATIONS

AB	Anchor Bible
AHw	W. von Soden, *Akkadisches Handwörterbuch*
AJSL	*American Journal of Semitic Languages and Literatures*
AnBib	Analecta biblica
ANET	J.B. Pritchard (ed.), *Ancient Near Eastern Texts*
AOS	American Oriental Series
ARMT	Archives royales de Mari, transcriptions et traductions
ATD	Das Alte Testament Deutsch
BASOR	*Bulletin of the American Schools of Oriental Research*
BBB	Bonner biblische Beiträge
BDB	F. Brown, S.R. Driver and C.A. Briggs, *Hebrew and English Lexicon of the Old Testament*
Bib	*Biblica*
BKAT	Biblischer Kommentar: Altes Testament
BZAW	Beihefte zur *ZAW*
CAD	*Assyrian Dictionary of the Oriental Institute of the University of Chicago*
CAT	Commentaire de l'Ancien Testament
CBQ	*Catholic Biblical Quarterly*
CChr	Corpus Christianorum
ConBOT	Coniectanea biblica, Old Testament
CSEL	Corpus scriptorum ecclesiasticorum latinorum
EKKNT	Evangelisch-Katholischer Kommentar zum Neuen Testament
EvT	*Evangelische Theologie*
EWNT	*Exegetisches Wörterbuch zum Neuen Testament*
FRLANT	Forschungen zur Religion und Literatur des Alten und Neuen Testaments
FVS	Diels–Kranz, *Fragmente der Vorsokratiker*
HAT	Handbuch zum Alten Testament
HBT	Horizons in Biblical Theology
HKAT	Handkommentar zum Alten Testament
HNT	Handbuch zum Neuen Testament
HSM	Harvard Semitic Monographs
HTKNT	Herders theologischer Kommentar zum Neuen Testament
HTR	*Harvard Theological Review*
IB	*Interpreter's Bible*
ICC	International Critical Commentary

IEJ	*Israel Exploration Journal*
Int	*Interpretation*
JANESCU	*Journal of the Ancient Near Eastern Society of Columbia University*
JAOS	*Journal of the American Oriental Society*
JBL	*Journal of Biblical Literature*
JCS	*Journal of Cuneiform Studies*
JNES	*Journal of Near Eastern Studies*
JSOTSup	*Journal for the Study of the Old Testament*, Supplement Series
KAI	H. Donner and W. Röllig, *Kanaanäische und aramäische Inschriften*
KAT	Kommentar zum Alten Testament
KHC	Kurzer Handkommentar zum Alten Testament
LCL	Loeb Classical Library
MARI	*Mari: Annales de recherches interdisciplinaires*
MeyerK	H.A.W. Meyer (ed.), Kritisch-exegetischer Kommentar über das Neue Testament
MGWJ	*Monatsschrift für Geschichte und Wissenschaft des Judentums*
MVAG	Mitteilungen der Vorderasiatisch-ägyptischen Gesellschaft
NABU	*Nouvelles assyriologiques brèves et utilitaires*
OBO	Orbis biblicus et orientalis
Or	*Orientalia*
ÖTK	Ökumenischer Taschenbuchkommentar
OTL	Old Testament Library
OTS	*Oudtestamentische Studiën*
PL	J. Migne (ed.), *Patrologia latina*
RB	*Revue biblique*
RevQ	*Revue de Qumran*
RivB	*Rivista biblica*
SBLSCS	Society of Biblical Literature Septuagint and Cognate Studies
SBT	Studies in Biblical Theology
TCS	Texts from Cuneiform Sources
TP	*Theologie und Philosophie*
TRE	*Theologische Realenzyklopädie*
TSK	*Theologische Studien und Kritiken*
TWNT	G. Kittel und G. Friedrich (eds.), *Theologisches Wörterbuch zum Neuen Testament*
TZ	*Theologische Zeitschrift*
UTB	Uni Taschenbücher
VD	*Verbum domini*
VT	*Vetus Testamentum*
VTSup	*Vetus Testamentum*, Supplements
WMANT	Wissenschaftliche Monographien zum Alten und Neuen Testament
WZKM	*Wiener Zeitschrift für die Kunde des Morgenlandes*
ZAW	*Zeitschrift für die alttestamentliche Wissenschaft*
ZTK	*Zeitschrift für Theologie und Kirche*

LIST OF CONTRIBUTORS

Yehoshua Amir is Emeritus Professor of Jewish Philosophy, University of Tel Aviv, Israel.

Yairah Amit is Senior Lecturer of Bible, Department of Bible, University of Tel Aviv, Israel.

Moshe Anbar is Professor of Bible, Department of Bible, University of Tel Aviv, Israel.

Ze'ev W. Falk is Professor of Talmudic Law, Hebrew University, Jerusalem, Israel.

Christofer Frey is Professor of Systematic Theology, Evangelisch-Theologische Fakultät, University of the Ruhr, Bochum, Germany.

Yair Hoffman is Professor of Bible and Head of Department, Department of Bible, University of Tel Aviv, Israel.

Gottfried Nebe is Professor of New Testament, Evangelisch-Theologische Fakultät, University of the Ruhr, Bochum, Germany.

Frank H. Polak is Lecturer of Bible, Department of Bible, University of Tel Aviv, Israel.

Nahum Rakover is Professor in the Hebrew University, Jerusalem, Israel.

Henning Graf Reventlow is Professor of Old Testament, Evangelisch-Theologische Fakultät, University of the Ruhr, Bochum, Germany.

Benjamin Uffenheimer is Emeritus Professor of Bible, Department of Bible, University of Tel Aviv, Israel.

Klaus Wengst is Professor of New Testament, Evangelisch-Theologische Fakultät, University of the Ruhr, Bochum, Germany.

JOSEPHUS ON THE MOSAIC 'CONSTITUTION'

Yehoshua Amir

When Josephus had to give an exposition of the Jewish law he always
had in mind, of course, the perspective of the educated Greek reader.
He gives two such expositions, one in the fourth book of his
Antiquities of the Jews, and one in the second book of *Against Apion*.
A comparison between these two summaries will be helpful in tracing
the ripening of Josephus's insight into the intricacies of the intellectual
task he had taken upon him. His endeavours in this area resulted in his
coining a new Greek term, *theokratia*, whose origin in Josephus seems
to have escaped many of those who use that word, be it in a depreca-
tory or in an affirmative sense.

In his *Antiquities* Josephus owed his readers an account of this
topic. From the time of Herodotos historiographic convention has it
that, whenever a historian introduces into his or her narration a
people not known or not sufficiently known to the ordinary readers,
the writer must interrupt the thread of the narration and explain
something about the mores and the way of life of that people. For the
average Hellenistic reader the Jews certainly fall under this definition;
and the best known fact about them would be that they have many
abstruse laws which they keep tenaciously. Since Josephus determines
that the laws kept by the Jews without the slightest change for all these
centuries are the laws of Moses,[1] he must then incorporate into his
work an account of these laws. This account is given by him in conclusion to the story of Moses' life.[2]

The object of the account is referred to both in the plural (οἱ νόμοι,
'the laws') and in the singular (ἡ πολιτεία, 'the constitution'), and as
this duplicity of expression appears more than once[3] it seems to be

---

1. *Apion* 183.
2. *Apion* 183.
3. For example *Ant.* 4.193, 194.

deliberate. We should therefore expect in Josephus's exposition not simply an enumeration of different laws but an account of the law as an organic whole. For Josephus as a historian, the concept of πολιτεία was a demanding and complex one that led him to new insights into the essence of the Jewish commonwealth. Yet, as we shall see, it took him time to grasp the profundity of his problem.

For the moment, he announces that in his survey he will restrict himself 'to those laws of us which touch our political constitution'.[4] The remainder he intends to leave for another book, which in fact was never written.[5] We are, then, entitled to expect in the following summary a certain systematic approach which will try to subordinate the material to a guiding principle or to let the laws appear as parts of an all-embracing order of a group life. It must be said that these expectations are only partly fulfilled by Josephus's exposition in *Antiquities*. But it should also be noted that what is missing here may be supplied in Josephus's second exposition, which will be considered later.

Josephus warns us immediately that he will content himself with concentrating on the Mosaic laws, found in many places in the Torah, without adding any material of his own, obviously in order to avoid the accusation of adding prescriptions of his own for apologetic reasons. As a matter of fact, such suspicion would not be altogether unfounded, for Josephus—following in this an older Jewish source, doubtfully ascribed to Philo—imputes to Moses a prescription ('One must point out the road to those who are ignorant of it',[6] amplified in *Apion* 211 by an injunction to furnish fire, water and food to all who ask for them) which is derived from identifiable Greek sources and has no real equivalent in the Torah. Nor is this the only case of his manipulation of the biblical text.

The only innovation he considers as his task 'consists in ordering everything according to its genus'. Yet it must be said that, unlike Philo, whose presentation of the law of the Torah in *De Specialibus Legibus* is really based on a calculated classification,[7] no classificatory principle can be discovered in Josephus's survey. We may doubt whether Josephus had a clear grasp of the methodological obligation

4.   *Ant.* 4.198.
5.   *Ant.* 4.198, and compare Thackeray's note in the LCL edition.
6.   *Ant.* 4.276; cf. *Apion* 2.211. As to the Greek sources cf. Philo, LCL, IX, p. 539, note to § 7.8; J. Bernays, *Gesammelte Abhandlungen*, pp. 261-82.
7.   See Philo, *Dec.* 154ff.

he should have taken on himself when he used the term 'genus'. It appears that all he really meant by concentrating the prescriptions of the Torah was to bring them together into a coherent and pragmatic presentation. If this is so, then we may say that he succeeded; his account is continuous, and lucid enough to make good reading, at least for most of the text. And we may add that in some places in his exposition we can discover an arrangement according to a leading viewpoint.

We can say that the starting point of Josephus's account is indeed well chosen. The view of the pervading unity of the πολιτεία of Moses, which will later become the focal point of Josephus's whole concept of the work of Moses, finds its clear expression in the stress he lays on the injunction to build a single holy capital, with one temple of God in it.[8] And it should be noted that the exclusiveness of this sanctuary is already here expressly motivated by the unity of God.[9] Philo, some generations previously, had said the same thing in very similar words: 'Since God is one, there should be only one temple',[10] and, *pace* Philo's English translator,[11] I think it obvious that Josephus is influenced here by the older author's formulation. Nevertheless, there is a nuance in Josephus's formulation that is not found in Philo, expressed in his statement, 'For God is one and the people of the Hebrews is one'. The full meaning of this addition, which in its present context seems somewhat out of place, will become evident later. Yet it may be said in anticipation that Josephus gives Philo's theological statement a 'sociological' twist by means of his addition.

I would not maintain that such a sociological interpretation was deliberately chosen. It is not clearly stated that the unity of the temple is a highly efficient tool for welding together into a united nation the people participating in its worship. Certainly, two paragraphs later we read that the pilgrimage to Jerusalem was instituted 'to promote by thus meeting and feasting together feelings of mutual affection'. That should be an excellent continuation of the thought implied in the former sentence. Yet if we had here a clear-cut line of argument, how could it be that this line was rudely interrupted by the following paragraph: 'Let him that blasphemes God be stoned, then hung for a day, and buried ignominiously and in obscurity'. In terms of the

8. *Ant.* 4.199.
9. *Ant.* 4.201.
10. *Spec. Leg.* 1.67.
11. See Colson's note to *Spec. Leg.* 1.67 (LCL, VII, p. 618).

continuity of thought suggested above this passage is quite irrelevant. Its appearance here strongly indicates that the sociological argument suggested above is ours more than Josephus's. If the coherence guaranteed by the inner structure of the Mosaic state had been the central point that Josephus wanted to bring home to his readers in this passage, he would easily have been able to avoid such an intrusion of irrelevant material. It would appear, then, that the sociological implications of the unity of God, or the uniting power of the one temple, were felt rather than clearly understood by Josephus.

There is another feature of the *Antiquities'* account of the Mosaic legislation that may be surprising to readers familiar with the parallel report in *Against Apion*: although our report starts with the presentation of an institution central to this πολιτεία we have to read on for a long time, through various injunctions of all kinds, including daily prayers, prohibitions against wearing linen and wool together and prescriptions concerning the court of justice, until we hear anything about the way this πολιτεία is governed. That question arises only incidentally in the course of a discussion of the biblical law of kingship.[12] Quite in line with what seems to be the plain meaning of the biblical text, Josephus sees the choice of a king not as obligatory but as optional. More than this: from his own addition to this statement it becomes clear that he considers such a step definitely not commendable. I will not here enter into the question of whether Josephus could see his position as supported by the biblical story of the election of the first king of Israel. Josephus himself formulates his position by the very words with which he introduces his discussion of political systems: 'Aristocracy, with the life that is lived thereunder, is indeed the best: let no craving possess you for another polity'.[13] Here, unequivocally, we have Josephus's political credo. Obviously, at this stage in his intellectual development he considered the πολιτεία of Moses to have been an aristocracy, although he must have (grudgingly) admitted monarchy as a permissible, if not commendable, alternative.

The aristocratic ruling class in charge of his πολιτεία would of course by the priesthood of Jerusalem. We may well assume that the Jerusalem priesthood at large tended to see itself as an aristocratic class destined to rule, and that this was where they inserted themselves

12. *Ant.* 4.223.
13. *Ant.* 4.223.

into the accepted political categories of the Hellenistic-Roman world. Certainly, Josephus the priest had grown up absorbing this view of society as part of the spiritual atmosphere he sprang from. If this is how Josephus was wont to see himself, it is understandable that he came to assume that the whole of the Mosaic πολιτεία was cut to fit the role that the priesthood had to play in it. Thus, Josephus's definition of Moses' πολιτεία as an aristocracy is exactly what we would have expected from him. Indeed, the remarkable feature in the passage under consideration is not its political content, that is Josephus's aristocratic credo, but rather the fact that that credo does not stand at the head of 'our political constitution' as a declaration of principle; instead, it is brought in in the course of the discussion of a particular point of Moses' legislation.

Josephus would certainly have accorded his declaration a more important place, had he, at the time of writing, been aware of all the implications of his self-imposed task of delineating the image of a πολιτεία founded by Moses out of the wealth of biblical commands regulating the whole of human existence, both collective and individual. As soon as he understood the implications he would have realized that in order to cope with such a task he would have to delve much deeper into political theory than any previous historian had been required to. It goes without saying that such a theory was available solely in the context of Greek philosophy. I cannot here go into the question of whether, or to what extent, such Greek concepts were appropriate to the biblical themes onto which they were grafted. Our question, instead, is: whence did Josephus draw the concepts he found suitable for characterizing the Mosaic πολιτεία, and how did he use them in order to present to his Greek audience an impressive, or at least acceptable picture of Judaism? Questions of this kind are obviously not to be addressed to the account given in the *Antiquities* but rather to the later and more mature account contained in *Against Apion*.

Against Apion, unlike Josephus's other books, is a piece of apologetics from beginning to end. Throughout, Josephus finds himself in a bitter debate with a hostile Hellenistic environment. We find here a wealth of venomous fabulistic constructions of Jewish history, composed by anti-Jewish writers of various origins, accompanied by calumnies, suspicions and detractions, all countered by Josephus's arguments, which combine advocacy, sophistication and irony.

Anyone living with the trauma of the futility of verbal defence against anti-Semitism will find a book like this rather depressing; its redeeming feature is its final part, where Josephus turns from negative to positive apologetics. The turning point in his representation is reached when he declares that, instead of refuting faulty descriptions of the Jewish law, 'I want to state briefly, to the best of my ability, the whole constitution of our policy and its details'.[14] In this exposition we find the famous, or perhaps notorious, term *theokratia*; this term became accepted into political philosophy usage, but as noted above there has been little scholarly consideration of the term's origin or of the methodological role Josephus assigns it.

What is new in this second exposition of the Mosaic legislation is stated in Josephus's introductory declaration, quoted above: he wants to give a brief account of the Jewish constitution as a whole and in detail. In this account, then, he will begin with considerations about the general character of the Mosaic legislation and only afterwards go on to specific laws. The first part of this two-part structure extends (after a short preface) from §151 to §189, and then follow 'the precepts and prohibitions of our Law'. Such a general account is not found in *Antiquities* and so we have to infer for ourselves Josephus's underlying motives. Here, in Josephus's last book, we find an author who succeeded, while based at the Imperial Court in Rome, in widening his intellectual horizons and steeping himself in philosophical problems. Now, when he is confronted by a problem of political philosophy, he no longer approaches it haphazardly but tries to deal with it methodically, even going so far as to coin a new word in a language that is not his mother tongue. The character of this second exposition does seem to indicate that Josephus has now acquired a methodological consciousness of the intricacies of his problem.

First of all he holds, as regards the aim of the present book, that an evaluation of the Mosaic legislation must be the core of positive apologetics for the Jewish people, for it is common knowledge that the Jewish people adhere to this law, being 'the most law-abiding of all the nations'.[15] According to Greek political thought the value of a legislation is, first of all, a function of the personal standard of its author, the legislator. That means for Josephus that he must assign to

14. *Apion* 2.145.
15. *Apion* 2.150.

Moses a place within the highly admired class of the great legislators of the ancient world. For the Hellenistic reader this was not a new idea, and later I shall look at a non-Jewish list of legislators of worldwide renown which includes Moses. This is why glorification of the personality of Moses was one of the central aims of Jewish-Hellenistic literature and why calumnies against him as an impostor or as a sorcerer are a prominent topic of anti-Jewish literature. The portrait of him drawn here by Josephus stresses his unselfishness in using his immense prestige not for buttressing a dominant position for himself but for persuading the people to accept his excellent code of laws. Among the great lawgivers, celebrated all over the Greek world, Moses stands out as prior to them all, since he composed his laws before the word νόμος even existed in the Greek language. It must be stressed that calling Moses a legislator is for Josephus much more than a matter of terminology. Against the Jew-baiters he maintains that Moses was 'one such as the Greeks boast of having had in Minos and later legislators'.[16]

Moses, then, is here definitely placed in the category of legislators holding worldwide esteem. As the senior of this category, he may well be considered wiser than the rest, but fundamentally he faces the same task. He has to organize a state, and so he has, first of all, to decide what form of government he will install. Before Josephus goes on to examine the specific solution of this problem ascribed to Moses, then, it is made clear that the establishment of government is part of Moses' task in his capacity as legislator.

On the face of it, Moses would have to choose between a limited number of possible constitutions. It is true that there are innumerable varieties of political organization in different countries, but we can sum all of them up into three cardinal forms: 'Some peoples have entrusted the supreme power to monarchies, others to the ruling of a few and others to the majority'.[17] This division as the cornerstone of all constitutional reasoning had held good since the time of Greek culture. Yet Josephus continues: 'But our legislator had no regard to any of these things, but ordained our government to be what may be termed—at the cost of doing violence to the language—*Theokratia*, assigning the sovereignty and the power to God'.

This is a surprising statement that has to be carefully analysed. First

16. *Apion* 2.161.
17. *Apion* 2.164.

of all, taking into account the passage of *Antiquities* considered above, we would expect Josephus to say that the second of the three alternative solutions, rule by a few, or aristocracy, is the best form of government. In the case of the Jewish community, as we saw, this ruling class was identified as the priesthood. If Josephus simply wanted to find an easy way to explain Judaism to Greek readers he had only to reaffirm his earlier opinion. We must conclude, then, that he was no longer satisfied with that view. Undoubtedly, a shift had occurred in his view of the fundaments of Moses' legislation. This was not necessarily a shift in Josephus's own political opinions, for we shall see that his very high estimation of the priesthood and its primary function in the community reiterates itself within the new frame of reference now initiated. He must however have realized that the high ranking of the priesthood in Moses' system was itself in need of a strong grounding.

Josephus must have found himself in a difficult position when he became aware that he could no longer easily identify himself with one of the conventional types of political organization, nor even formulate for himself a combination of these, as was usual in the historical and the political literature and practice of the time. All these positions must have seemed to him superficial, not going to the root of Moses' intention. He was therefore forced to coin a new word to bring home to Greek readers the essence of Moses' πολιτεία. The apologetic tone accompanying the introduction of this word, the phrase 'at the cost of doing violence to the language', seems to me to be a clear proof that this is not an already-existing word. Coining a new Greek word would not have been straightforward for Josephus; while Philo likes to display his mastery of each detail of idiomatic Greek, Josephus confesses not to have a full command of that language, and so he must have felt the situation to be a drastic one.

Translators of and commentators on *Against Apion*, justly baffled by this neologism, have done their best to assuage their uneasy feelings about it. The French commentator Reinach remarks: 'So, this word must be an invention of Josephus—or of his source'.[18] The latter alternative, usually offered in a less than confident tone, seems not to be very helpful. If this assumed source were an author of some renown, Josephus would not have felt the need to apologize for the

---

18. *Flavius Josephus, Contre Apion: texte établi et annoté par Th. Reinach et traduit par Leon Blum* (Paris: Société des Editions 'Les Belles Lettres', 1930), p. 86 n. 5.

word; and if it were an obscure author, we might as well credit
Josephus himself with the neologism. The English translator
Thackeray writes: 'The word was apparently coined by Josephus; the
idea goes back to the Old Testament'.[19]

These last words deserve careful examination. Thackeray does not
claim that the Hebrew Bible contains any term that could be translated
or even paraphrased by *theokratia*. Nor could we say that Josephus
would have been able to find in the Hebrew or Aramaic of his own
time any term that could be considered as an equivalent to that word.
We might perhaps think of מלכות שמים. But it should be noted that in
postbiblical language the title מלך, referring to God, always has
cosmological rather than national associations. Our prayerbook, for
instance, speaks of מלך העולם or of מלך על כל כל הארץ but not of מלך ישראל.
It is not only humankind that has to take upon itself the yoke of
מלכות שמים but the angels, too. So this term from the postbiblical Jewish
tradition stems from a root very different from the principle of a
guiding authority for welding together a community as a political
entity.

What Thackeray really has in mind, of course, is that in the world
of the Hebrew Bible the basic relation between God and Israel is that
between a king and his people,[20] a relation that makes the legitimacy
of a human king over Israel problematic. And the main expression of
God's kingship is indeed his giving commands to his subjects, both to
individuals and to the people as a whole. It is certainly correct to say
that in Josephus's new-found term an echo of this biblical idea comes
to the fore. I would also say that it is not completely absent from his
earlier presentation of the Mosaic law in *Antiquities*. When he there
formulates his strictures against choosing a king, he says: 'For God
suffices as a ruler'.[21] That formulation has discernible biblical over-
tones.[22] But it should also be noted that in this sentence Josephus
avoids the word 'king' and uses a more neutral word, ἡγεμών
('ruler'). I imagine that this was a conscious choice and that the statement was intended to be theological, with no reference to the
πολιτεία. It is precisely at this point that *Against Apion* takes a step

19. Josephus, LCL, I, note a.
20. Here I am indebted to M. Buber, *Königtum Gottes* (Berlin: Schocken
Books, 1932).
21. *Ant.* 4.223.
22. Cf. 1 Sam. 8.7.

further. Where in *Antiquities* we find only a somewhat vague statement of theological stricture, in *Against Apion* we find, with the
introduction of a new term, a constitutional definition in a political
discussion. The view implicit in Josephus's new word had already
been adumbrated in *Antiquities*, but only now does it become the
cornerstone of a political conception.

Recalling the centrality of the kingship of God in the Hebrew Bible
is not, however, to deny the novelty of Josephus's concept. I have
tried for the sake of clarity to translate Josephus's own definition of
his term *theokratia* as literally as I can: 'assigning the sovereignty and
the power to God'. Who is the subject of this action of assigning? It is
Moses as the legislator. According to the Greek theory, every constitution is the work of a person who conceived it and carried it through;
the legislator. This legislator's task is to assign to each element of the
state its specific role, according to the legislator's overall plan of the
state. So, to put it bluntly, if Moses is the legislator of the Jewish
commonwealth, it is he who gave God his appointment as the
sovereign of this state. I deliberately choose this extreme formulation
in order to highlight the oddity of Josephus's construction, which
seems to be the consequence of grafting a religious concept onto a
secular background. Even if we agree, then, with Thackeray's statement that 'the idea goes back to the Old Testament', we have to allow
that we have here a very novel and not unproblematic transformation
of this biblical idea.

On the other hand, we must not assume that in the context of Greek
political thought religious belief is an unknown factor in the shaping
of a state's constitution. The opposite is true. We find in the thought of
the sophist Critias an extreme analysis of the connection between
religion and political constitution;[23] he argues that politicians found it
impossible to enforce the laws because people always broke them in
secret with the confidence that their wrongs would not be discovered,
and so politicians invented religion in order to deter wrongdoers by
the belief that there are gods who can see all their deeds and will
punish them, even if no human eye will detect their misdeeds. The
belief in religion as a convenient device for politicians remained
widespread even where its intrinsic truth was not denied. From an
author who was strongly influenced by Stoic philosophy[24] we have a

23. See *FVS*, p. 88: Critias B25.
24. Strabo 16.39.

long list of famous legislators who told their respective peoples that they had received their laws from certain gods. This list is concluded by the sentence:

> Whatever may be the truth of what they told, by people it was believed and taken as facts, and therefore they were honoured as prophets (μάντεις) and were found worthy to get a kingdom, and both in their lifetime and after their death it was accepted that they brought to us the messages and directions of the gods.

It should be noted that this list of lawgivers includes Moses; in fact, it is in the course of a discussion of Moses and his deeds that this whole theme comes into discussion. Small wonder, then, that Josephus too was aware of this approach. He expressly compares Moses with the great lawgivers of the Greeks and states: 'Among these some attributed their laws to Zeus, others traced them to Apollo and his oracle at Delphi, either believing this to be the fact or hoping in this way to facilitate their acceptance'.[25]

Attributing laws to the gods was known to the Greeks as a common practice of all the lawgivers and could not be considered a distinguishing mark of Moses, even though the biblical narration reports unequivocally that God revealed his commands to Moses and to Israel. With this discussion in mind, Josephus himself reports in *Antiquities* the divine revelation of Mount Sinai with the cautious remark: 'Of these happenings each of my readers may think as he will; for my part, I am constrained to relate them as they are recorded in the sacred books'.[26] It is remarkable that Josephus himself is very careful not to commit himself in this respect. We have to say that so far he puts Moses on a par with the rest of the great lawgivers.

Yet there is one detail in his description that seems to secure for Moses a special status. He says about Moses that 'having first persuaded *himself* that God's will governed all his actions and all his thoughts, he regarded it as his primary duty to impress that idea upon the community; for to those who believe that their lives are under the eye of God all sin is intolerable.[27] The end of this sentence recalls the view that the people's belief in a godhead is a guarantee of its keeping the laws, and up to this point even Critias the sophist would have agreed. Yet Moses, as he is portrayed by Josephus, is not primarily

25. *Apion* 2.162.
26. *Ant.* 3.81.
27. *Apion* 2.160.

concerned with the pragmatic uses of the people's believing in the supremacy of God's will but with his own belief. It is true that when he endeavours to spread this belief among the people he takes account of its role in securing the keeping of the laws, but it is of the highest importance for him that this belief is not only useful but also true. Josephus does not develop this further, but by making the point that Moses persuades firstly himself and only later the people, he must have wanted to suggest that this raises the issue above the merely pragmatic level.

But are we entitled to see Josephus as here inaugurating a Jewish as against a Greek philosophy of politics? When he says that 'in the world at large' we find accepted the three types of polities which are mentioned, but that Moses had no regard for these things, it looks indeed as if Josephus wants to present Moses as opposed to all other human communities. But such an attitude would not be typical of Josephus, who always tries to place Judaism inside rather than outside the community of humankind.

Furthermore, we should note that a sweeping rejection of all the existing forms of state constitutions does not isolate Josephus—or Moses—in the realm of philosophical thought, for this is exactly the point of departure of Plato. It is well known that Plato develops his picture of an ideal order of society through an examination and rejection of all the existing orders of political life, enumerating, of course, the same basic types of states as Josephus. In his late book *Laws* Plato repeats this rejection and argues that the very names 'aristocracy', 'democracy' and so on designate those parts of society that dominate the other parts. These systems of state organization therefore cannot be acceptable, for a genuine πολιτεία must be a unity and not a society divided between a dominating and a subjugated class. A correct form of communal life would not have the name of the *demos* or the *aristoi* who form the ruling class, but the name of the god who maintains a just rule over the whole society. Plato goes on to relate the myth of such a god, Kronos, who once, long ago, ruled over a happy society. If we supply a name for such a polity it could not be other than *theokratia*, but unfortunately Plato did not explicitly use the term. I can only state it as my own hypothesis, then, that Josephus's new word was actually coined in continuation of the ideas found here in Plato's last work.[28]

28. I argue for this in my article 'Theokratia as a Concept of Political

We now come to the final question: how is Josephus's *theokratia* to work in practice? For, after all, it is not a mythological state like that of Plato, ruled by a god, but a human society, ordered by a legislator. A πολιτεία, even a theocracy, must be considered a human construct. The ideal state as described by Plato in the *Republic* is guided by the idea of the Good. According to Josephus, Moses declared piety, instead, to be the leading principle of his state. How is this principle to ensure the inner unity of the state, secured by Plato by his development of the idea of the Good?

Josephus's first answer is that Moses the lawgiver taught the whole people to hold the same opinions about the godhead and to keep the same divine commands.[29] But that is not all. We have to take into consideration that the content of this common belief is the belief in *one* God. Strictly speaking, it is not even monotheism as such that seems to Josephus to be Moses' central achievement. He is only too ready to identify Moses' 'notions of God' with those of the bulk of Greek philosophers.[30] But unlike Philo, for whom Moses is primarily 'the greatest of all philosophers', who attained the highest possible knowledge of the divine, Josephus portrays him as the creator of a historical reality. For those philosophers

> addressed their philosophy to the few, and did not venture to divulge their true beliefs to the masses... whereas our lawgiver, by making practice square with precept, not only convinced his own contemporaries, but so firmly implanted this belief concerning God in their descendants to all future generations that it can not be moved.[31]

In other words, Moses' uniqueness consists in his making his actions square with his thought, making his concept of God into the motive force of his political action, and so allowing monotheism to become the vitalizing principle of the political order he established. Monotheism as a political enterprise is an idea never envisaged by Greek philosophers. Josephus can only imagine that they lacked the 'courage'[32] needed for such a venture. I believe that this charge involves a gross misunderstanding of the nature of the monotheistic

Philosophy', *Scripta Classica Israelica* 8–9 (1989), pp. 83-105.
29. *Apion* 2.181.
30. *Apion* 2.168.
31. *Apion* 2.169.
32. *Apion* 2.169.

trend in Greek philosophy, although I cannot go into the arguments for this here.[33]

The social aspect of this universal monotheistic belief is expressed through an idea already familiar to us from *Antiquities* but only now falling into place exactly: 'A temple common to all, for the God common to all'.[34] It should be noted that in the Greek here the noun 'temple' governs a double genitive: the temple is, simultaneously, the temple of God and the temple of all the people. This peculiar construction expresses with remarkable exactness the idea of the temple as conceived by Josephus the priest. By being the one temple of the one God, this temple was the common property of the whole people of God united by it and made by it into one people.

Josephus adds the Greek proverb 'similar always likes similar'. This refers to the three-way relationship between the one God, the one temple and the one people. Here we are at the heart of the sociological message of monotheism. The institutional expression of this sociological extension is for Josephus the one body of priests, with the High Priest at its head, which administers the principal affairs of the community.[35] That this transposition is all too simplistic and leads to untenable results is true enough, but it is a pity that this consideration has overshadowed the theoretical merits of Josephus's methodological approach and has obscured what is in fact a serious attempt at defining the essence of Jewish communal life within the framework of Greek political theory. The inner 'harmony' (συμφωνία) of the state, strived for by the philosophers, is reached by Moses' approach.[36] We find here the belief, widespread in Hellenistic Judaism, that the ideals which Greek thought has established in theory can be achieved in practice by means of Israel's Torah.

I shall end by mentioning a telling example for interpreting a detail of the Mosaic law as a practical solution of a problem that remained open in the discussion of Greek theory. Plato believed that it is not enough to enforce laws by administrative means; the lawgiver must

---

33. Cf. my article 'Die Begegnung des biblischen und des philosophischen Monotheismus als Grundthema das jüdischen Hellenismus', *EvT* 38 (1978), pp. 2-19.

34. *Apion* 2.193.

35. *Apion* 2.185.

36. *Apion* 2.179.

explain the necessity of the laws to the people.[37] Josephus, in relation to this, poses the question whether instruction in the laws should be imparted by teaching or by practical exercise—the former being more or less identified as the Athenian method and the latter as the Spartan method. Josephus holds that Moses laid very great stress on exercising his citizens in the law from childhood on, 'leaving nothing, however insignificant, to the discretion and caprice of the individual', but simultaneously he set apart one day in the week, the Sabbath, on which they 'should desert their other occupations and assemble to listen to the law and to obtain a thorough and accurate knowledge of it'.[38] So he included within the law itself a special device to secure its theoretic side—exactly the spiritual moment that was postulated by Plato as a necessary supplement to enforcing the laws. Here Moses is clearly presented as securing the practical implementation of ideas that the Greek philosophers had only theorized about.

37. *Laws* 722b.
38. *Apion* 2.173-74.

LITERATURE IN THE SERVICE OF POLITICS: STUDIES IN JUDGES 19–21

Yairah Amit

Introduction

Literature has always been susceptible to involvement in political struggle, so the political mobilization of biblical literature should occasion no surprise. Politics and theopolitics—the subjects of our conference—actually encompass most of the biblical literature, because this literature interprets developments and behaviour as functions of the interaction between the individual or the nation and God. Prophecy, laws, historiography, biblical poetry and even the wisdom literature deal clearly and openly with political subjects related to the history of the kingdom, the fate of the nation, the conduct of its rulers, relations between the nation and its surroundings, rules of conduct toward the king and so on. Moreover, with the aid of a principle such as that of dual causality every political act can be understood as the political consequence of divine will; that is, as being theopolitical in nature.[1] In other words, in the biblical literature even non-mention of God does not divest political events of their theopolitical significance. It can therefore be stated that in biblical literature politics and theopolitics are in most cases one and the same.

The literary subject with political or theopolitical implications that I have chosen to discuss is the anti-Saul polemic hidden in chs. 19–21 in the book of Judges. As we know, Saul was the first ruler of the kingdom of Israel. He was appointed to that office because of public pressure as well as divine election—an event of theopolitical significance (1 Sam. 8–12). He was killed as part of the struggle with the Philistines, as foretold by God through his prophet Samuel (1 Sam. 28–31). His surviving son, Ish-Boshet, failed to establish his hold on

---

1. See my article 'The Dual Causality Principle and its Effects on Biblical Literature', *VT* 37 (1987), pp. 385-400.

the kingdom (2 Sam. 2–4). Rule passed to David, who was also appointed by the will of the people (2 Sam. 5.1-3) as well as divine election (1 Sam. 16.1-13). The dynasty of David was long-lived and continued to reign in Judah until the time of Yehoyachin and Zedekiah (2 Kgs 25); according to 1 Chron. 3.17-24, David's descendants were known even seven generations afterwards. The change of dynasties obliged theopolitical historiography to explain the choice of David and his house and to paint Saul in a light that would cause his departure from the stage of history to be understood as a religiously unavoidable step.

The biblical literature had to contend, therefore, with the question of what disqualified the first ruling house and why the house of David was worthy of being established. Both overt and covert means were used in this attempt. Following some others,[2] I maintain that chs. 19–21, at the end of the book of Judges, constitute a polemic against Saul and his supporters. Taking that as my point of departure, I have described this polemic as a hidden one and have formulated an approach to establishing the existence of such a polemic. Moreover, according to my opinion this polemic was attached to the end of the book in order to prepare the readers, as they followed the historical sequence, for the change in dynasty and to shape their opposition to the king from the city of Gibeah in the tribe of Benjamin.[3]

In order to make my case, I shall first try to clarify why the story that opens with the rape of the concubine in Gibeah is a hidden polemic against Saul and his followers. Afterwards, I shall address the question of why the biblical narrator made use of the technique of hidden polemic.

Judges 19–21 as a Hidden Polemic against Saul and his Followers

In my essay 'Hidden Polemic in the Conquest of Dan: Judges 17–18',[4] I have tried, first, to define this literary tool which I call 'hidden

---

2.   See notes 17-20 below.

3.   For a detailed discussion about the place of chs. 19–21 in the book of Judges see my work 'The Art of Composition in the Book of Judges' (Hebrew; dissertation, Tel Aviv University, 1984), pp. 126-45, and my article 'The Ending of the Book of Judges', in *Proceedings of the Ninth World Congress of Jewish Studies*, (Hebrew; Division A; Jerusalem: World Union of Jewish Studies/Magnes/ Hebrew University, 1986), pp. 73-80.

4.   *VT* 60 (1990), pp. 4-20.

polemic', secondly, to describe the dangers accompanying its use, and thirdly to design the critical system or the criteria for its discovery. Here, I will make the following observations on these points.

1. As a definition, we may say that stories having a hidden polemic are stories that do not use direct means but employ only hints or signs to take a stand on a particular subject, which is the cause of the polemic, and about which different opinions have been expressed in the biblical literature. One of the most important messages of these stories is their hidden censure or approval.

2. The danger in this definition is that it affords an opening for unlimited interpretations, which may at times stray widely from the actual significance of the story. Conceivably, it would be possible for different readers to argue that a particular story conceals a polemic against a whole variety of things. The ensuing unfettered exegetical association and the legitimization of interpretations would hinder understanding of the writings rather than facilitate their clarification. As we all know, it is difficult to escape this danger even in the sphere of interpretation of the overt and not the hidden.

3. How can these dangers be avoided? It seems to me that in order to avoid different and unintended interpretations and to direct his readers to the polemical issue, the biblical author must have inserted various signs throughout his text. These are the indirect means the author has employed to shape the hidden polemic. The exegete who maintains that some story contains a hidden polemic must therefore point to the existence of a number of elements whose interweaving in the fabric of the story was meant to hint at the polemical subject: obviously the way to identify a hidden polemic is to find the scattered hints.

Furthermore, in order to avoid the danger of discovering hidden polemic in a text where none exists, I would impose two additional restrictions on myself as exegete. First, the polemic argument must be based on other writings in the Bible which testify openly to the presence of controversy surrounding the particular subject. In other words, it is important to show that the phenomenon being dealt with has given rise to polemic in other biblical contexts as well. Secondly, the interpreter should find supporting evidence for the subject of the polemic in the exegetic tradition in order to be certain that the hidden polemic interpretation being attributed to a particular text is not his or her own invention in the interests of his or her own interpretative purposes. This last limitation would also ensure that the interpretation is faithful to the tradition of simple literal analysis and does not digress into homiletic or allegorical interpretation.

Thus far we may summarize by saying that in order for any text to be interpreted as including hidden polemic, it needs to meet the test of the following four criteria:

1. Avoidance of explicit reference to the phenomenon which the author wants to censure or advocate.
2. The existence of signs, no matter how odd or difficult, used by the author to develop the polemic, so that, in spite of the absence of specific references, the reader finds sufficient landmarks to reveal the polemic.
3. Additional evidence from biblical material regarding the existence of open polemic in connection with the same phenomenon.
4. Reference to the implicit subject of the polemic in the exegetical tradition.

Examination of Judges 19–21 in the light of these four criteria indicates that this text does contain a hidden polemic.

The First Criterion
It is clear that the first criterion, avoidance of explicit reference to the subject of the polemic, is met in this passage, since Saul and his house are not mentioned.

The Second Criterion
To meet the second criterion we must find in the passage various signs, the indirect means of alluding to Saul.

The First Sign. We may take as the first sign the use of the names of places connected, according to what is related in the book of Samuel, to central events in the life of Saul.

1. The name that keeps recurring throughout the incident is that of Saul's city Gibeah, which is referred to 22 times. In the entire Bible this name is mentioned eight more times: six times in Samuel (1 Sam. 10.1, 26; 14.2; 22.6; 23.19; 26.1) and twice in Hosea (9.9; 10.9); as 'Gibeah of Saul' four more times (1 Sam. 11.4; 15.34; 2 Sam. 21.6; Isa. 10.29); as 'Gibeah of Benjamin' six times (1 Sam. 13.2, 15;

14.16; 2 Sam. 23.29 [= 1 Chron. 11.31], and see Judg. 20.4) and as
the 'hill of God' (*Gibe'at 'elohim*) once (1 Sam. 10.5). It should be
noted that this list does not include texts in which the names 'Geba',
'Gibeah' and 'Gibeon' are confounded.[5] Still, we see that the number
of times that Gibeah is mentioned in the text under discussion is far
greater than the number of times it appears in the rest of the Bible as
a whole.

2. Yabesh-gilead is mentioned in our story as the one and only
city which did not come to the assembly at Mizpah; it was therefore
punished by a kind of ban, and four hundred virgins found there
were taken to be wives of the remnants of the tribe of Benjamin
(Judg. 21.1-14).[6] This story hints at the existence of ties of tribal
kinship between Yabesh-gilead and Benjamin. As we know, Yabesh-
gilead is connected with the history of Saul from his ascendancy to
power (1 Sam. 11), when he came to its rescue against Nahash the
Ammonite, until his death, when it was precisely its people who came
out to pay their last homage to Saul and his sons and bury them on
their land (1 Sam. 31.11-13; 2 Sam. 21.12-14; 1 Chron. 10.11-12).
Moreover, residents of Yabesh-gilead showed loyalty to Saul and his
house even after his death, and they did not respond to David's appeal
to them to recognize him as king (2 Sam. 2.4b-7).

3. In his search for his father's asses, Saul arrived at Ramah, the
city of Samuel, and there he was anointed king for the first time
(1 Sam. 9–10.16).[7] It was also to Ramah that David fled from Saul
(1 Sam. 19). In our story Ramah is mentioned as the place that the
Levite did not reach (Judg. 19.13). It is presented only as a possible
option for lodging, not even practical, since by the time they had
reached Jebus, 'the day was far spent', and when they reached Gibeah,

---

5.   See A. Demsky, 'Geba, Gibeah and Gibeon—"An Historico-Geographic
Riddle"', *BASOR* 212 (1973), pp. 26-31. A detailed discussion about the city of
Gibeah, its location, its history and its role in Israelite tradition is to be found in
P.M. Arnold's 'Gibeah in Israelite History and Tradition' (PhD dissertation, Emory
University, 1986).

6.   See B. Mazar, 'Yabesh-gilead', *Encyclopaedia Biblica*, III (Hebrew;
Jerusalem: Bialik Institute, 1958), pp. 459-61. See also my interpretation in
M. Greenberg and S. Ahituv (eds.), *Mikra Leyisra'el* (Tel Aviv: Am Oved, forth-
coming).

7.   On the identification of the site of Ramah see Z. Kalai, in *Encyclopaedia
Biblica*, VII (Hebrew; Jerusalem: Bialik Institute, 1976), pp. 373-74.

identified with Tell al-Ful,[8] 'the sun went down unto them'. Thus, it would seem that mention of Ramah, located north of Gibeah, was meant to help set the geographical coordinates as those of Saul's era. In other words, the city of Ramah does not serve the needs of the story but rather the needs of the polemic alone; its mention seems forced, and I therefore list it here.

4. The selection of Saul as king enjoyed public recognition after Samuel convoked all of Israel to come to the ceremony at Mizpah where the tribes of Benjamin and of Saul were singled out (1 Sam. 10.17-27).[9] According to what is recounted in Judges, the entire nation gathered at Mizpah before it went to war against Benjamin (20.1-3). There they also swore not to give their daughters as wives to the tribe of Benjamin (21.1). But Mizpah is mentioned only as a preliminary meeting place, not as the place from which they departed for war or to which they returned when they met to discuss the rehabilitation of the tribe of Benjamin. Thus, it would seem that its mention, too, is forced, intended as a hint of the geographical reference points of Saul's era.

5. It is worth noting the connection between the name 'Rock of Rimmon' (Judge. 20.45-47; 21.13), the refuge of the six hundred of Benjamin, and the pomegranate (rimmon) tree on the outskirts of Gibeah (1 Sam. 14.2), where Saul was staying with exactly six hundred men, is unavoidable.[10]

6. I would also note that Benjamin, the tribe of Saul, is mentioned as a tribe or a tribal area 172 times in the entire Bible, of which 42 instances (about 25 per cent) occur in our story.

8. See note 5 above and I. Finkelstein, *The Archaeology of the Period of the Settlement and Judges* (Hebrew; Tel Aviv: Hakibbutz Hameuchad, 1986), pp. 52-55.

9. Mizpah is identified with Tell en-Nasbeh. For the report of the last excavations see Finkelstein, *Archaeology*, pp. 56-59.

10. The identification of Rock of Rimmon with a rock close to modern Rammūn, which is located four miles east of Bethel, is almost generally accepted. See G. Cohen, 'Rock of Rimmon', *Encyclopaedia Biblica*, V (Hebrew; Jerusalem: Bialik Institute, 1968), pp. 1051-52. Thanks are due to my student Sinthia Edinburg who drew my attention to this sign.

The Second Sign. The description of the Levite's deeds makes a number of allusions to Saul.

1. The Levite walked with a pair of donkeys (Judge. 19.3); and Saul was looking for his father's asses (1 Sam. 9.3).

2. An old man from the hill country of Ephraim hosted the Levite (Judge. 19.16); and Samuel, who was an old prophet from the hill country of Ephraim, hosted Saul (1 Sam. 9.22-26).

3. The Levite got advice from his servant (Judg. 19.11) and, in retrospect, it would have been better had his suggestion been adopted (19.12-14). Saul's servant boy also gave him sound advice (1 Sam. 9.6-8).

4. Like Saul who cut a yoke of oxen into pieces in order to announce the war and to assemble an army (1 Sam. 11.7), the Levite cut up the corpse of the concubine in order to announce what happened in Gibeah and to gather the people together (Judg. 19.29). In the case at hand, the means by which the announcement was conveyed suited the accompanying threat: 'thus shall be done to (your) cattle'. But the Levite's action is strange: what could be understood from receiving the severed hand of a woman? Thus, in this instance as well, cutting up the concubine would seem to be a forced motif, whose purpose was to remind the reader of Saul's action.

The Third Sign. This is the motifs connected to war.

1. The people were gathered and went out after Saul 'as one man' (1 Sam. 11.7). In the days of the war in Gibeah the entire community was also assembled together 'as one man' (Judg. 20.1).

2. The exaggerated numbers are also similar. In Saul's time 330,000 people gathered (1 Sam. 11.8), and during the war at Gibeah 400,000 came together, not counting the men of Benjamin.

3. Of Benjamin six hundred remained; Saul too remained at Gilgal (1 Sam. 13.15) and at the outskirts of Gibeah (1 Sam. 14.2) with six hundred followers.

4. Although there are textual problems, it is interesting to mention that according to the Massoretic text the Ark of God took a part in the war of Michmas (1 Sam. 14.18) as well as in the war of Gibeah (Judg. 20.27-28).[11]

---

11. Many researchers prefer the LXX version of 1 Sam. 14.18, where the Ark of God is not mentioned, and explain the mention of the Ark in Judg. 20.27-28 as a late gloss. See the critical commentaries.

The Fourth Sign. A detailed exposition of exemplary hospitality precisely in Bethlehem in Judah constitutes the basis for a negative analogy with Gibeah. On the one hand, mention at the beginning of the story of Bethlehem in Judah, the city in which David was both born and anointed king, and mention later on of his capital Jebus (that is, Jerusalem), and on the other hand the frequent mention of Benjamin and Gibeah, the birthplace and capital city of Saul, along with the cities of his anointment, Ramah and Mizpah, would seem to be not simply a matter of chance. I am convinced that creation of this analogical pattern in the course of the exposition was intended to intimate that the groups of names of cities represent persons and juxtapose the one whose origin and capital are Gibeah with the one whose origin was Bethlehem and whose capital was Jerusalem. There is no doubt that readers who found themselves between the two cities would prefer the hospitality of Bethlehem to that of Gibeah.

Considering all these factors it would seem that the incident of the concubine in Gibeah points to Saul, making it a hidden polemic. The author employs every means to cast the most negative light possible on Saul's origin. He weaves analogical threads between the reception of guests in Gibeah and that in Sodom, thus suggesting to the reader that Saul's city Gibeah is worse even than Sodom, since in Sodom the threatened rape did not occur, whereas the rape in Gibeah actually took place and even ended in murder, and the tribe of Benjamin was not prepared to punish the city but rather shielded it and afforded it protection.

The Third Criterion

The third criterion relates to the presence of the subject of the polemic in other biblical writings. The relations between Saul and David and the reasons for preferring David are a matter which occupied both the author of the book of Samuel and the author of Chronicles. It is thus a subject of importance in biblical historiography. However, there is a great difference between the ways in which the subject of the establishment of the monarchy in Israel is treated in these two books.

Study of the description of the period of Saul's rule in the book of 1 Samuel reveals a particularly complex literary structure. The progress of events in this period is similar to the stages described by

Aristotle in his analysis of tragedy.[12] First of all we can trace the principle of the tragic direction of the transition from extreme happiness and success to the opposite pole of failure and calamitous end. Saul goes from the extreme of anointment as king (1 Sam. 9–11) to the opposite pole of tribulation and death (ch. 31).

Moreover, in the evolution of Saul's kingdom we can even identify five stages, corresponding to the elements which Aristotle attributes to the tragic plot: fateful error, terrible deed, peripety or unexpected reversal, recognition and suffering.[13] The fateful error occurred at Gilgal, prior to the battle of Michmesh, when Saul despaired of Samuel's coming on the seventh day and failed to wait for a few more minutes (1 Sam. 13.8-12). Because the error here is one of judgment and assessment with no hint of malicious intent, the reader is led to identification with the tragic hero and a feeling of compassion towards him. The terrible deed, which although not malicious could not be remedied, occurred in the war with Amalek, when Saul was not only responsible for not keeping God's commandment and for violating the interdiction, but also tried to save his own skin by casting the guilt onto the people (1 Sam. 15.9-15).[14] The proclamation of the prophet, 'The Lord has this day torn the kingship over Israel away from you and has given it to another who is worthier than you' (v. 28) marks the reversal of fortune (see vv. 27-35). From this point onward a chain of events unfolds which leads Saul, in the most natural way, to his tragic end. The first event in the series is the anointing of David as king and his appearance in the royal court (ch. 16). The stage of Saul's recognition or comprehension is marked by David's successes, starting with the victory over Goliath (ch. 17) and continuing with

12. Aristotle, *Poetics* (LCL edn), chs. 7, 13. To the application of Aristotle's theory on Saul's story and the description of his life as tragedy, see S. Halperin, 'Saul's Kingdom—The Tragedy of the First Israeli King', in *Samuel and Saul: The Prophet and the King (Studies in the Book of Samuel)* (Hebrew; Jerusalem: Kiryat Sefer, 1986), pp. 52-60. I accept her argument but not her system of application, which is different from the one suggested by me.

13. S. Halperin, *On Aristotle's 'Poetics'* (Hebrew; Tel Aviv: Hakibbutz Hameuchad, 2nd edn, 1984), pp. 81-135. Halperin observes that 'while Aristotle does not call them stages and does not even present them in this order, according to his argument, it is clear that this is their significance and their order' (p. 83).

14. It should be noted that the stage of the terrible deed which follows the fateful error usually encompasses the error, so that the two stages appear as one in the tragic structure. See Halperin, *On Aristotle's 'Poetics'*, pp. 100-101.

Saul's attempts to harm David (18.8-9, 15, 28-29). From this stage onward a long period of suffering commences, with Saul the king behaving like a hunted man, suspecting those closest to him, and occupying himself with a futile pursuit of David (chs. 19–27). Saul's tragic life ends with the failure in the war with the Philistines on Mount Gilboa (chs. 28–31).

The author of the book of Samuel thus organizes his stories in a sequential narrative which keeps the structure of tragedy and affords the readers materials that will enable them to understand Saul and to identify with him, to feel his pain and share his suffering, to feel compassion for him and finally to be moved by his resignation as he goes forth to his final battle.[15] Thus it happens that although Saul, even according to the book of Samuel, has violated the divine order, the readers show understanding for him and do not censure him categorically. The literary structure which accords a tragic dimension to the unfolding events prevents a one-sided, negative portrayal of Saul.

In contrast with the description in Samuel, the author of Chronicles follows a different course. This author barely deals with the kingdom of Saul. He begins his account of historical events with the death of Saul as the background for transfer of the kingdom to David. Still, he does not merely describe a leadership vacuum but justifies Saul's death. According to him, Saul sinned toward God in not having fulfilled his command and, moreover, he had consulted a ghost to seek advice and did not seek the advice of the Lord. Because of these grave transgressions, he was punished and the monarchy transferred to David (1 Chron. 10.13-14). The presentation of events by the author of Chronicles may thus be regarded as an attempt to formulate a partisan historical picture, completely different from that suggested in the book of Samuel.[16]

We find that the question of the change of ruler and the need to justify the choice of the house of David was an issue which occupied the biblical literature not only at the time it occurred or shortly afterward, that is, at the end of the second millennium or the beginning of

15. See for example Josephus, *Ant.* 6.14.4. On the tragic hero see D. Krook, *Elements of Tragedy* (New Haven and London: Yale University Press, 1969), ch. 3, 'The Tragic Hero', pp. 35-65.

16. Onesidedness can also be seen in Ps. 78, which avoids any mention of the kingdom of Saul and emphasizes the choice of David and the preference of Judah over the tribe of Ephraim (vv. 67ff.).

the first millennium BCE, but also during the era of the Second Temple, when the book of Chronicles was written (the fourth century BCE).

The Fourth Criterion

As to the fourth criterion—presence of the hidden subject of the polemic in the exegetic tradition—Judges 19–21 is described by some German researchers of the previous century as an anti-Saul political tradition; thus first Auberlen,[17] followed by Gudemann[18] and Graetz.[19] It is interesting to mention that this approach has acquired only few supporters in contemporary studies.[20]

Why a Hidden Polemic?

The use of the technique of the hidden polemic raises the question of why any subject should be dealt with in an indirect manner rather than openly. It is possible to adopt the censorship solution, but in order to do so it is necessary to reconstruct the reasons which made it necessary to move the polemic underground. However, in the case before us, the struggle to consolidate the rule of the house of David was open and unconcealed, and this would have obviated the necessity for a hidden polemic. David did not shrink from exploiting the famine as a pretext for sending the descendants of the house of Saul to their deaths at the hands of the Gibeonites (2 Sam. 21). He brought near him only those who could not threaten his rule, such as Michal the barren or Mephiboshet, the lame son of Jonathan. The behaviour of Ziba,

17. See C.A. Auberlen, 'Die drei Anhänge des Buches der Richter in Ihrer Bedeutung und Zusammengehörigkeit', *TSK* 33 (1860), pp. 536-68. See also H.W. Jüngling, *Richter 19: Ein Plädoyer für das Königtum* (Rome: Biblical Institute Press, 1981), pp. 8-11.

18. M. Gudemann, 'Tendenz und Abfassungszeit der letzten Kapitel des Buches der Richter', *MGWJ* 18 (1869), pp. 357-68.

19. H. Graetz, *Geschichte der Juden von den ältesten Zeiten bis auf die Gegenwart* (Leipzig, 2nd edn, 1891), I, pp. 319-21.

20. See, for example, F. Crüsemann, *Der Widerstand gegen das Königtum* (WMANT, 49; Neukirchen–Vluyn: Neukirchener Verlag, 1978), p. 164; B.Z. Dinur, in *Studies in the Book of Judges* (Hebrew; Jerusalem: Kiryat Sefer, 1966), pp. 485-86; B.Z. Lurie, in *Studies in the Book of Judges*, pp. 463-79; and *idem*, *Saul and Benjamin* (Hebrew; Jerusalem: Kiryat Sefer, 1970), pp. 179-81; T. Rudin-O'Brasky, 'The Appendices to the Book of Judges (Judg. 17–21)', in *Beer Sheva*, II (Hebrew; Jerusalem: Magnes/Hebrew University, 1985), pp. 141-65 and especially pp. 151-65.

servant of Mephiboshet, and Shimei the son of Gera during Absalom's revolt is indicative of the open existence polemic. With the division of the kingdom, it would seem that the house of Saul had ceased to be a subject of polemic of any kind, and for the most part the polemic was conducted openly against the Northern Kingdom and its rulers who did not belong to the house of Saul. Nor is there even a hint that during the First Temple period the remnants of the house of Saul constituted any threat to the rule of the house of David in Judah. One study does raise the hypothesis that during the Second Temple period an attempt was made to rehabilitate the first monarchy in Israel, for example via the friendly attitude toward the house of Saul in the book of Esther, in which Mordecai is represented as the one who completes what Saul was unable to do.[21] Thus it was precisely 'Mordecai, son of Yair son of Shimei son of Kish, a Benjaminite' (Esth. 2.5) who fought and took revenge on Haman the Agagite. But Abramsky, the researcher who raises this hypothesis, notes himself that

> there is no way to answer the question of whether this thought reflects an existential stirring, following the Return [to Zion], in support of the rehabilitation of the house of Saul and popular anticipation of its renewal or return in some form or to know whether there was any real expectation that the descendants of the house of Kish during that [late] period would take action [in such a direction].[22]

It would seem, therefore, that the place to search for the reason for this literary polemic is the sphere of rhetorical strategy. From the perspective of biblical historiography it would seem that someone was bothered by the literary construction of the book of Samuel which fosters understanding, compassion and even sympathy for Saul. This editor decided to try to influence readers by planting earlier material which would change the interpretation put upon what is related in the book of Samuel. It appears that the role of Judges 19–21, immediately preceding the book of Samuel, is to reinforce the negative aspect of all that is connected with Saul, to blur the tragic effect, and thus to make it easier for readers to understand the reasons for the change in regime and the preference for David.

The question then arises why this rhetorical strategist employed

21. S. Abramsky, 'Return to the Kingdom of Saul in the Books of Esther and Chronicles', in *MILET: Studies in Jewish History and Culture* (Tel Aviv: Everyman's University, 1983), pp. 39-63.

22. Abramsky, 'Return to the Kingdom of Saul', p. 60.

hidden rather than open means. It would seem to me that two reasons can be found for this, one tactical and the other theological.

Tactically, the hidden polemic is preferable since as an indirect technique it avoids the danger inherent in polemic of arousing immediate opposition, while at the same time making a cumulative impression and shaping the reader's attitudes, producing a suitable setting for the story to come. In this way the author creates a negative atmosphere around all that is related to Saul.

Theologically, the use of an open polemic in this case would probably have aroused wonder concerning divine election. By making the polemic hidden and directing the attack against Benjamin and Gibeah, the impression is created that the chosen one from Benjamin has indeed been afforded an opportunity, but, 'Sin couches at the door' (Gen. 4.7), and as one who has resided in this particular city, it is not surprising that he has failed.

But the literary evidence reveals that neither the tragic form, avoiding the one-sidedness of the book of Samuel, nor the sophisticated technique of the hidden polemic employed by the author of Judges 19–21 appealed to the author of Chronicles. In this political issue he preferred the technique of an open and clear form. It may even be that his rejection of the ambivalent attitude of the book of Samuel, and of the limited influence of the polemic which preceded it, served as motivation for the one-sidedness of his own book, distinguished by its selectivity and organization of materials that are manifestly pro-David and anti-Saul.

'THOU SHALT MAKE NO COVENANT WITH THEM'
(Exodus 23.32)

Moshe Anbar

The Mari texts cover a highly eventful period of numerous political
upheavals in which a role was played by monarchs of powerful kingdoms and rulers of small city-states. Political events of worldwide
impact, as well as the everyday life of the ruling classes and the
common people, are reflected in the texts.

The Mari archive contains some fifty 'prophetic texts'. Since 1947,
the time when Georges Dossin presented Adolphe Lods with the first
Mari prophetic text, Mari prophecy and its relation to biblical
prophecy has become an essential part of the discussion of the origins
of Near Eastern prophecy in general and of biblical prophecy in
particular.

Here I shall discuss one theme that appears in these texts, namely the
desire of prophets to influence the foreign politics of the state. To
illustrate this, I choose one episode from the history of Mari, prophecies opposing the alliance with Ešnunna. Sammetar, a high official
at Mari, wrote the following to his lord Zimri-Lim in the year 1770
BCE:

> [2]Say [1]to my lord: [3]Thus (says) Sammetar [4]your servant: [5]Lupāḫum, the
> *āpilum* of Dagān [6]came to me from Tuttul. These are the [7]instructions
> (*tēmum*) that my lord [8]gave him in Saggarātum: '[9]"Entrust me" to Dagān
> of Terqa'. These instructions [10]he brought, and thus they answered him:
> '[11]Wherever you go, success ("good heart") [12]will meet you. A battering
> ram [13]and a siege tower are given to you. They will march [14]at your side.
> They will help you.' [15]This message (*tēmum*) [16]they gave him in Tuttul.
> [17]And as soon as he returned from Tuttul, I sent him to Dīr, and he
> brought to Dirītum [18]my bar (of a city-gate). [19]Previously he brought a
> *širānum*-vessel and said (to the goddess): '[20]the *širānum*-vessel is not in
> good repair, as a result, the water [21]leaks. Strengthen the *širānum*-vessel'.
> [22]Now, he brought my bar (of a city-gate) [23]and this is the message (the

goddess) sent him with: '[24]God forbid that you will trust the peace (*salīmum*) [25]of the man of Ešnunna, and because of that [26]be negligent. [27]Your guards [28]should be stronger than previously'. [29]And (Lupāhum) said to me: [30]'God forbid that the king [32]should make peace (*napištam lapātum* "touch the throat") [31]with the man of Ešnunna without asking the god'. As previously, [33]when the Bini-Yamina descended [34]and settled in Saggarātum and I told the king: [35]'Do not slaughter a foal (*ḥâram qatālum*) of the Bini-Yamina. [36]Because of the noise made by the members of their tribes, [37]I will expel them and the river will finish them for you. [38]Now, without asking the god, [39]he must not make peace'. [40]This is the message (*tēmum*) that Lupāhum told me. [41]After him, the next day, [42]a *qammatum* of Dagān of Terqa [43]came to me and thus she said to me: '[44]Beneath the straw the water flows! [45]They write [you] continuously regarding peace (*salīmum*) proposal. They send you continuously [46]their gods while they are planning [48]in their heart [47]a second lie! [49]The king [50]must not make peace ("touch his throat") without asking the god'. [52]She asked for [51]one simple *laḥrum*-garment and a nose-ring and I gave it to her and [53]in the temple of Bēlet-Ekallim [54]she handed over her prophecy (*wûrtum*) to the high priestess Inibšina. The message [that (...)] [55]she told me [56]I sent to my lord. My lord should take counsel, and act according [57]to his great kingship.[1]

The letter sent by Sammetar dates to the month of Heshwan of the sixth year of Zimri-Lim (1770 BCE). We know the exact date thanks to a small tablet stating that on the seventh of this month Lupāhum received one sickle of silver 'when he went to Tuttul' (M. 11436).[2] In the previous year an Ešnunnean expeditionary force marched to the south of Jebel Sinjar and the triangle of the Ḫabur, Idamaraṣ, reaching Šubat-Enlil (Tell Leilan) in the month of Heshwan.[3] After a short period they were driven, with the help of Zimri-Lim, from this area and returned to their country, whence Ešnunna sent another expeditionary force, this time to the south of Mari, conquering its border fortresses. But this force was also driven back to its country. Following these events, in the months of Ab (1770 BCE) peace negotiations began between Ešnunna and Mari. This period of negotiations is reflected in our letters.

---

1.   J.-M. Durand, *Archives épistolaires de Mari I/1* (ARMT, 26.1; Paris: Editions Recherche sur les Civilisations, 1988), pp. 426-29.

2.   In Durand, *Archives épistolaires de Mari I/1*, p. 396.

3.   M. Anbar, *Les tribus amurrites de Mari* (OBO, 108; Freiburg/Göttingen: Universitätsverlag/Vandenhoeck & Ruprecht, 1991), pp. 61-62.

Line 5. Lupāḫum was an *āpilum* of the god Dagān. *āpilum*[4] is derived from the root *apālum,* 'to answer a question, to respond'; he is an 'answerer'. We know of an *āpilum, āpiltum* of the gods or goddesses Dagān, Adad, Ninḫur-saga, Nin-egal, Ḫišamītum, Marduk, Dirītum and Šamaš. An *āpilum* can undertake missions in state affairs, he can bring forward the demands of a deity in questions of patrimony, and he can prophesy against foreign nations. The *āpilum* explains the signs of the extispicy, and prophesies while drunk. His prophecies could be verified through the sending of the hair and hem. A *bārûm*-diviner verifies the credibility of the *āpilum* by divination performed in the presence of the hair and hem of the *āpilum*.

Lines 7-15. Zimri-Lim sent Lupāḫum to Tuttul asking him to consult Dagān, the god of the Middle Euphrates, regarding a war Zimri-Lim is going to face. The answer is favourable for Zimri-Lim.

Lines 17-23. On arriving from Tuttul Lupāḫum is sent to Dīr in the southern part of the district of Mari. Every time he goes to the goddess of Dīr, Dīritum, he brings with him a symbolic object. In the past he brought a leaking vessel, symbolizing the unstable situation of the country; now he brings the bar of a city, probably Mari, symbolizing the need to strengthen the defence of the city and kingdom.

Line 22. '...he brought my bar (of a city-gate)': this repeats the image of line 18.[5]

Lines 24, 31-32, 39, 45, 50. By good chance, we possess the text of the treaty between Ibāl-pī-El II, the son of Dāduša, the king of Ešnunna, and Zimri-Lim, the king of Mari. This document is called 'the big tablet' or 'the tablet of the life of the god' (*tuppum rabûm, tuppi nīš ilim*).[6] In this treaty Zimri-Lim qualifies Ibāl-pī-El as his father, *abī* (A.361.11.15′, 111.1′, 3′, 8′, 10, 12′[7]). A treaty between two parties is concluded in two stages: in the first stage 'small tablets' or 'tablets of the touching of the throat' (*tuppum ṣeḫrum, tuppi lipit*

4. Cf. Durand, *Archives épistolaires de Mari I/1*, pp. 396-98.
5. Cf. M. Anbar, 'La "Reprise"', *VT* 38 (1988), pp. 385-98; *idem*, 'La Reprise', *NABU* 103 (1989); add. XXVI 199.30-32, 38-39, 384.19′, 24′; 480.11, 16; A.1025.4, 10 (*MARI*, VI, p. 337); A.4002.19, 22 (*MARI*, VI, p. 79 n. 205); A.4026.15-16 (*MARI*, VI, pp. 49-50); Deut. 1.1, 5; 1 Sam. 6.15; Josh. 24.27; 2 Sam. 24.17 (//1 Chron. 21.17; 2 Chron. 6.12-13; 1 Kgs. 18.31-32a).
6. Cf. 'La petite tablette' and 'la grande tablette', *NABU* 98 (1991).
7. D. Charpin, in *Marchands, diplomates et empereurs: Etudes sur la civilisation mésopotamienne offertes à Paul Garelli* (Paris: Editions Recherche sur les Civilisations, 1991), pp. 141-45.

napištim) are exchanged and each king is 'touching his throat',
napištam lapātum, as we read in a letter sent by a servant of Zimri-
Lim who was sent by him to Ešnunna: 'now our lord sent to his father
(the king of Ešnunna), his gods, his big standards (with divine
symbols) and us, his servants, to make the touching of the throat and
to tie forever the fringe of father and son (*sissikti abim u mārim*)'
(A.3354+.17-20[8]). When two parties who intend to conclude a treaty
stay in their own countries without meeting each other, each party
sends its gods to the other party to take an oath in their presence.

In the second stage 'big tablets' are exchanged and each party
swears by the life of the god (*nīš ilim*), as we learn from another
letter sent to Zimri-Lim: 'The Prince [that is, the king of Ešnunna]
has just sworn by the life of the gods. My lord should be happy. After
this letter, I will lead to my lord the gods of my lord, the gods and the
messengers of the Prince... and we will organize the oaths by the life
of the gods' (A.2028.4-12[9]).

Lines 23-28. Presumably he is conveying to the goddess Dīritum,
whose city is located in the south of Mari, the message he got in Tuttul
from Dagān urging her not to trust the peace proposals of the man of
Ešnunna and not to neglect the defence of the southern borders of the
kingdom of Mari, from where an eventual attack by Ešnunna could
come.

Lines 29-32, 33-40. The question is to what sort of oracle the
āpilum is referring. One has the impression that he is referring to
extispicy. If this is the case, we have a very important indication,
namely, that divination is held in higher regard than prophecy.

Lines 32-37. Lupāḫum is referring to a previous prophecy
concerning the Amurrite tribe Bini-Yamina. He is referring probably
to the negotiations following the suppression of their rebellion in the
third year of Zimri-Lim (1773-1772).[10] The peace treaty he is mentioning is accompanied by a symbolic act of slaughtering a foal
(*ḫâram qatālum*). This practice is mentioned a few times in the Mari
texts; for example, we read in a letter about a treaty concluded
between the Bini-Yamina and the kings of Zalmaqum (the region in
the north of Ḫarrān): 'Asdi-takim (the king of Ḫarrān) and the kings

8. Charpin, in *Marchands, diplomates et empereurs*, p. 163 and n. 60.
9. Charpin, in *Marchands, diplomates et empereurs*, p. 163 and n. 62.
10. Anbar, *Les tribus amurrites de Mari*, p. 59.

of Zalmaqum and the *sugāgū* (the sheiks) and the elders of the Bini-Yamina have slaughtered a foal in the temple of Sîn of Ḫarrān'.[11] In our letter the *āpilum* promises, in the name of the god, to get rid of the Bini-Yamina. The reason for their extermination is not without interest, because the same reason for a punishment is given in Atramḫasis (for example II.i.4[12]): 'The god got disturbed with their uproar'.

Lines 41-50. A *qammatum*-prophetess[13] also warns Zimri-Lim against an alliance with Ešnunna; he should not conclude a treaty without first asking the god.

Lines 51-52. The *qammatum*-prophetess is paid for delivering the message in the same way that a messenger is paid.

Lines 53-54. The prophetess had also communicated her prophecy to the priestess Inibšina. Now, it so happens that we possess the letter of Inibšina containing this message:

> Say to my Star: Thus (says) Inibšina:... Now, a *qammatum* of Dagan of Terqa came to me [10]and thus she said to me: 'The peace (*salīmātum*) (proposals) of the man of Ešnunna are treacherous, because beneath the straw the water flows! And into the net [15]that he is weaving I will gather him. I will destroy his town and I will indeed destroy his property, dating from old age'. [20]This she told me. Now, guard yourself, without a divination (*têrtum*) [25]do not enter the city. [25]Thus I heard saying: by himself... Do not... by yourself.[14]

In the Mari archive we find another prophecy against the peace with Ešnunna:

> Say to my Lord: Thus (says) Kānisān your servant: [5]My father Kibri-Dagān [wrote me] to Mari [say]ing: [I heard] the things [that] were done [in the temple of Dagān], thus they/he s[aid to me]: [10]'Bene[ath the straw] the water flows! He went, the god of my lord, he delivered his enemies into his hands'. Now [15]a *muḫḫum* is calling repeatedly in the same way as before. This Kibri-Dagān wrote me...[15]

Line 5. Kibri-Dagān is the governor of Terqa.

Line 15. *muḫḫūtum, muḫḫûm*[16] is from the root *maḫûm*, 'to

11. XXVI. 24.10-12.

12. W.G. Lambert and A.R. Millard, *Atra-ḫasīs* (Oxford: Clarendon Press, 1969), pp. 72-73.

13. Durand, *Archives épistolaires de Mari I/1*, p. 396.

14. XXVI. 197.

15. XXVI. 202.

16. Durand, *Archives épistolaires de Mari I/1*, pp. 386-88.

become frenzied, to go into trance'.[17] The word is equated in a commentary of *šumma ālu* with *šegû*: to be wild, to rave.[18] Indeed, in a passage from Hosea we read אֱוִיל הַנָּבִיא מְשֻׁגָּע אִישׁ הָרוּחַ (Hos. 9.7): 'The prophet is mad, the inspired fellow is raving'.

Let us sum up the information we have gathered from the three letters concerning the prophecies against a peace with Ešnunna. The prophecies are delivered by three kinds of prophets of Dagān of Terqa: a *qammatum*, an *āpilum* and a *muḫḫum*, who promise that Zimri-Lim will defeat his enemy. The prophecies were delivered in Terqa and Tuttul. The question I would ask here is why the clergy of Dagān object to the peace treaty with Ešnunna. As we are dealing with pagans nobody will pretend that הַנִּסְתָּרֹת לַיהוה אֱלֹהֵינוּ וְהַנִּגְלֹת לָנוּ וּלְבָנֵינוּ עַד־עוֹלָם ('The secret things belong unto the Lord our God: but those things which are revealed belong unto us and our children for ever' [Deut. 29.28]). There must be a logical explanation for their objection. It would be out of the question to suppose that they had better information than the king of Mari, or that they had spies in the court of Ešnunna, who revealed to them the real intentions of the king of Ešnunna. In the documents published so far I have found no explanation for their attitude. The only explanation I can suggest is based on the fact that the prophets insist that Zimri-Lim will act only after he has consulted the god. It seems to me that the clergy of Dagān, the god of the Middle Euphrates, wants to insure its influence on Zimri-Lim by obliging him to act only after having consulted the god through them and thus securing the prominent position of their temple in the Kingdom of Mari.

Future events show that the prophets were right and that Zimri-Lim was wrong. After few years of peace between Ešnunna and Mari, in 1765–1764 BCE Ešnunna accompanied Elam in once again invading the area in the south of Jebel Sinjar.[19]

Let us turn now to the Bible. Here we find many examples of prophets trying to intervene in the foreign affairs of the state. I will look at one in particular which has some similarity with the Mari case. In 1 Kings 20 we read that Ben-Hadad, the king of Aram who besieged Samaria, offers Ahab, the king of Israel, a treaty, whereby Ahab will become his vassal (vv. 3, 18). Ahab rejects this offer, a

17. *CAD*, pp. 115b-116a.
18. *AHw*, p. 1208b.
19. Anbar, *Les tribus amurrites de Mari*, pp. 67-68.

war breaks out and Aram is defeated by Israel. The next year Ben-Hadad goes up to Aphek to fight Israel and again he is defeated by the king of Israel, who captures the city of Aphek. The king of Aram pleads for peace and the king of Israel replies 'he is my brother' (אחי הוא, v. 32), that is to say a partner in a treaty between equals. The representatives of Ahab reply using the same term, 'Thy brother Ben-Hadad' (אחיך בן־הדד, v. 33). Ahab concludes the conversation with the words 'I will send thee away with this covenant' (ואני בברית אשלחך). And we read: 'So he made a covenant with him, and sent him away' (ויכרת־לו ברית וישלחהו, v. 34). But the prophets opposed this covenant, saying, 'Thus saith the Lord. Because thou hast let go out of thy hand a man whom I appointed to utter destruction, therefore thy life shall go for his life, and thy people for his people' (ויאמר אליו כה אמר יהוה יען שלחת את־איש־חרמי מיד והיתה נפשך תחת נפשו ועמך תחת עמו, v. 42). Future events showed that once again, as in the Mari case, the prophet proved to be right.

In the Mari case there is not the slightest doubt that the actual order of events was as I have described. In the example from the Bible, on the other hand, it is very likely that we are dealing with a fictitious prophecy, composed perhaps years after the events in order to transmit a theological message: 'the prophets of the God of Israel are true prophets. They proved that they can predict the future, so, Children of Israel, listen to them and be guided by their instructions'.

Concerning the attitude of the classical prophets to Israel's international treaties, I would like to quote from A. Rofé's *Introduction to the Prophetic Literature*:

> Seeing that the Lord had appointed Assyria as the instrument by which He was to castigate Israel, the Assyrian threat should obviously not be countered by a military pact against her, above all not by an alliance with Egypt (Isa. 28:14-22; 30:1-5, 6-7, 8-14, 15-18: 31:1-3). Isaiah was consistent in his opposition to all political treaties. As early as the year 733 BCE, in the days of Ahaz, when the king was about to turn to Assyria for help (Isa. 7–8), the prophet contested this move. The majority of prophets through the generations share this standpoint: Hosea, Isaiah, Jeremiah, Ezekiel, down to Trito-Isaiah who proclaims the sending of envoys and tributes to foreign kings as a sin of the past (Isa. 57:9). This attitude, no doubt, reflects a certain lack of realism on the prophets' part: they demand the state to be administered not by politics but by faith. And even if the end of Israel and Judah seems to have justified the prophetic demand for

'splendid isolation', nevertheless it was the coalition headed by Achab which in 853 halted the Assyrian onslaught, thus giving Israel and Judah a respite of some hundred years.[20]

In this paper I have examined aspects of the role of prophecy in two cultures, second-millennium BCE Mari and first-millennium BCE Israel, in the belief that such a comparison can lead us towards a better understanding of the phenomenon of prophecy in both these particular contexts and in general.

20. A. Rofé, *Introduction to the Prophetic Literature* (Hebrew; Jerusalem: Academon, 1992), p. 70 (this is an 'Authorized Version', done by the author himself, whom I would like to thank for this translation).

RELIGION AND STATE IN ANCIENT ISRAEL

Ze'ev W. Falk

The Time of the First Temple

In ancient Israel there was no clear separation between religion, morals, law and politics; all were parts of one comprehensive system of norms. The question whether the notion of separation between state and religion existed during the First Temple period is actually an anachronism, since the terms were still unknown and undifferentiated.

Nevertheless, our own differentiations can help us in the understanding of ancient phenomena, events and statements, perhaps beyond the understanding of the ancient speakers themselves. According to the definition of Huizinga, history is the 'report of a culture about its past'. It is therefore part of the present, showing how the present has become what it is. In this sense, we may ask ourselves whether the present differentiation of religion and state has its antecedents in ancient Israel.

The kings of Israel, like those of other nations, made use of religious concepts, just as they built temples, to legitimize their rule, as well as to care for the spiritual needs of their subjects. Although religion usually existed independently of the king, by building the sanctuary and maintaining it he got a say in its ritual and appointed its priests. This was a factor in the lack of differentiation and the integration of state and religion.[1]

However, while the pharaoh of Egypt was himself seen as the deity, the king of Israel could at best be considered to be a viceroy of God

1. Cf. J. Pedersen, *Israel: Its Life and Culture* (Oxford: Oxford University Press, 2nd edn, 1964), pp. iii-iv, 238; A. Bentzen, 'The Cultic Use of the Story of the Ark in Samuel', *JBL* 67 (1948), p. 37-53; G.W. Ahlström, *Royal Administration and National Religion in Ancient Palestine* (Leiden: Brill, 1982).

or his anointed representative.[2] God was the true ruler of Israel and no human being could, originally, be recognized beside him.[3] True, in court etiquette and in poetic language the king of Israel was sometimes called 'Son of God',[4] but matters of the king and those of God were clearly distinguished.[5]

Moreover, a separation of state and religion is implied by the existence of a hereditary priesthood and a charismatic prophecy next to, and sometimes in opposition to, the king of Israel.[6] Accordingly, beside the authority of Moses existed that of Aaron, beside that of Joshua that of Elazar and beside that of Barak ben 'Avinoam that of Deborah. Gideon's refusal to accept the crown of Israel was based on the concept of God being the true king of the people,[7] which is a rejection of the secular state altogether.

A similar attitude is reflected in the description of Samuel's opposition to Saul.[8] The text accuses the king of having failed to inflict the divine punishment on Amalek,[9] of having taken priestly office without the authorization of the prophet[10] and of participation in foreign cults.[11] The common element in all these accusations is the supremacy of religion over the head of state. This was the ideological basis for a differentiation between 'divine matters' and 'matters of the king', which sometimes led to clashes between them.

2. Ps. 2.7; 45.7; 89.27; 1 Chron. 28.5; 29.23; 2 Chron. 9.8; but cf. 1 Sam. 8.7.

3. Judg. 8.23; 1 Sam. 8.8; Deut. 17.18-19.

4. 2 Sam. 7.14; Ps. 2.7; 89.27.

5. A.R. Johnson, 'Hebrew Conceptions of Kingship', in S.H. Hooke (ed.), *Myth, Ritual and Kingship* (Oxford: Clarendon Press, 1958), p. 204-35; R. deVaux, *The Bible and the Ancient Near East* (London: Darton, Longman & Todd, 1971), p. 152; M. Weinfeld, *Deuteronomy and the Deuteronomistic School* (Oxford: Oxford University Press, 1972), p. 80; J.A. Wilson, *Authority and Law in the Ancient Orient* (JAOSSup, 17; Baltimore: Johns Hopkins University Press, 1954), p. 98.

6. Cf. S. Ettinger, 'Kawim letoledot hametach ben kehunah umekukhah bahistoriah hayehudit', in S. Gaffni and S. Motzkin (eds.), *Kehunah umelukhah: Yachasey dat umedinah beyisrael uva'amim* (Jerusalem: Shazar Centre, 1987), pp. 9-20.

7. Judg. 8.23; cf. M. Buber, *Königtum Gottes* (Berlin: Schocken Books, 1932).

8. 1 Sam. 8.7-22; 10.17-19.

9. 1 Sam. 15.10-35.

10. 1 Sam. 13.9-14.

11. 1 Sam. 28.3-25.

However, in the ideal situation—perhaps best exemplified by David's rule—the king played both the religious and political role and derived his legitimacy from prophecy.[12] He sometimes participated in priestly cult[13] and used the members of the priestly class for both divine and royal affairs.[14] They were listed among the civil service.[15]

Throughout the building of the Temple King Solomon expressed the legitimacy of his monarchy and the special character of this holy place.[16] However, this system of state religion did not prevent him from showing tolerance towards foreign religions imported through his political marriages.[17]

Perhaps as a result of this new emphasis on religion the king stopped acting as priest, leaving this office to professionals. Another reason could have been the insight that the killing of human beings by and on behalf of the king no longer permitted him to function as the priest.[18]

In the Northern Kingdom the legitimacy of the king was derived from a direct divine or prophetical intervention,[19] which called for a greater integration of religion and state than that in Judaea. If the status of the king was guaranteed by succession from his father, although ultimately based on the covenant with the House of David, there could be greater independence of the political from the religious power.

Jeroboam's policy may be described as a form of state religion. He declared the sanctuaries of Dan and Bethel royal places of worship, acted himself as priest, appointed a new family to priesthood and intercalated the year to differentiate between the festivals in the

12. 1 Sam. 16.1-13; 2 Sam. 7.4-17.

13. 2 Sam. 6.12-23; 8.18; Ps. 110.4. Cf. G. Widengren, *Sakrales Königtum im AT und im Judentum* (F. Delitzsch Lecture, 1952; Stuttgart: Kohlhammer, 1955); A.R. Johnson, *Sacral Kingship in Ancient Israel* (Cardiff: University of Wales, 1955); R. deVaux, *Ancient Israel* (New York: McGraw–Hill, 1965), pp. 111-14; S. Herrmann, *A History of Israel in OT Times* (London: SCM Press, 2nd edn, 1981), p. 161.

14. 1 Chron. 26.30.

15. 2 Sam. 8.17; 20.25; 1 Chron. 18.16.

16. 2 Kgs. 11.17.

17. 1 Kgs. 11.5-10.

18. Cf. Exod. 20.22; 1 Chron. 22.8.

19. Cf. A. Alt, *Kleine Schriften zur Geschichte des Volkes Israel*, II (3 vols.; Munich: Beck, 1954), pp. 116-34.

Northern Kingdom and those celebrated in Judaea. His successors
Omri and Ahab promoted Canaanite religion, to integrate the non-
Israelite elements of their population and to foster diplomatic relations
with their neighbours.[20] But instead of true tolerance, the Northern
Kingdom under their rule oppressed the religion of Judaea and its
prophets. Amos was not allowed to preach in the sanctuary of Bethel
because it was a Royal Temple,[21] and it remained such an institution
even after the destruction of Israel by Assyria.[22]

The integration of religion and state can be traced in the Southern
Kingdom. King Joshaphat of Judaea was said to have created a
Supreme Court of Justice under the presidency of the priest, for the
adjudication of 'divine matters' and under the presidency of the
'Nagid of the House of Judaea' for the adjudication of 'royal
matters'.[23] King Joash of Judaea was introduced into his office both by
a covenant with God and a covenant with the people,[24] which may
express his authority by religion as well as by the state.

On the other hand a tendency of separation can also be noted. King
Uziah of Judaea was criticized by the writer of the book of Kings for
religious tolerance granted to the local sanctuaries competing with the
Temple of Jerusalem, while the book of Chronicles criticized his
attempt to assume a priestly office beside his kingship.[25]

But the integration of religion and state persisted. King Zedekiah is
said to have united the political with the religious authority. The priest
is appointed by him as a kind of royal officer for the administration of
the Temple.[26] Likewise, after the Babylonian exile Nehemiah appointed
the Levites as guards at the gates of Jerusalem on the Sabbath,[27] but
this was done according to the Persian king's authorization, which
referred to 'the divine laws' together with 'the royal laws'.[28]

In conclusion, we may ask whether the failure of the prophets to
prevent the spreading of foreign religions in Judaea and Israel was not

20. 1 Kgs 16.31; 2 Kgs 3.2.
21. Amos 7.13.
22. 2 Kgs 17.26.
23. 2 Chron. 17.7-9.
24. 2 Kgs 11.17.
25. 2 Kgs 15.4-5; 2 Chron. 26.16-23.
26. Jer. 20.1; 29.26.
27. Neh. 13.22.
28. Ezek. 7.26.

the result of the integration of religion and state. Perhaps a clear-cut separation between the two would have given the religion of the God of Israel a better chance.

The Hasmonean Times

The Hasmonean Revolt was a fight for religious freedom and for the right to be different from majority culture. It was basically a fight for the separation of Jewish religion from the Hellenist state. Since the official High Priest had been appointed by the Hellenist regime, the Hasmoneans seized the office and declared their religious independence. The religious self-government was then extended to political self-government, and the Hasmonean rulers themselves were accused by the Pharisees of religious oppression.

On the 18th of Elul 141 BCE Simon, the brother of Juda Maccabee, convened an assembly of the priests and elders to be appointed as president, 'Sar-Am-El', and High Priest for life, until the assent of 'a true prophet'.[29] This assembly was what the rabbis later called 'the Court of 71' or 'the Great Synedrion', and the rule was established that 'a King or a High Priest can be appointed only by a Court of 71'.[30] This forum was composed of priests, Levites and Israelites and represented the rabbinic as well as the civil leaders.

His son, Jochanan Hyrcanos, also combined the religious with the political office. By means of a professional army he was engaged in much warfare, and the rabbis declared that 'an optional war can be made only with the consent of the Court of 71'.[31] Because of the integration of religion and state, the Edomites were forced to convert to Judaism, against the opinion of the rabbis.[32] The rabbis demanded his resignation from the priesthood, which would have meant separation of religion and state.[33] The Sadducees, on the other hand, knowing the king was on their side, supported the integration of the religious and political establishments. This system continued under his son Juda Aristobul, who also proselytized the enemy population by force.[34]

---

29. 1 Macc. 14.27.
30. 1 Kgs 8.12-21.
31. *m. Sanh.* 1.5.
32. Josephus, *Ant.* 13.9.1.
33. *b. Qid.* 66a; Josephus, *Ant.* 13.10.5-6; *War* 1.2.8.
34. Josephus, *Ant.* 13.11.1, 3.

Rabbinic criticism of this union of priesthood and kingship was expressed by an annual recital in the Temple on the Day of Atonement of Jacob's blessing: 'The scepter shall not depart from Judah'.[35] Rabbinic jurisprudence noted the discrepancy between its expectations and the political reality. It was said that the king was not permitted to function as a judge and could not be sued in a rabbinic court.[36] This formulation dates either from the time of Alexander Jannaeus or from that of Herod (first century BCE). On the other hand, the rabbis were realists and recognized the royal right of punishing insurgents,[37] of expropriation for the king's highway[38] and other measures of government violating rabbinic law.[39]

The ultimate conflict between the rabbis and the king occurred under the rule of Alexander Jannaeus. His ritual legitimacy to act as High Priest was denied and he was publicly asked to resign.[40] Under the rule of his widow Salome Alexandra the office of High Priest was separated from that of the king and the Pharisaic rites were respected in the Temple. However, the fight between religious and political authorities went on, so that in 90 BCE a group of Pharisees petitioned the Syrian king Demetrius III to rule over the Jewish people rather than let a Jewish secular king rule over them.[41] A similar petition was presented to Pompeius in 63 BCE,[42] and to Augustus in 4 BCE.[43]

Both the Pharisees and the Essenes near the Dead Sea constructed religious worlds of their own, disregarding the political reality. This was the ideological basis of separation, at least as long as the circumstances did not permit the total change of the Jewish state under the rule of religion.[44]

35. Gen. 49.10; Naḥmanides *ad loc.*; b. *Yom.* 53b; y. *Šeq.* 6.1; b. *Qid.* 66a.
36. m. *Sanh.* 2.2.
37. b. *Sanh.* 49a.
38. m. *Sanh.* 2.4.
39. Cf. R. Tsevi Hirsch Chajos, 'Din melekh israel', in *Collected Works of R. Tsevi Hirsch Chajos*, I (Jerusalem, 1958), pp. 43-49; S. Federbusch, *Mishpat hamelukhah be-israel* (Jerusalem: Rav Kook Institute, 1952).
40. Josephus, *Ant.* 13.13.5; *War* 1.4.4; m. *Suk.* 4.6; t. *Suk.* 3.16.
41. Josephus, *Ant.* 14.1.
42. Josephus, *Ant.* 14.3.2.
43. Josephus, *Ant.* 17.11.2; *War* 2.6.1.
44. Cf. G. Weiter, *Jewish Theocracy* (Leiden: Brill, 1988); Gaffni and Motzkin, *Kehunah umelukhah*.

THE BIBLICAL TRADITION IN THE PERSPECTIVE OF POLITICAL THEOLOGY AND POLITICAL ETHICS

Christofer Frey

1. *The Problem*

Everyone interested in the biblical Scriptures tends to read his or her own private Bible. Charismatic Christians prefer biblical texts with a communitarian emphasis characterizing the congregation as the body of Christ; believing Ecologists prefer Psalm 104—usually without the final exhortation that sinners should be extinguished from the earth (Ps. 104.35). These are but two examples. This selective reading of the Bible discloses a kind of a hidden analogy to the idea of the saints who, according to Max Weber, give concrete form to the abstract monotheistic God in the view of—for example—knights (St George), carpenters (St Joseph), and so on.[1] Is this variety of religious interest and concentration in the reading of the Scriptures necessary, or does it deserve a well-founded theological critique? The following considerations in the form of a simple, clearly focused essay aim to investigate this particular problem in an even more specific form, by examining the use of biblical passages or biblical metaphors for political interests, especially for legitimation of values and positions. Christian tradition has developed a certain type of political theology ever since Christianity became a state religion, starting with Varro, Eusebius and Augustine, but critical scepticism about the political use of Scriptures has been demonstrated as well.[2]

---

1. See M. Weber, *Wirtschaft und Gesellschaft* (ed. J. Winckelmann; Berlin: Kiepenheuer&Witsch, 1964), pp. 317-488, esp.pp. 368-488.Compare G. Künzlen, *Die Religionssoziologie Max Webers* (Sozialwissenschaftliche Abhandlungen der Görres-Gesellschaft, 6; Berlin: Duncker & Humblot, 1980).

2. See for example P. Koslowski, 'Politischer Monotheismus oder Trinitätslehre?', *TP* 56 (1981), pp. 70-91; R. Maurer, 'Thesen zur politischen Theologie', *ZTK* 79 (1982), pp. 349-73.

2. *Political Ethics or Political Theology?*

In the 1970s the discussion of 'political theology' was re-established, especially on the German academic scene.[3] But it should be compared with 'political ethics', an academic trend which developed in the same period.[4] *Political ethics* is a more general notion defining a particular area of ethics, whereas *political theology* is the name for certain widely differing agendas which could be subsumed to ethics as well as to ideology (the latter being a system of ideas intended to legitimate particular interests, not to reveal the truth of a hitherto often hidden reality).

The distinction between political ethics and political theology has been particularly emphasized by a German liberal Protestant, the theologian Trutz Rendtorff.[5] In criticizing a certain type of political theology he evaluates political ethics as the only adequate conception for the modern world. He distinguishes Christianity and church; the latter defines a particular societal institution, whereas the former refers to a social way of life, which emancipated itself from church as well as from church-related institutions and transformed itself into the secular morality of certain (especially European) modern societies of a liberal–democratic type.[6] The idea of a development of liberty is used to present Christianity as the progress towards its own ethical stage and towards an era of universal historical fulfilment.[7] Churches—as institutional bodies—can no longer claim a theocratic legitimation in order to dominate the legislation and the moral code of a given society.

What is the impact of the Bible on this historical theory of political

---

3. See H. Peukert (ed.), *Diskussion zur 'politischen Theologie'* (Mainz: Matthias Grünewald; Munich: Chr. Kaiser Verlag, 1969).

4. T. Rendtorff, 'Politische Ethik oder "politische Theologie"?', in Peukert (ed.), *Diskussion*, pp. 217-30.

5. T. Rendtorff, *Christentum zwischen Revolution und Restauration: Politische Wirkungen neuzeitlicher Theologie* (Munich: Chr. Kaiser Verlag, 1970).

6. T. Rendtorff, 'Kirche und Gesellschaft im Kontext neuzeitlichen Christentums', in H.D. Wendland (ed.), *Sozialethik im Umbruch der Gesellschaft* (Göttingen: Vandenhoeck & Ruprecht, 1969), pp. 77-89.

7. Cf. the idea of Ernst Troeltsch not of an absolute Christian truth, but of a culmination of Christian history and the development of culture in Europe: see *Der Historismus und seine Überwindung* (Berlin: Pan Verlag Paul Heise, 1924).

ethics? Generally speaking the Bible is regarded as a document of
individual piety, which can be studied without institutionalized guide-
lines, and can fulfil its function as a source of personal inspiration.[8]
Various eclectic *political* ideas, rather than biblical passages, shape the
framework of this theory. The prevailing idea of present liberty,
however, could reflect the freedom of the law as lived by Jesus and
the freedom of the children of God who are adopted by their heavenly
father. The justification stated by Paul, the ancient rabbi, and the
rediscovery by Luther of the freedom of a Christian finally resulted in
the freedom of modern democratic societies.[9] Biblical ideas may be
alluded to, but biblical phrases are very rarely quoted; references to
the Bible are rather selective. And this is no coincidence.

But what is political theology in the view of Rendtorff? It has two
aspects: (1) the general political consequences of the idea of an all-
embracing God, and (2) the political legitimation, even the theoretical
self-defence, of a religious body as an institution inside a given
society. The second aspect, that of an institution-related political
theology, relies on an ontology of the political system as expressed in
holy orders and symbolized in religiously legitimized leaders (for
instance emperors or kings), all this being in contrast to modern and
democratic societies, which rely on a constitution and its enlightened
humanistic intentions.

The distinction between political theology and political ethics, as
presented by Rendtorff, is intended to defend his own view of history:
Rendtorff does not challenge the process of a Christian tradition starting from the Bible and transforming itself into modernity, nor does
he do justice to the recent discussions of political theology.[10]

3. *Political Theology: Some Approaches to a Variable Phenomenon*

The discussion of the manifold phenomenon of political theology could
point back to a Jewish heresy as well as to extremely problematic
vestiges of anti-Semitism.

---

8.   T. Rendtorff, 'Christentum ohne Kirche?', *Concilium* 7 (1971), pp. 406-
12.
9.   This idea was originally propagated by F. Gogarten, *Verhängnis und
Hoffnung der Neuzeit* (Stuttgart: Friedrich Vorwerk, 1958).
10.   T. Rendtorff, *Theorie des Christentums: Historisch-theologische Studien zu
seiner neuzeitlichen Verfassung* (Gütersloh: Gerd Mohn, 1972), esp. pp. 182-87.

Criticism of Israel's Theocracy

Not 'political theology' but the reverse attribution, 'theologico-politicus', describes the famous *Tractatus* by Baruch de Spinoza, the seventeenth-century philosopher expelled from the Portuguese Synagogue of Amsterdam.[11] Spinoza developed his critical thought exactly in the sense which was later explained as political theology, for he discussed and even challenged the legitimacy of the political authority to interfere in spiritual matters. Spinoza worked intensively to separate theology and philosophy.[12] To him it was evident that philosophy should provide political counsel and advocate particularly the freedom of opinion. But what was the end of a theology relying on the Scriptures? The true essence of God was to be attained by reason, and true happiness could be achieved by rational reflection much better than by faith.[13] Consequently Spinoza attacked the traditional exegesis of the Bible, which because of its origin and in its metaphorical character was adapted to the understanding of an uneducated people.[14] Spinoza, however, wanted to reconstruct the historical development of biblical texts; so he became one of the initiators of historical criticism (along with Hobbes, to whom he seems to owe many of his arguments).[15] He regarded the hidden truth of the Bible as rational: it can be discovered in the form of morality, in the light of natural reason. Did Spinoza defend political ethics or political theology? He developed a natural (but metaphysical) theology, thoroughly pantheistic, and in so doing he elaborated the foundation of freedom.[16]

What are his main points from the perspective of the Bible? The philosopher defined the ancient state of the Hebrews as a theocracy.[17] In their earliest period, the Hebrew people contracted directly with

---

11. B. de Spinoza, *Theologisch-politischer Traktat* (Philosophische Bibliothek, 93; Hamburg: Felix Meiner, 5th edn, 1955).

12. Spinoza, *Theologisch-politischer Traktat*, pp. 320ff.

13. B. de Spinoza, *Tractatus de intellectus emendatione/Ethica ordine geometrica demonstrata*, IV (ed. C. Gebhardt; Heidelberg: Carl Winter, 1926), pp. 31-34.

14. Spinoza, *Tractatus*, pp. 34, 55.

15. See R. Specht, *Baruch Spinoza* (Klassiker der Philosophie, 1; Munich: Beck, 1981), pp. 338-59.

16. Spinoza, *Theologisch-politischer Traktat*, pp. 252ff.

17. Spinoza, *Theologisch-politischer Traktat*, pp. 295ff.

God; God was the only governor, and religion and civil law were identical. All religious dogmas were in themselves legal pronouncements. Spinoza even speculated about the end of this particular form of Israelite theocracy; after the incident of worshipping the golden calf the order of Levites was institutionalized; their presence in Hebrew society interrupted the immediacy towards God.[18]

According to Spinoza modern states should not imitate ancient theocracy. None of the servants of a revealed religion could claim any right to interfere with affairs and agencies of the state.[19] But the original immediacy towards God is somehow recapitulated by the rational faith in a God, governing the social and political laws as well as the order of nature. Every human government must conform to the basic rational laws, while the individual is required to renounce his or her elementary rights of self-defence (a Hobbesian idea).[20] The older systems of political theology presuppose that politics requires theology, first of all revealed divine knowledge, then immediately perceived rational theology. But recent political theology, which is in some respects a parallel to Roman Catholic liberation theology, insists that theology cannot abstain from politics. Why?

To answer this question we may remember another heretical Jew, Ernst Bloch. He investigated the natural law tradition (which was also a theme of Spinoza) and emphasized its utopian perspective:[21] not human nature as an a priori, but humanity as a perspective of hope as the end of an all-inclusive exodus discloses the true aspirations of suppressed people. In his book *Atheism in Christianity*[22] (but curiously not *in Judaism!*) Bloch interprets the Hebrew and the Greek Bible in terms of an emancipating exodus which leads away from God and from the social and political estrangement of people. Job is regarded as an exponent of this type of rebellion; and therefore the question of theodicy is a cause of active anthropodicy.[23]

The Blochian approach had an impact on J.B. Metz, a left-wing

18. Spinoza, *Theologisch-politischer Traktat*, pp. 319ff.

19. Spinoza, *Theologisch-politischer Traktat*, pp. 350ff.

20. Spinoza, *Theologisch-politischer Traktat*, pp. 273ff.

21. E. Bloch, *Naturrecht und menschliche Würde* (Frankfurt am Main: Suhrkamp, 1961).

22. E. Bloch, *Atheismus im Christentum: Zur Religion des Exodus und des Reichs* (Frankfurt am Main: Suhrkamp, 1968).

23. Bloch, *Atheismus im Christentum*, pp. 148-66.

Catholic intensely interested in the problems of Latin America.[24]
Taking up the cause of the poor, he challenges institutionalized theology and recommends a new reading of the Bible. 'Memory of suffering' is his programmatic formula.[25] His diagnosis tries to uncover the
central problem of domination—domination over nature by modern
technical structures, domination by human beings over human beings.
All domination embarrasses, indeed obstructs the possible development of integrated life. Cross and resurrection are necessary as criteria of a truly political belief: the history of suffering remembered
and the eschatological fulfilment expected incite a practice, which
demands a knowledge and a critical perception first of the existing
reality, then of a possible better future.[26] Metz pronounces his protest
against a bourgeois (that is, Catholic) type of religion, which strait-
jackets belief in privacy and isolates the believer in his or her individual existence. Therefore he is attracted by Latin American grass-
roots Catholicism. While Metz centres his political theology around
the suffering and resurrection of Christ, Latin American liberation
theology often concentrates on the exodus tradition.[27] In contrast to
the kind criticized by Spinoza a new type of political theology is
presented and combined with a new and different interpretation of
biblical tradition. Spinoza interpreted the Scriptures in the sense of
historical criticism, resulting in the thesis that ancient Hebrew theocracy failed; he decided to replace the revelation of God to the
Hebrews by rational evidence of a universal God of providence,
governing nature as well as politics. The nature and essence of this
God is the major theme of this political theology. But the new programme of political theology presupposes that historical criticism is
exhausted; it proclaims the narrative reading of the Bible, which
offers a political mythology and serves as an instigation to social

24. J.B. Metz, *Glaube in Geschichte und Gesellschaft* (Mainz: Matthias
Grünewald, 1977).
25. J.B. Metz, 'Erinnerung des Leidens als Kritik eines teleologisch-technolo-
gischen Zukunftsbegriffs', *EvT* 32 (1972), pp. 338-52.
26. Metz, *Glaube*, pp. 5ff., 53ff., 79ff., 108ff.
27. See R. Frieling, *Befreiungstheologien: Studien zur Theologie in
Lateinamerika* (Bensheimer Hefte, 63; Göttingen: Vandenhoeck & Ruprecht, 2nd
edn, 1986); R.S. Chopp, 'Latin American Liberation Theology', in D.F. Ford
(ed.), *The Modern Theologians: An Introduction to Christian Theology in the
Twentieth Century*, II (Oxford: Basil Blackwell, 1989), pp. 173-92.

justice, an interpretation concentrated on the Old Testament. Often the immediate use of the Bible for the ends of politics in Christianity is accompanied by a shift of interest from the New to the Old Testament: social criticism recalls Amos, and—unfortunately—the preaching in Germany at the beginning of World War I called back into hostile minds the acclamations of God's justice as found in the Psalms.[28]

The Perversion of Political Theology
Everyone reads his or her own Bible; so the Scriptures can be misused for the legitimation and motivation of particular interests. Does politics need a theological (and even biblical) component? The philosopher of the Enlightenment could deny this. But a post-Enlightenment tradition of political theology could assert the need for this kind of legitimation. It is the consequence of modern nihilism. The rational evidence for a God and his orders failed; therefore politics needs a new mythology.

Spinoza's *Tractatus* was apparently influenced by Hobbes (*De Cive*[29]), whom Graf Reventlow considers heir to an Anglican humanism characterized by a strong rational tendency.[30] But while Spinoza advocates the rational evidence of the highest and all-embracing divine truth, Hobbes—at almost the same time—favours relativism: one religion is competing with another, and only authority can solve the problem of founding the law (*auctoritas, non veritas facit legem*).[31] Hobbes's political system is not built upon reason, but upon the ultimate political decisions. According to him human beings are moved by *interests* which must be co-ordinated by the political authority; reason is defined either as the capacity of rules or as the individual decision to follow them. Individual behaviour cannot be aggregated or synthesized into a social system by a theory, but only by decision and authority.

28. G. Brakelmann, *Der deutsche Protestantismus im Epochenjahr 1917* (Witten: Luther-Verlag, 1974), p. 323.

29. T. Hobbes, *De Cive* (ed. H. Warrender; Oxford: Basil Blackwell, 1983), ch. 16ff.

30. H. Graf Reventlow, *The Authority of the Bible and the Rise of the Modern World* (London: SCM Press, 1984), pp. 194-222.

31. T. Hobbes, *Leviathan* (ed. C.B. Macpherson; Harmondsworth: Penguin, 1968), ch. 26 (resp.: *Opera Latina*, III [ed. W. Molesworth; London: J. Bohn, 1841], p. 202).

A twentieth-century doctrine revives the Hobbesian assumption of the necessity of authority and claims a political theology which legitimates the secularized state by an underivable authority. This doctrine was defended by Carl Schmitt, a legal scholar dangerously inclined towards Nazism.[32] Schmitt proposed the following ideas as elements of his theory:

1. As there is no evident natural or rational foundation, every law is based on decisions of a sovereign.
2. Although the state in the twentieth century is secular, there remains a striking analogy between the essence of God and the constitution of the state.[33]
3. All exercise of power is legitimate by itself, because it contains a fundamental decision, be it theocratic, liberal, revolutionary, or anti-revolutionary (the latter being to Schmitt the main source of inspiration). In this Schmitt inherits an anti-revolutionary thesis of the nineteenth century.[34]
4. Liberalism, however, degenerates into technocracy and economic manipulation without dignity and authority, whereas theocratic ideas must be converted into a secular theology of political power.[35]
5. The Hobbesian state of nature can only be overcome *inside* a strong society, which defines itself by maintaining a specific *external* relation, by the difference between friend and enemy.[36]

32. C. Schmitt, *Politische Theologie: Vier Kapitel zur Lehre von der Souveränität* (Berlin: Duncker & Humblot, 1970); *idem, Der Leviathan in der Staatslehre des Thomas Hobbes: Sinn und Fehlschlag eines politischen Symbols* (Cologne–Lövenich: Hohenheim-Verlag, 2nd edn, 1982). Cf. K.-M. Kodalle, *Politik als Macht und Mythos: Carl Schmitts 'Politische Theologie'* (Stuttgart: Kohlhammer, 1973).

33. Schmitt, *Politische Theologie*, p. 49.

34. C. Schmitt, *Donoso Cortes in gesamteuropäischer Interpretation: Vier Aufsätze* (Cologne: Greven, 1950).

35. C. Schmitt, *Politische Theologie II: Die Legende von der Erledigung jeder Politischen Theologie* (Berlin: Duncker & Humblot, 1970).

36. C. Schmitt, *Der Begriff des Politischen: Text von 1932 mit einem Vorwort und drei Corollarien* (Berlin: Duncker & Humblot, 1963), p. 29. Schmitt interprets the term 'enemy' by the Latin *hostis* (not *inimicus*) and by the Greek πολέμιο (not ἐχθρός). For him it is not necessary to hate the political enemy.

6.   This existential political decision creates an order and a certain analogy between the powerful act of a deistic God and the authority in a modern state.

Schmitt's doctrine should be evaluated against the background of late antiquity:

1.   In a pagan *theologia politike* or *theologia civilis* a trans-mundane God or even a multitude of gods represented the ultimate legitimacy of emperors, kings and other political authorities.
2.   Early Christianity proclaimed the one transcendent God, who first of all challenged pagan gods and the authorities relying on them; but as an abstract entity this God could develop into the principle of legitimation of centralized power.[37]
3.   Augustine in his narrative, historically oriented account of the two states, the *civitas dei* of the redeemed and the *civitas diaboli* of the condemned, proved to be hostile to any theology of the empire and tried to transfigure all innerworldly power.[38]

Political theology as an attempt to enthrone politics as source and guarantee of sense is close to the negative aspect of stage 2. Schmitt conforms his theory to the position of an abstract monotheism, but secularizes it. Ancient Christian monotheism was expressed in trinitarian formulae, because it relied on the narrative tradition of the Bible and the deep conviction of God's self-revelation by events proceeding through history; but Schmitt, using monotheism as a vehicle for the explanation of power, is interested only in theological metaphors and in mythologies and not at all in the dynamics of social development. Thus, political theology created a possibility dangerous to many people, who felt threatened by nihilism.

37. Cf. E. Peterson, 'Der Monotheismus als politisches Problem', in *Theologische Traktate* (Munich: Kösel, 1951), pp. 45-147. See also A. Schindler (ed.), *Monotheismus als politisches Problem? Erik Peterson und die Kritik der politischen Theologie* (Gütersloh: Gerd Mohn, 1978).

38. Aurelius, *Augustinus: De Civitate Dei*, CSEL, XL.

4. *Reading or Exploiting the Bible*

Political theology is a variable arrangement of legitimating or delegitimating ideas concerning the sense and authority of a political order. Social and political structures may resemble particular views of the world, and this could deeply influence the understanding and interpretation of the Bible. By overemphasizing certain trends of ideas, differences and affinities appear:

1. Enlightened political theology tries to assure the authority of reason by a critical analysis or even dissection of biblical narratives.
2. The theology of liberation concentrates its use of the Bible on narrative Old Testament theopolitics.[39] It emphasizes God's action in history and especially messianic trends, the suffering of Christ and his overcoming of death as a proleptic event which is to be continued in an analogous history of his people.
3. Political ethics, not theology, tries to extract certain motives from the Bible and to extend them in certain topics, especially in liberal politics. The Bible is a source of personal certitude.
4. A secular type of political theology is centred on the question of authority and uses certain biblical metaphors as a means of legitimation.

A comparison of the third and fourth points demonstrates that political ethics and a secular political theology are somehow related; they are not opposed in the sense in which Rendtorff presented their bias. And a comparison of all four points raises a worrying issue: each position moves its adherents to rely on an eclectic tradition, either the history of freedom, especially relevant to individuals (see 3.), or the history of liberation as a common, social process (see 2.), or the authority of law and order strengthened by theological symbols (see 4.).

This raises anew the question as to how people read the Bible. The

39. A predecessor of this trend is P.L. Lehmann, *Ethics in a Christian Context* (New York: Harper & Row, 1963). Lehmann speaks of 'God's political activity in history'.

fundamental conviction of the Protestant Reformation was not the value of tradition itself, but the authority of the word of God preached and heard in continuity with biblical witnesses and in discontinuity with all misleading tradition. The word of God was held as the critical test of all attempts to legitimate one's particular view of faith and politics by a belief in an unbroken tradition.

God transcends all tradition, but can at the same time reveal himself by the word which is transported by tradition. But he will be experienced as a transcending personal force which renders all political powers relative. The famous passage of Rom. 13.1-7 should be interpreted in the following sense: God—the unique God revealed in Israel—annihilates all local gods, all divine or religious authorities assumed by local, provincial or central governments and administrations. God is the only God and degrades all other 'deities' to non-gods. He permits only a preliminary and continent authority.[40] The so-called doctrine of the two kingdoms of the Reformation emphasizes exactly this difference; it reveals an anti-theocratic tendency and undermines all kinds of authorities which tend to establish themselves as worldly guarantees of salvation.[41]

40. Cf. J. Blank, *Schriftauslegung in Theorie und Praxis* (Munich: Kösel, 1969), pp. 147-86.

41. The delegitimating force of the so-called 'doctrine of the two kingdoms' was elaborated especially by U. Duchrow, *Christenheit und Weltverantwortung* (Stuttgart: Klett, 1970), and E. Wolf, *Sozialethik* (Göttingen: Vandenhoeck & Ruprecht, 1975), pp. 267ff.

THE CONCEPT OF 'OTHER GODS' IN THE DEUTERONOMISTIC LITERATURE

Yair Hoffman

I

What was the concept of 'the other' in biblical Israel? The very question raises serious theoretical, historical and methodological doubts. Do all nations necessarily share a set of common concepts? Might a concept of 'the other' be one of them? Would a nation's concept of 'otherness' depend on the existence of a national self-image?[1] Did any such self-image exist in ancient Israel? Should this biblical period of more than 700 years be treated as a whole when such issues are concerned?

Another set of theoretical difficulties might be focused on the question: does a general, all-embracing, abstract image of 'otherness', unqualified in any specific aspect (for instance a certain nation, a specific culture or religion) exist in any society? Did it exist in ancient Israel? As to methodology, we might ask to what extent the Bible, or any elitist literature, adequately reflects popular or collective attitudes? Is there any methodological filter through which the biblical material could be sifted in order to separate the common, popular views from their image among the authors of the Bible? My personal interest in the biblical concept of 'the other' raises another set of theoretical problems: supposing, in spite of the above-mentioned questions, that such a concept did exist and is detectable, could it function as a mirror reflecting the self-image of the Israelite society ('tell me

---

1. The theory of the personal and collective image which is referred to in these words was suggested by K.E. Boulding, *The Image* (Ann Arbor, MI, 1956). His definition of an image of the individual is: 'what I believe to be true; my subjective knowledge. It is this image that largely governs my behavior' (*The Image*, p. 6). Accordingly the 'public image' is 'an image the essential characteristics of which are shared by the individuals participating in the group' (*The Image*, p. 64).

what you think of the other and I will tell you who you think you are')? And could such a self-image, such a *subjective* common knowledge of the Israelites, enlighten us as to the *objective* characteristics of ancient Israel and its neighbours?

Facing such a mass of theoretical hindrances one might well conclude that any investigation of the concept of 'the other' in biblical Israel should be postponed until satisfactory answers are provided to these questions. Nevertheless, this logical conclusion will not be adhered to in this paper, since its practicability stands in an inverse ratio to its theoretical correctness. First of all, theoretical speculations can hardly lead to any undisputed conclusion which will create a methodological common denominator for our discussion. Secondly, it is not for me, a biblical scholar, but for a sociologist to venture at reaching conclusions in the theoretical aspects of such matters. Therefore the abstract discussions have been put aside here, and, notwithstanding its flimsy theoretical base, the discussion will concentrate on the biblical investigation. However, another preliminary theoretical remark is still needed. Even if a *general* concept of 'otherness' did prevail in ancient Israel I doubt my ability to discern it. The investigation will therefore be limited to one part of the Bible in which a particular concept of the other may be seen: the Deuteronomistic (Dtr) image of alien deities. An attempt will also be made to examine whether an objective reality is discernible through the subjective concepts of Dtr; in other words, to see to what extent such an investigation of an 'image' can contribute to our understanding of the ancient Israelite religion.

II

The problems regarding the religion of Israel during the period of the First Temple can be focused (and thus, indeed, inevitably oversimplified) in one question: to what extent was it monotheistic? The range of scholarly opinions in this issue is too wide and the details too many to be even shortly summarized here. I will therefore mention briefly only two views which can delineate the extreme borders of the area in which the dispute in this issue is conducted: the views of Y. Kaufman and P. Lemche.

According to Kaufman[2] monotheism was inherent in the Israelite

2.   Y. Kaufman, *Toldot Ha'israelit* (4 vols.; Tel Aviv: Dvir, new edn, 1960

consciousness since the birth of the nation under the leadership of Moses. A non-monotheistic Israel never existed, and monotheism was always so deeply rooted in the nation's mentality that the Israelites never understood symbolic paganism (that is, the idea that idols simply represent the real gods) and mistook all idolatry as primitive fetishism.[3] Even Ezekiel and Second Isaiah did not understand the essence of paganism, and considered it fetishism.[4] Hence, Kaufman would say, condemnations and prohibitions of idolatry (for example in the commandment 'You shall not make for yourself any carved image', Exod. 20.4 = Deut. 5.8) actually refer only to cultic practices rather than being ideological polemics against polytheistic beliefs. Such a polemic was unnecessary. The chasm between monotheism and the Israelite image of paganism was so deep that syncretism could not have and never had existed in Israel, and the cult of Baal, adopted by a small minority of Israelites, was utterly separated from the cult of Yahweh.[5] Kaufman therefore claims that we should reject the idea, held by many scholars, that only with the exile did syncretism come to its end.[6] Among all the Israelite kings Menashe was the only real paganist, and 'he is indeed a riddle'.[7]

An utterly different picture is depicted by Lemche,[8] who by and large follows Wellhausen in his reconstruction of Israelite monotheism. He claims that the reign of David should be regarded as a '*terminus a quo* for the emergence of pan-Israelite ideology'.[9] Thus Yahwism as a common religion of the tribes of Israel could not possibly have emerged in any prior period. In fact, until the Deuteronomistic reform there was no distinction between Israelite and Canaanite religion, and Yahweh, originally 'a storm god and a war god',[10] was considered a national god just like Baal, parallel for example to Kemosh among the Moabites. He was not only identified

[1937–56]), I, pp. xxi-xliv; II, especially pp. 53-59, 111-38, 221-75; IV, pp. 9-54, 83-87.

   3.   *Toldot Ha'emunah Ha'israelit*, IV, pp. 76, 130.

   4.   *Toldot Ha'emunah Ha'israelit*, III, pp. 33, 84-86.

   5.   *Toldot Ha'emunah Ha'israelit*, II, pp. 221-25.

   6.   *Toldot Ha'emunah Ha'israelit*, VIII, p. 18.

   7.   *Toldot Ha'emunah Ha'israelit*, II, p. 234.

   8.   N.P. Lemche, *Ancient Israel: A New History of Israelite Society* (Biblical Seminar, 5; Sheffield: JSOT Press, 1988).

   9.   *Ancient Israel*, p. 108.

  10.   *Ancient Israel*, p. 255.

with Baal but also subordinated to El, the lord of gods.[11] Only later
did the prophets deny this identification, demanding that the Israelites
worship solely Yahweh.[12] Then the Deuteronomists and the reformed
prophets created the opposition between Yahwism and Canaanite religion,[13] which after the exile was developed into a monotheistic
belief.[14]

My purpose here is not to evaluate the evidences and the arguments
introduced by Kaufman and Lemche;[15] it is rather limited to an examination of the Deuteronomistic concept of alien deities, to see which
position, if either, it leads towards. The chronological setting of Dtr,
the first half of the sixth century, is a strategic junction in the history
of the religion of Israel, which makes such an examination worthy.

III

Some generalizing expressions are used in the Bible when foreign
deities are referred to. The most conspicuous are אל זר, אלהי נכר and
אלהים אחרים.

אלהי נכר is attested 13 times: in Dtr 5 times (Deut. 31.16; Josh. 24.20,
23; Judg. 10.16; 1 Sam. 7.3); in poetry twice (Deut. 32.12; Ps. 81.10);
in various other contexts 6 times (Gen. 35.2, 4; Jer. 5.19;[16] Dan. 11.39
[אלוה]; 2 Chron. 33.15; Mal. 2.11 [בת אל נכר]).[17] This distribution

11. *Ancient Israel*, p. 226.
12. *Ancient Israel*, pp. 246-47.
13. *Ancient Israel*, p. 249.
14. *Ancient Israel*, pp. 221-22.
15. Kaufman was not acquainted of course with the new data which probably
mention Yahweh and Ashera as a couple. See for example S.M. Olyan, *Ashera and
the Cult of Yahweh in Israel* (Atlanta: Scholars Press, 1988); B. Margalit, 'Some
Observations on the Inscription and Drawing from Khirbat el-Qom', *VT* 39 (1989),
pp. 371-75; *idem*, 'The Meaning and Significance of Asherah', *VT* 40 (1990),
pp. 264-97; W.H. Shea, 'The Khirbet el-Qom Tomb Inscription Again', *VT* 40
(1990), pp. 110-16. These data appear to count against Kaufman's theory, but
alone are not sufficient to nullify it.
16. Some scholars regard Jer. 5.18-19 as part of the Deuteronomistic editorial
layer of the book. See for instance W. Thiel, *Die deuteronomistische Redaktion von
Jeremiah 1–25* (Neukirchen–Vluyn: Neukirchener Verlag, 1973), pp. 97-99. See
also W. McKane, *Jeremiah*, I (ICC; Edinburgh: T. & T. Clark, 1986), pp. 126-27;
R.P. Carroll, *Jeremiah* (OTL; London: SCM Press, 1986), pp. 185-86.
17. In Jer. 8.18 we have בפסליהם בהבלי נכר when הבלי נכר is an apposition to
פסיליהם: their idols.

indicates that the phrase is not limited to one literary layer, and its 38 per cent dispersion in Dtr does not designate it as a typical Deuteronomistic phrase. This assertion will be appreciated later, when the expression אלהים אחרים is examined. The meaning of נכר in this expression and in the other constructions using נכר as an attribute is always the same: 'foreign'. Thus בן/בני נכר (18 occurrences): foreigner(s); אדמת נכר (Ps. 137.4): foreign land: מזבחות הנכר (2 Chron. 14.2): foreign altars. We must therefore conclude that the phrase אלהי נכר, although reflecting some idea of otherness, does not certify that these deities were considered an utterly different essence from the God of Israel. The same conclusion holds true in the case of the less common expression אל זר, which occurs only in a few poetical contexts: Ps. 44.21; 81.10 and also Deut. 32.16 (זרים, 'foreigners', meaning אלהים זרים, 'foreign deities').

Is this the case also with אלהים אחרים, 'other gods', apparently the most relevant phrase to this study, since it gathers all foreign deities under the umbrella of 'otherness'? It seems to testify that at least among those who used the phrase a certain concept of otherness relating to the deity prevailed; yet a clarification of the exact concept it conveys is still needed. First of all, attention should be paid to the dispersion of the phrase. אחרים as an attribute occurs 72 times in the Bible, referring to deities (אלהים) 62 times, garments (בגדים) 4 times, days (ימים) 3 times, and messengers (מלאכים), articles (כלים) and sons (בנים) once. Thus אלהים אחרים is certainly an idiomatic phrase, and its distribution proves it to be a Deuteronomistic one: it occurs 59 times (95 per cent) in Dtr[18] and only 4 times in non-Deuteronomistic texts: Hos. 3.1; Exod. 20.3, 23.13; 2 Chron. 28.25 (with no parallel in 2 Kgs).[19] What, then, did the Deuteronomist have in mind while

18. Deut.: 18; Josh.: 3; Judg.: 4; Sam.: 2; Kgs: 11; Jer.: 18; 2 Chron.: 3 (parallels of 2 Kgs). All the Jeremianic occurrences are in the prose sections of the book, either in long sermons (for example 7.6, 9, 18; 44.3, 5, 8, 15) or in shorter redactional extensions (for example 13.10; 19.4; 22.9). Both are widely recognized by scholars as Deuteronomistic. In addition to the references given above see: S. Mowinckel, *Zur Komposition des Buches Jeremia* (Kristiana: Jacob Dybwad, 1914), pp. 31-45; L. Stulman, *The Prose Sermons of the Book of Jeremiah* (Atlanta: Scholars Press, 1986), pp. 1-48.

19. The possibility that אלהים אחרים in Exod. 20.3; 23.13 is a later (Deuteronomistic) redaction is raised by some scholars, for instance M. Noth, *Exodus* (OTL; London: SCM Press, 1962), pp. 162, 190. See also Y. Hoffman, *The Doctrine of the Exodus in the Bible* (Tel Aviv: University of Tel Aviv Press,

moulding this idiom, whose very frequent usage indicates that it gained the lexical status of a common term?

BDB, under the entry אחר, writes: 'adj.: another...Often with the collateral sense of different...[or] that of strange, alien...especially in the phrase אלהים אחרים, other gods...particularly in Dt....& Deut. writers...'. This explanation, however, does not clarify whether the 'otherness' expressed by אלהים אחרים reflects the idea of an essential, absolute distinction between the real God of Israel and some non-existent deities worshipped by other nations; perhaps it reveals no more than a different point of view, just as in אל נכר; אלהי זר: they are *other* gods since they are not *ours*. A survey of אחרים shows that when attached to garments, days, messengers and articles it undoubtedly and clearly has a relative meaning: something different, yet of the very same kind. There is no reason to assume that in the phrase אלהים אחרים the attribute has a more distinctive meaning. Indeed, one might point to the well-known feature of the Hebrew Bible—the absence of sophisticated philosophical terminology—and claim that this eliminates a priori the possibility of finding sharp linguistic distinctions between absolute and relative.

However, such an argument loses its validity at least in verses in which אלהים אחרים is qualified by clauses such as אשר לא ידעת/ם אתה ואבותיך/כם ('which neither you nor your parents knew').[20] Such a clause indicates that when the Deuteronomist felt that the vagueness of אלהים אחרים prevented him from achieving more accuracy, he found a way of making the phrase less equivocal. What clarification, then, was aimed at by using this clause? Most commentators interpret אשר לא ידעת 'of which ye have had no experience',[21] a qualification which does not insist at all on the exclusiveness of Yahweh. It rather condemns the stupidity of breaching relations with God, whose grace and ability to save Israel have been proven, and turning to other

1983), pp. 116-21. For another possibility see below, note 22.

20. See Deut. 11.28; 13.3, 7; 28.64; 29.25; Jer. 7.9; 19.4; 44.3.

21. Driver's translation of Deut. 11.28. See S.R. Driver, *Deuteronomy* (ICC; Edinburgh: T. & T. Clark, 3rd edn, 1902), p. 132. Similarly D.Z. Hoffmann, *Deuteronomium I* (Hebrew; Tel Aviv: Nezach, 1960), p. 146; A.B. Ehrlich, *Mikra ki-Pheschuto*, I (Hebrew; Berlin: Poppelauer, 1899), p. 328. See also S.R. Luzzatto, *Commentary to the Pentateuch* (Tel Aviv: Dvir, 1965 [1871]), p. 526: 'you have not experienced their divine power, note that they are new, that you have never heard their names'.

deities, whose clemency and competence have not been tested. Apparently this argumentation might lead to either of two alternative conclusions: (1) the author accepted the existence of other deities and did not doubt their capacity to help their own peoples; (2) he denied the existence of any deity except Yahweh, but knowing that such a total nonexistence is unprovable and therefore unconvincing to the polytheistic mentality he chose a more practical form of argumentation. In either case it is clear that the audience for whom these words were intended did not deny the existence of other gods. Of the two alternatives the second is more doubtful. It is hardly plausible that the Deuteronomist would have made theological concessions (that is, not insisting unequivocally on the exclusiveness of Yahweh) on such a crucial issue for mere pragmatic reasons (the rejection of a foreign cult). My conclusion is, therefore, that the qualifying clause אשר לא ידעת verifies that by the phrase אלהים אחרים Dtr did not intend a conclusive denial of deities other than Yahweh.

If this is the case, what necessitated the creation of a new phrase adding nothing new to the already existent ones? A legitimate response here might be to reject the question, since no language is developed according to 'efficiency programmes', and therefore expressions sometimes emerge in spite of their apparent lexical superfluity. Nevertheless, in our case another answer is credible. I suggest that the creation of the expression אלהים אחרים reflects Dtr's vague feeling that a term was needed which could express the dichotomy, though not the absolute contradistinction, between Yahweh and all other gods. The Deuteronomist was not satisfied with the already existing relative phrases (אל זר; אל נכר) because they did not convey the sense of a sharp enough dichotomy.[22] The creation of a term was vital for the Deuteronomist who wanted to contrast other deities with Yahweh not on the level of existence, but on the level of potency. Such a dichotomy is expressed, for example, by a contemporary of the Deuteronomist, Jeremiah, who juxtaposed Yahweh and other deities using the metaphor of the fountain and the cistern: 'For my people have committed two evils: They have forsaken Me, the fountain of living water, and hewn themselves cisterns, broken cisterns, that can hold no water' (Jer. 2.13). At first sight, the claim that the distinction

22. If אלהים אחרים in Exod. 20.3 and 23.13 are not later additions, as suggested above, then it is possible that the Deuteronomist deliberately picked a phrase out of the Ten Commandments in order to make it a distinct term.

here refers to the level of potency, not of existence, seems to be refuted by v. 11: 'Has a nation changed its gods, which are no gods'. However, the second stich of this verse affirms my suggestion: 'but my people have changed their Glory for what does not profit'.[23] These words indicate that the apparent absoluteness in the expression 'no gods' (לא אלהים) is in fact a polemical device, and the real meaning of the phrase is: 'they are of no use for you'.[24]

Thus the concept of the 'other gods' expressed by the term אלהים אחרים is that they exist, they may even be helpful for their 'natural' worshippers, but not for Israel, which can be helped only by Yahweh. Such a concept of the other gods leads indirectly to the belief that Yahweh is mightier than the other gods, and therefore it is not only immoral but also stupid for Israel to transgress his covenant. The concept of the sovereignty of Yahweh over all deities, though not his exclusiveness, and the idea that it is legitimate for each nation to worship its own gods, are well attested in Deut. 4.19. Here Israel is warned not to worship the sun, the moon and the stars, whom the Lord has 'allotted (חלק) unto all nations under the whole world'.[25]

IV

In post-Deuteronomistic, that is late exilic and post-exilic, writings אלהים אחרים is attested only once.[26] This can be explained by my

---

23. ועמי המיר כבודו בלא יועיל. Probably כבודו ('their glory') is an emendation of כבודי ('my glory'). This is one of the תיקוני סופרים (scribal emendations) which are mentioned in some rabbinic sources; see for example *Mek.*, Shira 4, in which 11 emendations are listed; *Ochla Weochla* (ed. Z. Fransdarf, 1824), p. 113: '18 words were amended by Ezra'. On this phenomenon see for example D. Barthelemy, 'Les Tiqqune Sopherim...', in G.W. Anderson and P.A.H. de Boer (eds.), *Congress Volume Bonn 1962* (VTSup, 9; Leiden: Brill, 1963), pp. 285-304; C. McCarthy, *The Tiqqune Sophrim and other Theological Corrections* (OBO, 36; Göttingen, Vandenhoeck & Ruprecht, 1981).

24. For a recent discussion of the metaphor in this verse see M. Fishbane, 'The Well of Living Water', in M. Fishbane and E. Tov (eds.), *Sha'arei Talmon* (Winona Lake, IN: Eisenbrauns, 1992), pp. 3-16. It seems that Fishbane too understands the metaphor as referring to the Lord's saving power in contrast to the impotence of the idols: 'Only God...is the fount of salvation' ('The Wall', p. 6).

25. See also Deut. 29.23-25 (English 29.24-26): to the nations' astonishing question why the Lord punished Israel so furiously the answer would be that they worshipped אלהים אחרים, 'Gods whom He had not allotted (חלק) to them'.

26. 2 Chron. 28.25. See note 20 referring to qualified occurrences of the phrase.

suggestion that the term was not intended to express unequivocal, absolute denial of deities other than Yahweh: the late authors, whose monotheistic faith was more crystallized and refined, refrained from using a term which seemed to them too ambiguous and not sharp enough. The most conspicuous example is Second Isaiah, and because of the importance of his attitude I allow myself a short diversion from the main subject of the discussion, Dtr.

Absolute monotheism is expressed in Isaiah 40–55 in various ways, the two most noticeable being declarations and comparisons. Declarations such as 'I am He. Before Me there was no God formed, nor shall there be after Me' (Isa. 43.10); 'I am the first and I am the Last. Besides Me there is no God' (Isa. 44.6; see also 44.8; 45.5-7, 21; 48.12, among others)[27] denote unambiguously the exclusiveness of Yahweh. The comparisons made by this prophet are very illuminating. Since other Gods do not exist, to whom can he compare Yahweh? Thus in a paradoxical way the prophet makes the comparison by claiming that no comparison is possible: the rhetorical question 'To whom then will you liken God? Or what likeness will you compare to Him' (40.18) is followed by a parodic description of the idols' makers (40.19-20) in order to prove the futility of their deities.

The same tactics of controversy can be found in Isa. 44.8-20. Another sophisticated way of overcoming the difficulty of comparing incomparable entities is to compare prophecies uttered by Yahweh's messengers with prophecies of the idolators: only the former have come true (see for example Isa. 41.21-29; 45.18-22; 46.8-11). Never in his monotheistic utterances does this prophet use the term אלהים אחרים. A most interesting example of this intentional avoidance is: 'I am Yahweh, that is my name and my glory I will not give to another (אחר), nor my praise to graven images (פסילים)' (42.8). Here it is clear that the prophet deliberately avoids using the term אלהים אחרים, expressing by the poetic parallelism his view that the אחר is not a deity but a graven image![28] If my understanding of אלהים אחרים in Dtr is correct then the lack of this term in Second Isaiah not only reflects the prophet's total denial of other deities; by the same token it indicates

---

27. C. Westermann, *Isaiah 40–66* (OTL; London: SCM Press; Philadelphia: Westminster Press, 1969), p. 26, uses the phrase 'self-glorification statements' regarding these and similar declarations.

28. On the prophet's utterances against the idols see R.J. Clifford, 'The Function of Idol Passages in Second Isaiah', *CBQ* 42 (1980), pp. 450-64.

that his vehement monotheistic preaching was not directed only or even mainly towards the Babylonians among whom he was living, but rather towards his own people, the exiles. It was not a missionary attempt to convert pagans but rather an educational need to refine Israel's religious faith. He therefore refrained from using a well-known term because its ambiguity jeopardized the prophet's attempts to lead Israel towards the theological stage of absolute, real monotheistic faith. To this conclusion we will return later on.

V

Theological concepts in Dtr are not solely expressed in definite terminology but also in stories, speeches and historico-philosophical remarks or sermons. Hence, our investigation of the Deuteronomistic concept of other gods should not be limited to phraseology and terminology. Yet, since it is impossible to analyse here every single chapter within the Deuteronomistic corpus, I will refer only to three representative passages, one of each type.

1. *Story*

The Deuteronomistic story most relevant to our subject is the episode of Elijah's clash with the Baal prophets on Mount Carmel, 1 Kings 18. What concept of Baal is expressed here? From its very beginning the story seemingly juxtaposes Yahweh and Baal as two alternative deities: 'How long will you falter between two opinions (שתי הסעיפים)? If Yahweh is God follow Him but if Baal—follow him' (1 Kgs 18.21). And a test is then arranged to prove who is the real God.

However, attention should be paid to the two points: first, the story does not mention any deities other than Yahweh and Baal; secondly, the words of Elijah in his prayer just before the test are 'Let it be known this day that you are God *in Israel*' (v. 36). Hence, when the test is concluded with the clear victory of Yahweh, and the whole people admits that 'Yahweh is the God! Yahweh is the God' (v. 39), the real meaning of this declaration is, in fact, that Yahweh and not Baal is God *in Israel*. The divine essence of Baal outside Israel is neither denied here nor, of course, confirmed, since it is irrelevant to the story. However, the lack of any absolute denial of other deities as a whole, the absence of a conclusive claim to the uniqueness of Yahweh, is definite in the story. Since its sole intention is the total refutation of the divine power of Baal in Israel it is only natural that no use of the generalizing term אלהים אחרים is made.[29] Hence, this story fits into the picture outlined above regarding the Deuteronomistic concept of אלהים אחרים. Baal, as one of the 'other gods', might exist, but for Israel he is utterly useless. In fact he is even harmful, causing the nation to go astray from its real God—the only one whose saving power has been proven.

2. *Speech*

Speeches by eminent figures are one of the most important literary devices used by the Deuteronomist to convey his ideas.[30] Is not the whole book of Deuteronomy—the literary, theological and stylistic source of Dtr—built as a speech of Moses?

An appropriate example of a Deuteronomistic speech which reveals a concept of the other gods is Joshua 24.[31] Joshua's speech begins with a historical review starting from Israel's forefathers, Terah and Abraham, who were dwelling 'on the other side of the river' serving 'other gods', when the Lord took Abraham to the land of Canaan

29. Rofé, who claims that this story expresses a clear monotheistic view, does not pay attention to the fact that the whole story does not refer to foreign deities other than Baal. His suggestion is to ascribe the story to Yahweh's loyalists in the time of Manasseh, just before the Josianic Reform. This assumption might be right but it is independent of the monotheistic interpretation of the story. See A. Rofé, *The Prophetical Stories* (Jerusalem: Magnes, 1982), pp. 159-62. See also H.H. Rowley, *Men of God* (London: Nelson, 1963), pp. 37-65, who correctly rejects the monotheistic interpretation of the story.

30. For example Josh. 23 (Joshua); 1 Sam. 8.10-18; 12.6-25 (Samuel); 1 Kgs 11.29-39 (Ahijah the Shilonite). The Deuteronomistic prose sermons of Jeremiah (for example Jer. 7; 44) should also be included within this category.

31. There is no need to discuss here the attribution of the speech to Dtr. Whether it is original to Dtr or simply a Deuteronomistic edition of a previous source, I believe that it is 'presented to us in Deuteronomistic dress' (R.D. Nelson, *The Double Redaction of the Deuteronomistic History* [JSOTSup, 18; Sheffield: JSOT Press, 1981], p. 95). Soggin too agrees that 'the work of the Deuteronomic editor reappears throughout the text'. See J.A. Soggin, *Joshua* (OTL; London: SCM Press, 1972), p. 23. Noth regards the chapter as one of the 'Deuteronomistically edited passages'. See M. Noth, *The Deuteronomistic History* (JSOTSup, 15; Sheffield: JSOT Press, 2nd edn, 1981), p. 23. For a recent comprehensive study of Josh. 24, which advocates its affinity to Dtr, see M. Anbar, *Josué et l'alliance de Sichem (Josué 24.1-28)* (Beitrage zur biblischen Exegese und Theologie, 25; Frankfurt: Peter Lang, 1992).

(Josh. 24.2-3).[32] Abraham is neither condemned for serving other gods nor is there even a hint that he was stupid to do so. Then, after describing the saving actions of Yahweh until that moment (Josh. 24.5-13) Joshua urges his audience to decide which deity they choose to worship—Yahweh or 'the gods that your fathers served on the other side of the river or the gods of the Amorite in whose land you dwell' (v. 15). When the people utterly reject the latter two possibilities, recounting the miraculous saving acts of Yahweh, Joshua warns them that Yahweh is a jealous God, who will not forgive any apostasy, but they nevertheless firmly stick to their decision: 'No, but Yahweh will we serve' (v. 21). In the whole speech there is nothing to suggest that the author (or his literary representative, Joshua) intends to convey the idea that the other gods do not exist. Once again the only argument is: whether or not they exist the other gods' ability to assist Israel has never been proven and therefore for Israel there is only one God.

3. *Historiographical Retrospections*

Blending historico-philosophical retrospections into the historical reviews is another characteristic of Dtr.[33] Like the speeches, indeed even more effectively, this literary tactic enables the author to make a separation between preaching and recording history; mixing the two might discredit the reliability of the latter or diminish the effectiveness of the former. Being the explicit authority for interpreting the events, the author here can express his ideas as directly and clearly as he wishes. An example of such a passage which sheds light on our subject is Judg. 2.11-23. The *leitmotiv* here is that during the period of the Judges Israel's religious apostasy caused national afflictions and calamities, and it was Yahweh alone who saved the nation. The author mentions Baal (2.11, 13) and Ashtoret (2.13), and 'other gods from among the gods of the people who were all around them' (2.12), and there is no denial whatsoever of their existence. They are simply depicted as impotent where Israel is concerned, unlike Yahweh. Yahweh's fury is due to Israel's transgression of the covenant (2.20), not its serving nonexistent gods. The logical conclusion of such a

32. Soggin (*Joshua*, p. 232) correctly directs attention to the similarity between the alternative put before the people here and that in the story of Elijah on Carmel, mentioned above.

33. See for example Judg. 2.11-23; 17.6 (= 18.1a; 19.1a; 21.25); 1 Kgs 16.19; 2 Kgs 17.7-23; 18.5-7; 21.2-16; 23.25-27; 24.2b-4, 20.

presentation is that Yahweh is capable of manipulating the other
nations to act according to his plan (that is, punishment) for Israel,
while the other deities can do nothing to obstruct him. The superiority
of Yahweh is therefore evident, but not necessarily his exclusivity. It
is obvious, however, that such a concept of the other gods' limited
potency is an irreversible step towards the monotheistic ideology.

None of the other Deuteronomistic passages mentioned above
reflects a different concept of other gods.

VI

The passages discussed above represent the majority of Deuteronomistic writings regarding the existence of deities other than
Yahweh. Yet there are also some writings in Dtr which seem to
deflect from this line, transmitting clear and unambiguous messages of
monotheism.

In some writings the foreign deities are referred to not with the
attribute אחרים but by a sharper polemic style: they are called מעשה ידי
אדם עץ ואבן, 'the work of man's hands, wood and stone', 'which neither
see nor hear nor eat nor smell' (Deut. 4.28. See also 28.36, 64;
29.16, and 2 Kgs. 19.18, which will be discussed later). The
exhibition of the other deities as less than human beings should be
understood not only as a sharp irony, but should also be seen against
the background of the concept expressed in Gen. 1.26-27. Anthro-
pologically, people have created their gods in their own shape;
therefore, if an idol is inferior to human beings (it cannot see or
hear), it is definitely not God. So there can be no doubt that these
expressions, which do not refer to any certain deity, really mean to
deny the existence of any deity except Yahweh. As to the historical
background of these passages, unlike the previously discussed
Deuteronomistic writings, which have no obvious exilic background
and could be considered pre-exilic,[34] these passages presuppose the
exile. They even know that in exile Israel will worship other gods.

---

34. The view that two Deuteronomistic authors are discernible in Dtr was raised
by Kuenen, adopted by others, and has gained a wide support following Cross's
advocacy and elaboration of the theory. See F.M. Cross, *Canaanite Myth and
Hebrew Epic* (Cambridge, MA and London: Harvard University Press, 1973);
Nelson, *Double Redaction*; R.E. Freedman, *The Exile and Biblical Narrative*
(Atlanta: Scholars Press, 1981).

The exilic origin of these writings is therefore obvious, and widely accepted by scholars.[35]

What conclusions should be drawn if indeed unequivocal denials of other deities are found only in exilic Deuteronomistic passages? First of all, we can conclude that the exiles did worship idols—the exilic author would never have ascribed to Moses false prophecies (that is, that the exiles will worship other gods). This conclusion reaffirms our reading of Second Isaiah's polemics against idolatry as directed to the exiles and not towards the Gentiles.

A second conclusion is related to Kaufman's claim that biblical references to foreign deities as 'wood and stone' prove that Israel never understood the real essence of paganism, equating every idolatry with fetishism. If the main bulk of Dtr does not totally deny the existence of other gods, but only challenges their potency, and if a total denial is typical only of exilic Dtr, this may be seen as refuting Kaufman's view that symbolic idolatry was not understood among the Israelites because of their deep-rooted inherent monotheistic mentality.

Nonetheless, is it really the case that pure monotheistic messages are totally absent in pre-exilic Dtr? The most famous example that could undermine this assumption, a verse which has achieved the status of Jewish monotheistic credo, is the *Shema*: שמע ישראל יהוה אלהינו יהוה אחד (literally: 'Hear Israel, Yahweh is our God, Yahweh is one', Deut. 6.4). Although it does not mention alien gods, which is our subject here, it must not be overlooked in this context. The question is whether monotheism is implicit in these words or has been read into them during the ages by a particular, but not the only possible, interpretation.[36] I prefer the former option, admitting that the reasons are not

35. To mention only few out of many, see for example G. von Rad, *Deuteronomy* (OTL; London: SCM Press, 1966), pp. 50, 173, 176, 178-81; Noth, *Deuteronomistic History*, pp. 58-59; B. Peckham, *The Composition of the Deuteronomistic School* (Atlanta: Scholars Press, 1985), p. 62 n. 134; H.W. Wolff, 'Das Kerygma des deuteronomistischen Geschichtswerks', *ZAW* 73 (1961), p. 182; Cross, *Canaanite Myth*, pp. 274-89; E.W. Nicholson, *Deuteronomy and Tradition* (Philadelphia: Fortress Press, 1967), p. 35.

36. 'The question here is in what sense the pred. 'one' is to be understood. Does it express the *unity* of Jehovah, declaring that He is in His essence indivisible, cannot—like Ba'al and Ashtoreth, for instance, who are often spoken of in the plural number (e.g. 1 Sam. 7:4...)—assume different phases or attributes, as presiding over different localities, or different departments of nature, and cannot further be united syncretistically... with heathen deities; but is only known under the one

purely academic. Since the monotheistic interpretation of the verse contradicts nothing in the context, then one must be arrogant, even impertinent, to disregard the historical-cultural status of this interpretation simply in order to support one's own developmental scheme.

The second option can in any case fit with my line of argument providing we adopt one of the following assumptions: (1) that the *Shema* is a late post-exilic interpolation, intended to hammer a monotheistic declaration into Moses' own speech; (2) that the development of the monotheistic conviction within Dtr (let alone within Israel as a whole) was too complicated to be accurately and completely traced back. Thus it is possible that declarations about the exclusiveness of Yahweh did not exactly correspond to a deep and genuine awareness of their comprehensive religious implications. We might also think about our own Western civilization, with a history of 2000 years of monotheistic patterns of faith. We all know persons who regard themselves as pure believers in the One Almighty God, yet at the same time believe in all kinds of superstitions, from astrology to touching wood, which seem to contradict the very essence of monotheism. I suggest that this second explanation is methodologically preferable, and closer to the historical truth. It is methodologically wrong to use the option of interpolation just to sustain a shaky speculation. The integrity of using this option is even more doubtful when the argumentation demands that more than one verse be regarded as a later addition, which is indeed the case here. Besides Deut. 6.4 there are other Deuteronomistic monotheistic declarations, whose exilic origin cannot be certified, although neither can it be refuted. Deut. 4.35 reads: 'To you it was shown that you might know that Yahweh is God, there is no other besides Him'. Verse 39 reads: 'Yahweh is God in heaven above, and on the earth beneath there is no other'.[37] Deut. 32.21 reads: 'They

character by which He has revealed Himself to Israel...? Or does it denote the *uniqueness* of Jehovah, representing Him as God in a unique sense, as the God with whom other 'Elohim' can be compared, as the only Deity to whom the true attributes of Godhead really belong...? The second interpretation gives the higher and fuller meaning to the term...' (Driver, *Deuteronomy*, pp. 89-90). Von Rad (*Deuteronomy*, p. 63) also suggests two possible interpretations of אחד, but neither is really monotheistic. For a relatively recent discussion of this אחד see J.G. Janzen, 'On the Most Important Word in the *shema* (Deut. 6.4-5)', *VT* 37 (1987), pp. 280-300.

37. The problem of Deut. 4 and its origin is discussed in all the commentaries to the book. See also A.D.H. Mayes, 'Deuteronomy 4 and the Literary Criticism of Deuteronomy', *JBL* 100 (1981), pp. 23-51.

have provoked Me to jealousy by what is not god', and towards the
end of this poem we find 'Now see that I, even I am He, and there is
no God beside Me' (Deut. 32.39). In Josh. 2.11 the author ascribes the
following words to Rahab: 'For Yahweh your God He is God, in
heaven above and on earth beneath'. In 1 Kgs 8.60 a clear monotheistic creed is ascribed to Solomon: 'That all the peoples of the earth
may know that Yahweh is god, there is no other'.

It seems that through the clouded Dtr writings some patches of clear
evidence illuminate an uneven process which ended as unequivocal
monotheism in the exilic period. Before the exile some Deuteronomistic authors expressed the exclusiveness of Yahweh in credo-like
declarations, which did not correspond to the concepts of other gods
expressed by the very same authors. To put it differently, the
prevailing Deuteronomistic concept of other gods as real (though
impotent for Israel) deities contradicted Dtr's concept of the uniqueness of Yahweh, but both coexisted side by side. Is such a symbiosis
absurd? No, it is just a human paradox, and therefore an intelligible
reality.[38]

VII

Towards the end of this paper I would like to refer to another story
which reflects the dialectical character of our subject: 2 Kings 18–19
(= Isa. 36–37), in particular the speech directed by Rabshakeh to King
Hezekiah (2 Kgs 18.19-25; 29-35) and the prayer of Hezekiah (19.15-
19). In Rabshakeh's speech the Deuteronomistic author[39] is trying to

---

38. An example of a paradoxical monotheistic phrasing is 'there is none like you
and no God besides you' (אין כמוך ואין אלהים זולתך; 2 Sam. 7.22). S. Japhet discusses this paradox here and in some other verses in Chronicles; *The Ideology of the
Book of Chronicles* (Jerusalem: Mosad Bialik, 1977), pp. 42-52. She suggests that
the (non-monotheistic) phrase אין כמוך lost its original meaning, interpreted as 'there
is no one besides you'. Yet it is possible that in 2 Sam. 7.22 the words ואין אלהים
זולתך were added in order to nullify the possible implications of אין כמוך. For a
monotheistic rephrasing of non-monotheistic verses see S. Löwenstamm, *Kiriat
Sefer* 39 (1964), p. 50. He compares Ps. 95.3 to 96.5-6 and 96.7-9 to 29.1-2.

39. The obvious Deuteronomistic origin of this speech was recently emphasized
by E. Ben-Zvi, 'Who Wrote the Speech of Rabshakeh and When?', *JBL* 109
(1990), pp. 79-92. For a comprehensive study claiming that the story of the 701 war
was composed among proto-Deuteronomistic circles during the reign of King Josiah
see R.E. Clements, *Isaiah and the Deliverance of Jerusalem: A Study of the*

think as an Assyrian, and thus the author's concept of the Assyrian's concept of the Israelite faith is reflected. Rabshakeh is depicted as a polytheist who believes in Yahweh's sovereignty in the land of Israel, which is attested in the words 'Have I now come up without Yahweh against this place to destroy it? Yahweh said to me: Go up against this land and destroy it' (18.25). The response of Hezekiah's officials to these words is: 'Please, speak to your servants in Aramaic...and do not speak to us in Jewish (יהודית) in the ears of the people who is on the wall' (18.26). This request shows that according to the author's understanding the Jerusalemites shared the religious concept of Rabshakeh about the supremacy but not the exclusiveness of Yahweh. The fact that the author does not interpolate any remark of his own to refute or diminish this concept indicates that he himself tended to favour it. The conclusion of the story confirms this reading: Sennacherib was defeated, which proves that he was sent by Yahweh, but not to conquer Jerusalem. Hence, the intention of the story is not to deny the existence of other deities, but to prove Yahweh's supremacy and his special commitment to Jerusalem and its temple. This is also exemplified clearly in the second speech of the Assyrian official, 2 Kgs 18.29-35. His claim that no god was able to save his nation from Assyria, and Yahweh is not an exception, is intentionally stressed just to be refuted by the end of the story—the salvation of Jerusalem.[40] Therefore, the difference between the author's image of Yahweh and his concept of the Assyrian's image of Yahweh is focused only in the interpretation of Yahweh's historical plan, while the existence of other deities (which are impotent in Judaea) is not challenged, but represented as a common denominator to Rabshakeh and the author.

A more definite idea is conveyed by Hezekiah's prayer. Here the (retrospective) fact that Jerusalem, unlike the cities of other nations,

---

Interpretation of Prophecy in the Old Testament (JSOTSup, 13; Sheffield: JSOT Press, 1980).

40. There is an apparent discrepancy in Rabshakeh's argumentation. In his first speech he declares that Sennacherib was sent by Yahweh to destroy the land, while in the second speech he denies Yahweh's ability to save Jerusalem. But in fact there is no contradiction here: the author differentiates between the destruction of the land, which indeed happened, and the occupation of Jerusalem, which was avoided. Both arguments, however, retrospectively establish the idea of the supremacy rather than the uniqueness of Yahweh.

was saved is exhibited as a proof of the nonexistence of deities other than Yahweh, 'for they are no gods, but the work of man's hands, wood and stone. Now therefore, Yahweh our God save us from his hand that all the kingdoms of the earth may know that you are alone Yahweh the God' (2 Kgs 19.18-19). The different concept of the other gods in this second part of the story can be explained in one of the following ways. 1. Both parts of the story were written by the same author. But in the first part he did not raise the idea of the uniqueness of Yahweh, his literary game being to 'quote' Rabshakeh, who could not possibly think in monotheistic terms. If this interpretation is correct then our author appears as a sophisticated personality, gifted with a great awareness of the delicate nuances of the gradual process leading from polytheism to monotheistic thinking. By no means does it accord with Kaufman's claim that the Israelites did not understand at all the essence of paganism. 2. Hezekiah's prayer was composed by a later Deuteronomist,[41] whose firm monotheistic belief urged him to add Hezekiah's unequivocal words stressing the uniqueness of Yahweh. If this is the case then a gradual development towards a more refined monotheism is discernible within the Deuteronomistic work. No definite proof can be presented to support either explanation, yet both fit into our suggested model, that monotheistic declarations and polytheistic concepts of other gods paradoxically did not exclude each other. It is therefore needless here to speculate on the literary background of Hezekiah's speech.

VIII

Our search for the concept of 'the other' in ancient Israel has been very limited: not in Israel but in a single biblical layer, Dtr; not a general concept but a more specific one, other gods; not a comprehensive overview of these deities—their 'personal' characteristics (for instance jealousy, kindness, justice)—but only the specific question of their existence or nonexistence. Therefore, our conclusions must be limited too, and by no means do they allow any general statement

41. About the concept of two Deuteronomistic layers, raised by Kuenen and supported by Cross, see note 34. Holding this view Peckham classified most of Rabshakeh's speech in 2 Kgs 18.19-30 as Dtr 1, while Hezekiah's prayer in 2 Kgs 19.15-19 is classified as Dtr 2 (see *Composition of the Deuteronomistic School*, figure 7).

about ancient Israelite monotheism. Yet I believe that some contribution has been made by focusing on this specific point. It has helped to refute the notion that monotheism was inherent in the psyche of the Israelite nation. Israelite monotheism should rather be depicted as a thread which was gradually spun from many yarns, not necessarily of the same length, strength, material or colour. Only two of them have been examined here. One, the concept of other gods, weakened slowly but persistently the image of other deities in Israel. The second, glorifying declarations, sometimes exaggerated (considering the basically polytheistic mentality of the declarer) about Yahweh, accelerated the process by pointing at its terminal, logically inevitable goal.

Coming back to the question raised at the beginning of this discussion, it is clear that our conclusions are closer to Lemche's model of the development of the Israelite religion than to Kaufman's. Nevertheless, they do not cohere with all of Lemche's specific arguments, such as the equation of Yahweh and Baal and the subordination of Yahweh to El until the Deuteronomistic reform. Such specific arguments should be examined in detail, which is beyond my task here. However, my investigation has raised serious doubts not only as to our ability to differentiate between 'stages' in the development of Israelite monotheism and its struggle with all kinds of paganism but also as to the very existence of such clear stages.

REFLECTIONS ON THE RELATIONSHIP BETWEEN THEOPOLITICS, PROPHECY AND HISTORIOGRAPHY

Yair Hoffman

I

Max Weber, discussing the relationship of religion to politics, wrote:

> Every religiously grounded unworldly love and indeed every ethical reli-
> gion must, in similar measure and for similar reasons, experience tension
> with the sphere of political behaviour. This tension appears as soon as
> religion has progressed to anything like a status of equality with the
> sphere of political associations. To be sure: the ancient political god of the
> locality, even where he was an ethical and universally powerful god,
> existed merely for the protection of the political interests of his followers'
> associations.[1]

Without using the word 'theopolitics' Weber has illuminated here the
dialectic essence of this term. It combines two theoretically contradictory elements: the idea of eternity and the idea of ephemerality; the
aspect of the spiritual and the mundane aspect of human existence. Yet
I wonder if one of these can exist without the other. In trying to clarify the exact meaning of the term 'theopolitics' I searched for a
definition and could not find one, either in Weber's work or in
biblical or general encyclopaedias, not even in philosophical dictio-
naries. Perhaps a more thorough search could have proved more
fruitful, yet the fact that in more than a few relevant books no such
definition exists may not be a mere oversight. Be that as it may, I had
no other choice but to examine the meaning of the term myself. This
paper is therefore devoted to some reflections on the nature and
essence of biblical theopolitics. By 'politics' I shall generally mean
what is now called 'foreign affairs'. Only one of the biblical examples
will refer to domestic policy.

1. M. Weber, *The Sociology of Religion* (London: Methuen, 1965 [German
edn 1922]), pp. 223-45.

In order to focus the discussion and make it more productive I shall divide the main question, 'what is theopolitics?', into three smaller ones:

1. Is it related to the interaction between *theos* ('god') and politics, or to that between theology—the systematization of the major ideas of a given religious faith—and politics? In either case the relevance of theopolitics to prophecy is obvious.

2. Does 'theopolitics' imply the determination of politics by the supposed will of God, as the only criterion for making political decisions, or does it imply the manipulation of religion, which is a powerful factor in human life, in order to justify purely political decisions?

3. How sharp and definite are the borders between these possible alternative descriptions of theopolitics? If they are vague and unclear—as I shall claim—then the distinction between prospective and retrospective religious justifications for a certain policy would be unclear too. Thus a possible connection between theopolitics and historiographical thinking (not necessarily historiography as a literary genre) might be detected.

II

The simplest way of engaging in theopolitics, according to a combination of the first two possible definitions given above, is to approach the deity whenever a political decision is to be taken. There are many examples of such a procedure. Thus Ezekiel describes the king of Babylon as one who 'stands at the parting of the road at the fork of the two roads, to use divination: he takes the arrows, he consults the images, he looks at the liver' (Ezek. 21.26 [English 21.21]). We have, of course, the so-called Mari prophetic letters. In ancient Rome, too, there were the augurs, whose task was to announce the wish of the gods by interpreting various natural phenomena. Can we really say that these apparently purely religious procedures had no political elements? Certainly not in the case of the Roman augurs. At least towards the end of the republic they gained substantial political power, which explains why the office was cancelled as soon as the republic came to an end and the emperor became the sole ruler. Allow me to speculate a little about the way such direct consultations with the gods were made, by referring to some examples from the ancient Near Eastern sources.

When Mesha of Moab wrote in the middle of the ninth century ויאמר לי כמש רד הלתחם בחורנן (line 14) or ויאמר לי כמש לך אחז את נבה על ישראל (line 32)[2] he declared that he had been acting 'theopolitically', following Kemosh's orders. But was he indeed doing that? Did Mesha really believe that Kemosh had told him to act as he did? It is very likely that the answer is yes. Mesha probably consulted Kemosh through his Baru, Muhum, Nabi or priest before each battle. However, he would certainly not have agreed to accept a negative answer from his God while capitalizing on his previous victories and trying to gain as much as possible from them. I assume that if he had received a negative answer he would have posed his questions to Kemosh again and again, until the omens gave him the desired advice: go and fight against Nebo, or Howranan.

Should he then be considered a cynical manipulator of his own religious faith? Not necessarily. He was probably convinced that Kemosh would always give him the best advice, and, therefore, if the answer he received was not 'good' enough, that is, did not meet his own expectations, it was probably and naturally regarded as a misinterpretation of Kemosh's wishes, or as an invitation to rephrase the question. If this was indeed the case, can it be considered as the practice of theopolitics? The answer is yes, if the term means a theologization of political decisions, that is, the need to support each political step with religious arguments. However, if it means a policy dictated by purely religious motives the answer is no. The difference between these two possible meanings of 'theopolitics' is of course crucial. Yet there is a third possible explanation of Mesha's assumed process of making decisions: that he fought against Hawronan or whoever without first consulting Kemosh. Having won the battle he would reach the conclusion that it had been his god who had told him to fight (who had planted the idea in his mind before the battle) and that is exactly what he engraved on his stele. In such a case one might ask how far theopolitics is from (retrospective) historiography?

A biblical parallel of the case of Mesha is the famous story in 1 Kings 22; King Ahab, capitulating to King Jehoshaphat's demand, inquires for the word of God, asking four hundred of his prophets

2. *KAI*, II, p. 169: 'Und Kamosh sprach zu mir: Geh, nimm Nebo gegen Israel; und es sprach Kamosh zu mir: Steige hinab, kämpfe gegen Hawronan'.

whether or not he should fight the Arameans in Ramot Gilad. Michaihu Ben Yimla is not asked, since the king knows that Michaihu's answer will not please him. And when, because of Jehoshaphat's insistence, Michaihu is nevertheless asked, his interpretation of the real wish of God is rejected. The historicity of this story is irrelevant to my argument, since the story itself is evidence of the ambivalent attitude towards theopolitical oracles: they were essentially important, yet their advice was accepted only so long as it fitted the king's expectations.

One of Cyrus's famous inscriptions tells of Nabunaid, King of Babylon:

> He interrupted in a fiendish way the regular offerings... The worship of Marduch the king of the gods, he changed into abomination, daily he used to do evil against his city... He tormented its inhabitants with corvee-work without relief, he ruined them all. Upon their complaint the lord of the gods became terribly angry... He scanned and looked through all the countries searching for a righteous ruler willing to lead him [Marduch] in the annual procession. He pronounced the name of Cyrus, king of Anshan, declared him to be the ruler of all the world... He made him set out on the road to Babylon going at his side like a real friend... He delivered into his hands Nabunidus...[3]

Judged by modern standards no one would hesitate to define these declarations as mere propaganda; that is, a clever use of the religious feelings of the Babylonians aimed at establishing Cyrus's standing as the chosen king of their city. Is it not the case that in fact the conquest of Babylon was planned many years in advance, as part of an overall political project to establish a Median–Persian empire? Nevertheless, it is not too implausible that Cyrus did consult Babylonian priests, who encouraged him in the name of Marduch. If this was the case, then when the above inscription was written Cyrus and his contemporaries could have retrospectively considered the conquest of Babylon the accomplishment of the gods' will, that is as a theopolitical event.

II

With the background of these examples I would like to examine four biblical passages related to the question of theopolitics in ancient Israel.

3. *ANET*, pp. 315-16.

1. *Isaiah 7*

Rezin of Aram and Peqah of Samaria attack the Jerusalem of King Ahaz, probably in 734 BCE. Isaiah is sent by the Lord to Ahaz, proclaiming

> הישמר והשקט אל תירא ולבבך אל ירך משני זנבות האודים העשנים האלה...לא
> תקום ולא תהיה. כי ראש ארם דמשק וראש דמשק רצין ובעוד ששים וחמש שנה יחת
> אפרים מעם. וראש אפרים שומרון...אם לא תאמינו כי לא תאמנו
>
> Take heed, and be quiet; do not fear or be fainthearted because of these
> two smoking firebrands...it shall not stand neither shall it come to
> pass...for the head of Aram is Damaskus and the head of Damaskus is
> Rezin, and within sixty-five years shall Ephraim be broken from being a
> people, and the head of Ephraim is Shomron...if ye will not believe
> surely ye shall not be intrusted (Isa. 7.4-9).

This prophecy was later proved to have been mistaken, since only 13
years and not 65 were needed for Assyria to destroy both the kingdoms of Aram and of Samaria.[4] Therefore if the phrase '65 years' is
not a later interpolation[5] this discrepancy between the promise and the
historical reality can strengthen the assumption that we have here the
authentic prophecy, if not the exact *ipsissima verba* of the prophet. In
fact even if we decide that the exact number of years is a late interpolation, the policy that the prophet demands from the king is obviously
not to surrender to the Aram–Ephraim coalition since it is powerless.
Such a policy under those circumstances had nothing to do with religious views. It was rather a realistic evaluation of the weakness of
these two nations, who four years previously had been forced by
Tiglath-Pileser III to raise a heavy tribute to Assyria.[6] The imminent
self-caused disintegration of the Israelite Northern Kingdom, in which

4.   Rashi, Kimhi and Ibn-Ezra suggested counting the 65 years from the days of
Amos, who proclaimed the end of the Northern Kingdom and Damascus. Others
suggested reading בעוד שש וחמש שנה, 'within six and five years' (6+5=11), which
brings us very close to the destruction of Samaria in 721.

5.   See G.B. Gray, *Isaiah I–XXVII* (ICC; Edinburgh: T. & T. Clark, 1912),
pp. 119-20; O. Kaiser, *Isaiah 1–12* (OTL; London: SCM Press, 1972), p. 94.
They, among others, consider v. 8b as an interpolation referring 'to an event in 671.
At that time Essar-haddon settled a foreign ruling class in Samaria...' (Kaiser, *Isaiah
1–12*, p. 94).

6.   2 Kgs 15.19-20; *ANET*, p. 283: 'I received tribute from...Razon of
Damascus, Menahem of Samaria...'; 'As for Menahem I overwhelmed him like a
snowstorm and he...fled like a bird alone and bowed to my feet. I returned him to
his place and imposed tribute upon him to wit: gold, silver, garments...'

four dynasties had changed in the preceding short period of only
twelve years, was also clear enough. Under such circumstances 'be not
afraid of these two kingdoms' has nothing to do with theopolitics.
However, scholars suggest that the prophet's encouragement also
included another political advice, or rather warning: do not make
contact with Assyria, do not ask for its military aid. *This* element of
the proposed policy is regarded by many scholars as theopolitical. To
use Buber's words,

> What here prevails is indeed a special kind of politics, theopolitics, which
> is concerned to establish a certain people in a certain historical situation
> under the divine sovereignty so that this people is brought nearer the
> fulfilment of its task, to become the beginning of the kingdom of God.[7]

Such a policy, says Buber, was the fulfilment of the idea of being
'holy' (קדוש), that is, 'separated', and this is the link between Isaiah 7
and the call vision in the previous chapter, where the prophet heard
the heavenly קדוש קדוש קדוש—'sanctus, sanctus, sanctus'. Kaiser follows
Buber when he says that a covenant with Assyria was regarded by the
prophet as a 'violation of exclusive loyalty to a God who does not tolerate other gods'.[8]

The difference between such a theopolitics and the above-mentioned
examples of Mesha and Cyrus is decisive. The king is called here to
base his policy on religious principles whose theological validity is independent of any temporary *realpolitik*. The adherence to faith in God
is exhibited as a theoretical guide which could and should be translated
easily into a practical policy. Ignoring the Aram–Ephraim danger and
yet avoiding any commitment to Assyria, the threatening shadow over
the whole region, was a policy which could have been justified only by
religious, theological but otherwise illogical reasons.

However, this was not necessarily the prophet's suggestion. Scholars
who claim otherwise base their conclusions upon the assumption that
chs. 7–8 are an original prophetical entity; they also refer to some
other prophecies, mainly ch. 30. But some doubts can be raised as to
the validity of this argumentation.

In the first place, it is doubtful whether anyone can pinpoint any
clear, unequivocal phrase in Isaiah 7–8 in which an alliance with

---

7. M. Buber, *The Prophetic Faith* (New York: Harper & Row, 1960), p. 135.
He calls his discussion of this episode 'The theopolitical hour' (pp. 126-54).

8. Kaiser, *Isaiah 1–12*, p. 92; his title for 7.1-9 is 'the hour of faith'.

Assyria is condemned. Indeed, following Ahaz's rejection of a heavenly 'sign', a prophecy about the future Assyrian occupation of Judah is made, but even here there is no direct or implied warning against an alliance with Assyria. In chs. 30–31 the people's reliance on Egypt is condemned as a sign of lack of faith in God, קדוש ישראל (30.15); yet it is methodologically wrong to draw conclusions from this undated prophecy about Isaiah's political standing towards Assyria in the year 734.[9] Secondly, the original integrity of chs. 7–8 is doubtful. It seems that the original literary unit was vv. 7.1-16 plus 8.1-4 (the מהר שלל חש בז prophecy), while vv. 7.17-25 and 8.5-9 (or 8.5-17) which mention the future Assyrian occupation were added later. Only then do the names מהר שלל חש בז, עמנואל make any sense, symbolizing the future redemption of Jerusalem and the destruction of the Northern coalition. There is no reason to suspect the Isaianic origin of all the literary units in chs. 7–8, including those which mention Assyria as a future conqueror. But the latter were probably intertwined retrospectively into the salvation prophecy of 734 in order to indicate that at that time Isaiah already anticipated the Assyrian occupation and to put the blame for this occupation on Ahaz's sinful policy.[10] The conclusion is, therefore, that there is nothing to prove that in 734 Isaiah made actual political demands on the basis of theoretical theological concepts. Certainly, theopolitical aspects may exist in Isaiah 7–8, but these are due to a historiographical retrospective editorial tendency.

A similar tendency can be detected in 2 Chron. 28.20-21, but here it is the author, not the editor, who is responsible for the theological interpretation of events. Unlike 2 Kgs 16.6-9, which tells us that after Ahaz declared his submission to Tiglath-Pileser the latter assisted him by conquering Damascus, the Chronicler claims that Ahaz's sinful policy was disastrous: 'So Tiglath-Pileser king of Assyria came to him

9. *Pace* Kaiser, *Isaiah 1–12*, p. 94.

10. According to 2 Kgs. 16.7 Ahaz sent a delegation to the Assyrian king, saying, 'I am your servant and your son. Come up and rescue me from the hand of the king of Aram and from the hand of the king of Israel who are attacking me'. It is suggestive that this historical datum, which could have strengthened the editor's view that it had been Ahaz's obstinate rejection of Isaiah's theopolitics which had initiated the Assyrian occupation, is not mentioned in the book of Isaiah, unlike the detailed story of the 701 war in chs. 36–37. This absence supports my claim that during the siege Isaiah did not express any objection to asking for Assyrian support.

and distressed him (ויצר לו) and did not assist him (ולא חזקו)...he did
not help him (ולא לעזרה לו)' (2 Chron. 28.20-21). ולא חזקו ולא לעזרה לו
resembles חזקיהו and עזריהו, which hints at the contrast between these
two righteous kings and Ahaz.

2. *Isaiah 36–37*

In these chapters the story of Sennacherib's siege on Jerusalem in 701
BCE is told. I have no intention of delving into the complexity of the
story or of pretending to know what actually happened there. For the
present purpose it is sufficient to rely upon obvious biblical data
which are confirmed by the Assyrian annals.

Hezekiah rebelled against Sennacherib, who therefore conquered
'all the fortified cities of Judah' (Isa. 36.1) and besieged Jerusalem.
This is confirmed by the annals:

> As to Hezekiah the Jew, he did not submit to my yoke. I laid siege to 46
> of his strong cities, walled forts and to the countless small villages in their
> vicinity and conquered them...Himself [Hezekiah] I made a prisoner in
> Jerusalem, his royal residence, like a bird in a cage.[11]

Isaiah encouraged Hezekiah, promising him that the Assyrian king
would return to his land without conquering Jerusalem. The historical
truth was, in fact, that Jerusalem was not conquered. Yet in Isa. 37.33-
35 (= 2 Kgs. 18.32-34) a prophecy is quoted in which Hezekiah is
promised that Sennacherib 'shall not come into this city, or shoot an
arrow there, or come before it with a shield, or cast up a siege-
mound'. This prophecy was refuted by the events: a siege was
mounted, and the Assyrian king tells us about 'well stamped earth
ramps and battering rams'.[12] It is obvious, then, that Hezekiah's
rebellious policy against Assyria was supported, even encouraged, by
Isaiah *prior* to the siege on Jerusalem, *prior* to the occupation of all
the cities of Judah. The reason for such a policy can be understood not
only from the prophecy in chs. 36–37 but in fact from the belief
manifested throughout Isaiah that Jerusalem, the city of Yahweh, will
never be conquered by Assyria. His encouragement of Hezekiah in
telling him not to be afraid of Assyria, which could have been at least
one of the reasons that led Hezekiah to join a rebellion against
Assyria, if not to initiate it, was therefore based upon theopolitical

11. *ANET*, p. 288a.
12. *ANET*, p. 288a.

foundations. This policy proved to have been utterly wrong, since its consequences were tragic for the Judaean kingdom and its inhabitants, and it did not prevent Assyria from governing Judah for the next 60 or 70 years.

However, if it is not read by a detective or a critical scholar, who can compare evidence with the Assyrian annals, the book of Isaiah depicts a quite different historical picture. It is read as evidence of a great victory over the Assyrian power. By editing 37.33-35 after the story of the siege the editor succeeded in blurring the fact that the prophet's theopolitics had failed, thereby creating the impression that his prophecy came true, since, indeed, after 701 the Assyrians never again besieged Jerusalem.

Thus the comparison between Isaiah 7–8 and 36–37 has led to the conclusion that in the 734 conflict there was no real prophetic theopolitics; yet the editor of Isaiah's prophecies succeeded in creating the impression that the Assyrian occupation could have been avoided had an Isaianic theopolitics been adopted. On the other hand in 701 there *was* an Isaianic theopolicy, which Hezekiah adhered to, but it proved to be a mistake. This fact was mitigated, if not concealed, by means of a clever editorial and compositional work. I wonder if the detailed, argumentative, rhetorical character of the Rabshake's story should not be understood as a literary device designed to mitigate or conceal this discrepancy between the recommended theopolitics and the historical reality. In this story the disastrous consequences of Hezekiah's anti-Assyrian policy are ignored. The focus is only on the actual conquest of Jerusalem. The question whether or not it happens is claimed to be the sole criterion by which this policy should be measured. The retrospective character of such a criterion is obvious.

3. *Jeremiah*
Read as a whole the book of Jeremiah creates the clear impression that the prophet's pro-Babylonian attitude was purely theopolitical. The Lord chose Nebuchadnezzar to be his servant נבוכדנצר מלך בבל עבדי (25.9; 27.6) and to rule the world. In his call vision Jeremiah was told by the Lord that the calamity would come from the north, which on the background of the entire book is naturally understood as Babylon. Therefore Jerusalem should have willingly surrendered to the Babylonian dominion, that being God's decree. One of the obvious conclusions of the book is, therefore, that had the Judaeans accepted

Jeremiah's theopolitics Jerusalem would have been saved; the rejection of his prophetic theopolitics caused the destruction.

However, an analysis of the book's sources might raise some doubts as to the historical accuracy of this picture. In the poetical prophecies (Mowinckel's source A[13]) the only apparent case of theopolitics is the objection to reliance upon human treaties with Egypt or Assyria (2.18, 36). Yet this theological concept, probably influenced by Hosea's anti-treaty ideology, had nothing to do with practical policy. There is no indication whatsoever that Jeremiah either objected to or supported King Josiah's pro-Babylonian act against Pharaoh Necho in Megiddo. All that is said in these prophetic condemnations is that no human treaty can ever be a substitute for the covenant with God. The same holds true of the prophecies of the 'Enemy from the North': they are totally lacking any operative political implications, unless judged retrospectively. Hence, the entire body of *poetical* prophecies about Jerusalem and Judaea in chs. 1–45 has nothing to do with any kind of politics.

A different picture seems to be reflected in the relevant *prose* section of Jeremiah (25.1-14, 27, 28, 37, 38). In 25.9 and 27.6 Nebuchadnezzar is called by God עבדי ('my servant'), a term that expresses the prophet's theopolitics. In ch. 27 Jeremiah is ordered by God to send bonds and yokes (מוסרות ומוטות) to the ambassadors of the kings of Edom, Moab, Tyre and Sidon, who came to Jerusalem probably in 597, the inaugural year of Zedekiah,[14] to plan a rebellion against Babylon. To this symbolic act Jeremiah adds an explanation: it is God who has given those lands to Nebuchadnezzar, and therefore any disloyalty to the Babylonian king will be severely punished 'with the sword the famine and the pestilence until I have consumed them in his hand' (27.8). This theopolitical reasoning clarifies the operative conclusions which should have been drawn from the term עבדי.

Chapter 28 is dependent on ch. 27: the yoke episode and the theopolitical message are the same in both. Here too the root עבד is used (v. 14) to express the kind of relationship that God demands

13. S. Mowinckel, *Zur Komposition des Buches Jeremiah* (Kristiania: Jacob Dybwad, 1914). See also S. Mowinckel, *Prophecy and Tradition* (Oslo: Jacob Dybwad, 1946).

14. 'Jehoiakim' in v. 1 is a mistake, as is proved by vv. 3, 12 and 19-22. The whole verse is missing in G.

between Nebuchadnezzar and the rest of the world, including the animals (חית השדה).

The historical situation described in ch. 37 is the temporary removal of the Babylonian siege, after the Egyptian army marched from Egypt to assist Zedekiah. Jeremiah rejected the king's request to pray for the people and it is clear from the general context that his reasons were theopolitical: Zedekiah's rebellion against Babylon contradicted the prophetic theopolitical directions, and therefore it would fail and the city would be destroyed. The last advice of the prophet to his king is given in ch. 38: 'If you surely surrender to the King of Babylon's princes then your soul shall live and this city shall not be burned with fire, and you and your house shall live' (38.17).

Was this theopolicy authentic to Jeremiah, or was it a late exilic retrospective interpretation added to the book? Jer. 25.1-14 is commonly recognized as belonging to the Dtr layer of the book (Mowinckel's C); chs. 28, 37 and 38 are commonly categorized as part of the 'biographical' source (Mowinckel's B), while ch. 27 is classified C by Mowinckel[15] and some of his followers but is classified A, namely as authentic prophecies of Jeremiah, by Rudolph and seemingly by Bright.[16] Thiel considers all these chapters as having been heavily revised by the *deuteronomistische Redaktion*.[17]

Even if one does not agree with the critical conclusions about the sources of the book of Jeremiah one must realize that all the explicit theopolitical ideas are found in the prose sections, and none in the poetical prophecies denouncing Jerusalem and proclaiming its destruction. This correlation between a certain genre (prose) and a most important theological concept is best explained by the assumption that later contributors to the book of Jeremiah are responsible for ascribing such theopolitical ideas to the prophet Jeremiah. Chapters 37–38 convey a clear message: until the very last hours Jerusalem still had a chance of survival provided Jeremiah's theopolitics were adopted. This message might well be a retrospective answer to the tantalizing question of why Jeremiah, unlike Isaiah, did not succeed in

15. Mowinckel, *Zur Komposition des Buches Jeremiah*, pp. 8-10. See also R.P. Carroll, *Jeremiah* (OTL; London: SCM Press, 1986), pp. 529-37.

16. W. Rudolph, *Jeremia* (HAT; Tübingen: Mohr [Paul Siebeck], 1968), p. 173; J. Bright, *Jeremiah* (AB; Garden City, NY: Doubleday, 1965), pp. 201-203.

17. W. Thiel, *Die Deuteronomistische Redaktion von Jeremia 26–52* (Neukirchen–Vluyn: Neukirchener Verlag, 1981), pp. 5-10, 52-61.

preventing the national catastrophe. Yet this does not necessarily refute the authenticity of the message. Nor, even if the Jeremianic phrasing of the text is suspect, does it lead inevitably to the conclusion that it misrepresents Jeremiah's authentic views. The question therefore remains open: did the so-called biographer or Deuteronomist represent the prophet's ideas accurately, or is it his own, later, concept that has been introduced into the text?[18]

In order to answer this question another prophetic genre, which I have not yet mentioned, should be referred to: prophecies against foreign nations. The nine prophecies in Jeremiah (the one to Babylon will not be discussed here), all proclaiming calamities caused by an enemy, can be divided into two groups. The first includes five prophecies which reflect the concept that God has chosen one nation to govern the world, to be the Lord's 'Rod of Anger', if one adopts Isaiah's terminology: the two prophecies to Egypt (46.2-12, 13-26), the prophecies to the Philistines (47), the prophecies to Qedar and Hazor, the Arabian tribes (49.28-33), and to Elam (49.34-38). Judged by the historical background of the prophecies there can be no doubt that the victorious enemy described in them was identified by Jeremiah's audience as Babylon. It is true that only in one prophecy, that to Qedar, is Nebuchadnezzar mentioned by name in the main text (49.30), while in the others it is found only in the editorial superscriptions (46.2, 13) or conclusions (46.26). Yet, towards the end of the seventh century, when a northern enemy was referred to in prophecies to Egypt, to the Philistines, to the Arabs or to Elam,[19] it was

---

18. It is clear from my argumentation that I utterly reject the idea expressed by Carroll (*Jeremiah*, pp. 55-64) that there never was a historical prophet called Jeremiah, that he was simply a fictitious character invented by the 'Jeremianic School'.

19. See D.J. Wiseman, *Chronicles of Chaldean Kings (625–556 BC) in the British Museum* (London: The Trustees of the British Museum, 1956), p. 70: in the sixth year of Nebuchadnezzar (599 BCE) in the month of Kislev, he marched to Hatti-land, and from there he sent out his companies *mad-ba-ri irtedu-ma (amel) a-ra-bi ma-du-tu buši-šu-nu bu-li-šu-nu* ('and scouring the desert they took much plunder from the Arabs...'). In the Chronicle from Nebuchadnezzar's ninth year (see Wiseman, *Chronicles*, p. 72) the king of Elam is mentioned as Nebuchadnezzar's opponent who *ip-laḫ-ma, ḫat-tu imtaqut-šu-ma ana mati-šu i-tu[rra]* ('was afraid and, panic falling on him, he returned to his own land'). For a comprehensive discussion of Jeremiah's prophecies against foreign nations see Y. Hoffman, *The Prophecies*

absolutely clear which enemy the prophet had in mind.

In the second group of Jeremiah's prophecies against foreign nations (to Moab, 48; Amon, 49.1-6; Edom, 49.7-22; Damascus, 49.23-27) there is not even a hint as to the identity of the enemy.

I suggest the following interpretation of these data. During the first years of his mission Jeremiah, influenced by previous prophetic tradition, uttered prophecies of destruction upon foreign nations. These prophecies—against Moab, Amon, Edom and Damascus—express only a general theological idea about the supremacy of Yahweh in history.[20] Later, towards or after 605, when Jeremiah realized that Nebuchadnezzar was going to be the only great power in the region, he uttered the prophecies to Egypt, the Philistines and the Arabs, which express not only a general theological concept, but a more specific historiosophy shaped by monotheistic patterns of thinking: the *one* and only God has chosen *one* nation to execute his *one* comprehensive historical plan. Such a message at that time had a clear political implication in Judaea: do not oppose Babylon, accept its dominion willingly, since this is the Lord's decree!

Yet this political aspect is not explicit; neither Babylon nor Nebuchadnezzar is specifically mentioned. There are two reasons for this. The first is generic. Jeremiah's prophecies against foreign nations have oracular features, characterized by obscurity. The second is theological. Naming specific kings or nations might have blurred the principal theological aspects of the prophecies. The later editors were less sensitive to this reasoning, and interpreting (correctly) Jeremiah's prophecies with their historical background in mind, they added Nebuchadnezzar's name to the prophecies.[21] By doing

against Foreign Nations in the Bible (Hebrew; Tel Aviv: Tel Aviv University Press, 1977), pp. 108-31; 184-225.

20. The traditional nature of these prophecies is very easily perceived. The prophecy to Moab is a Jeremianic version of an ancient dirge lamenting the destruction of Moab, a duplicate version of which is found in Isa. 15–16. The prophecy to Edom is a literary assemblage with parallels scattered in Jer. 25.29; 48.40-41; 49.30; 50.13 (= 19.8); Obad. 1-6. Damascus was no longer an independent kingdom after the Assyrian occupation in 733, although the city still existed, including perhaps the 'Ben Hadad palaces' (49.27); this phrase is also used in Amos 1.3-5. Yet, in spite of their stereotypic features, the distinctive Jeremianic style is reflected in these prophecies. See Hoffman, *Prophecies against Foreign Nations*, pp. 117-22; 203-208.

21. Nebuchadnezzar is mentioned in the prophecy to Qedar and Hazor

so they introduced actual theopolitical aspects into the prophet's historiosophy. As we have already seen, this is exactly the tendency of the above-mentioned non-Jeremianic prose sections of the book.

We can now return to the issue of whether the theopolitics found in these prose sections adequately represents Jeremiah's ideas. It seems that an affirmative answer is in order. While in the direct prophecies to Judaea Jeremiah refrained from expressing any political opinion, in his prophecies against foreign nations after 605 he did express a concrete theopolitics, although not explicitly. The last step towards a real theopolitics, or rather 'theopolitization', was made by the editors retrospectively, both by introducing Nebuchadnezzar's name to the prophecies and by ascribing to Jeremiah explicit theopolitical preaching. Why did Jeremiah refrain from introducing his political ideas into the prophecies to Judaea? Was it perhaps because he learned a lesson from Isaiah, whose advocated theopolitics proved to be mistaken? I cannot answer this question. However, I do believe that the editors and the so-called 'Biographer' presented Jeremiah as a prophet who openly and unequivocally advocated a specific policy because they realized, retrospectively, that he was correct in his hints towards that policy in his prophecies against foreign nations. Such hindsight is historiographical in character, although it is expressed through 'biography'.

4. *Haggai 2.23*
The last example demonstrating the occasionally retrospective character of biblical theopolitics is the only one that relates to domestic policy. In Hag. 2.23 we read the following:

> In that day, says the Lord of hosts, I will take you, Zerubabel my servant, the son of Shealtiel, says the Lord, and will make you as a signet, for I have chosen you (ושמתיך כחותם כי בך בחרתי).

One can hardly ignore the connection between this and Jer. 22.24:

> As I live, says the Lord, though Coniah the son of Jehoiakim king of Judah were the signet on my right hand (חותם על יד ימיני), yet I would pluck you off (כי משם אתקנך).

(Jer. 49.30). In that instance it is difficult to determine whether the reference is original or editorial. Yet even if it is original it means that only in one case did Jeremiah himself decide to mention Nebuchadnezzar's name, in spite of the above-mentioned considerations. Perhaps he did so in order to stress to Jerusalem the relevance of a prophecy about the Arab tribes.

It is inconceivable that Haggai, meaning to encourage Zerubabel, would use the metaphor of a signet which had already lost its meaning by Jeremiah's prophecy. I therefore assume that Haggai was the first to use the metaphor. A counter-prophecy was then ascribed to Jeremiah and inserted into the prophetic anthology bearing his name, in order to nullify Haggai's theopolitical message. Both these prophecies, then, reflect a political polemic in Jerusalem in about 520 BCE. If this interpretation is correct, then Jer. 22.24 is another example of the retrospective character of some of the apparent theopolitical sayings in the Bible.

IV

The passages discussed in this paper in an attempt to achieve a better understanding of biblical theopolitics are by no means the only relevant ones, and not necessarily the best possible biblical examples. Perhaps a better way to understand biblical theopolitics would be to analyse stories of events such as the Josianic cultic reform, or the activities of Ezra and Nehemiah; but these are very complicated issues which cannot be discussed comprehensively in a short paper. However, I hope that my examples have shed some light upon biblical theopolitics.

What conclusions have been reached with regard to the opening question, 'what is theopolitics?' Is it related to the interaction between *theos* ('god') and politics? The answer is yes, in some cases. Yet in other cases it is also related to the interaction between *theology* and politics. Does the term imply the belief that politics are determined by the supposed will of God, the latter being the only criterion for making political decisions? Once again, the answer is in the affirmative in some cases, but in other cases it is better understood as a manipulation of religion, in order either to propagate a certain policy or to justify it retrospectively. In some cases, as we have seen, the retrospective combination of religion and politics becomes the mortar and straw out of which blocks for building a historiography are made. Hence, the answer to the third question—how sharp are the borders between the alternative possible definitions of 'theopolitics'— is at hand: there are hardly any borders. This vagueness is embodied in the very nature of such a dialectical combination between religion, politics and human beings' quest for certain, irrefutable formulae by which national life can be conducted.

CHRIST, THE BODY OF CHRIST AND COSMIC POWERS IN PAUL'S LETTERS AND THE NEW TESTAMENT AS A WHOLE*

Gottfried Nebe

1. *Introduction*

The theme of our (Jewish–Christian) conference 'Politics and Theopolitics in the Bible' is the problem of power and powers; power and powers in the human world and in relation to the might of God. If we look at the New Testament and the development of Christian religion we can say, starting with Jesus of Nazareth, that his appearance on earth, his work and his fate are connected to the problem of power. In the same way what is called in German the *Wirkungsgeschichte*[1] of Jesus, the history of Jesus beyond the end of his earthly life, deals with power and powers, with the might of God, with the power of the Christian church, with other powers in the world and the history of the world.

If we look at the historical Jesus, we see the problem of power on the one hand in Jesus' proclamation of the kingdom of God. Through Jesus the kingdom of God has come close, against the power and kingdom of Satan (see the catchwords βασιλεία τοῦ θεοῦ/τῶν οὐρανῶν, מלכות שמים; cf. especially Mk 1.14-15; 3.22-27; Lk. 11.20; 17.20-21). On the other hand the Jesus tradition of the Gospels presents us with the famous saying of Jesus: 'Pay Caesar what is due to Caesar, and pay God what is due to God' (see Mk 12.17 parr.). And if the apocalyptic message of the coming Son of Man also belongs to the proclamation of the historical Jesus (cf. especially Mk 8.38; Lk. 12.8-9), we find here too the problem of power: power relative to the last judgement and to a judgment of universal or cosmic dimensions (cf. also Mk. 13 parr.).

---

*   This is a revised, annotated and somewhat expanded version of my conference paper, read on March 2 1992.

1.   Cf. H.-G. Gadamer, *Wahrheit und Methode: Grundzüge einer philosophischen Hermeneutik* (Tübingen: Mohr, 1960).

Finally, we may ask, what do the concepts of the messiah-Christ and the Body of Christ mean here? It is clear that in the New Testament and certainly in the Gospels the concept and expectation of the messiah, the faith in Jesus as the Davidic messiah are important (cf. especially Mk 8.27-30 parr.; 12.35-37 parr.; Lk. 2.11; 24.25-27; Rom. 1.3-4). But it is debatable whether the concept of the messiah goes back to the preaching and self-identification of the historical Jesus himself.[2]

What does the conception of the Body of Christ—σῶμα Χριστοῦ— mean here? It is clear that in many parts of the New Testament and certainly in the Jesus tradition of the Gospels the concept of the Body of Christ is very important. Jesus underwent bodily suffering and was bodily raised from the dead (cf. Lk. 23–24 parr.; 1 Cor. 15). There is also the New Testament tradition of the Holy Communion, the Last Supper, where the body of Jesus is connected with a sacramental communion (cf. Mk 14.22-25 parr.; 1 Cor. 1.16; 11.23-26). Nevertheless it is remarkable that we cannot at first glance make clear connections between the central points of Jesus' proclamation and the concept of the Body of Christ, if by the latter is meant the physical body with its limbs and organs. It is on this aspect of the concept of the Body of Christ that I shall be focusing in this paper, and it is important to note that it appears not in the Gospels but in the Pauline letters: Romans, 1 Corinthians, Ephesians, Colossians. We may therefore see here a difference between the Jesus tradition of the Gospels and the figure of Jesus in the Pauline corpus.

In the history of Christian theology in the twentieth century, especially in Germany, this conception of the Body of Christ illuminated the problem of 'politics and theopolitics'. This is partly connected with the controversial theological dispute between Protestants and Roman Catholics.[3] But another question is, what are the relations between the concept of the Body of Christ and the concept of Jesus Christ as the sovereign of the cosmos, the κοσμοκράτωρ?[4] What can

---

2. On this subject cf. W. Wrede, *Das Messiasgeheimnis in den Evangelien: Zugleich ein Beitrag zum Verständnis des Markusevangeliums* (Göttingen: Vandenhoeck & Ruprecht, 4th edn, 1969); R. Bultmann, *Theologie des Neuen Testaments* (Tübingen: Mohr, 4th edn, 1961), pp. 26-34 (§4).

3. Cf. especially J.J. Meuzelaar, *Der Leib des Messias* (Assen: Van Gorcum, 1961), pp. 171-74, with reference to Karl Barth.

4. Cf. here E. Käsemann, *Paulinische Perspektiven* (Tübingen: Mohr, 1969),

we say here about the *Königsherrschaft Christi*, the kingly rule of Christ in cosmic dimensions, especially in connection with the relationship between the church and cosmic powers and political powers in the world? Is the concept of the Body of Christ a cosmic idea or an ecclesiastical one, belonging only to the understanding of the church? In this paper I will try to show that the latter view is correct; the New Testament, or Pauline, notion of the Body of Christ in the sense of a physical body with its limbs and organs is an ecclesiastical conception. Finally, we must examine the role of the designation 'messiah' in connection with this concept of the Body of Christ.

2. *Historical and Exegetical Approaches to the Subject*

I will begin with the idea of the Body of Christ and from that starting-point approach the issues outlined above. Again I should emphasize that I will be looking at the motif of the Body of Christ in the New Testament only in Romans and 1 Corinthians, and secondarily in Ephesians and Colossians. Romans and 1 Corinthians are undisputedly authentic Pauline epistles, but Ephesians and Colossians are controversial and in my opinion are not authentic. I therefore consider them Deuteropauline, and treat them in my paper after the authentic epistles of Paul.

If we look at this Body of Christ motif in the New Testament[5] we can see that in the two important passages 1 Corinthians 12 and Romans 12 Paul refers to the human experience of the body and its

pp. 178-210: 'Das theologische Problem des Motivs von Leibe Christi', esp. p. 183: 'Die Rede vom Christusleib ist die ekklesiologische Formel, mit welcher sich die hellenistische Christenheit zur Weltmission anschickte'. And Paul received that, as Käsemann supposes. In the famous 'Theological Declaration of Barmen' (31 May 1934) of the German 'Confessing Church' Jesus Christ's government of all fields of life is emphasized. And thesis 3 says, with ecclesiastical citation of Eph. 4.15-16 about the Body of Christ motif, and rejections: 'Wir verwerfen die falsche Lehre, als dürfe die Kirche die Gestalt ihrer Botschaft und ihrer Ordnung ihrem Belieben oder dem Wechsel der jeweils herrschenden weltanschaulichen und politischen Überzeugung überlassen'. See also, on the problem of 'Königsherrschaft Christi', E. Wolf, 'Königsherrschaft Christi und lutherische Zwei-Reiche-Lehre' (1964), in *Peregrinatio*, II (Munich: Chr. Kaiser Verlag, 1965), pp. 207-29.

5. Cf. E. Schweizer, 'σῶμα, σώματος, τό σῶμα', *EWNT*, III, pp. 771-72; 'σῶμα, σωματικός, σύσσωμος', *TWNT*, VII, pp. 1024-25; 'σῶμα, κτλ', *TWNT*, X, pp. 1276-78; 'χρίω, χριστός, κτλ', *TWNT*, X, pp. 1292-93.

limbs and organs. He says in Rom. 12.4-5: 'For just as in a single human body there are many limbs and organs (ἔχομεν), all with different functions, so all of us, united with Christ, form one body, serving individually as limbs and organs to one another'. In the same way Paul says in 1 Cor. 12.12: 'For Christ is like a single body with its limbs and organs, which, many as they are, together make up one body'.

These two passages clearly show the adaption of normal human experience to a figurative use. Paul obviously appeals to some kind of a general human agreement. We can trace this idea back to classical antiquity, for example to the work of Plato. The ancient Greeks had developed many conceptions of the body and its limbs and organs,[6] and we should notice them in the background of the Pauline passages.

A particularly important aspect of the classical concept of the body is the analogy made between human organizations or collectives and an *organism*. In this way the term 'body' (σῶμα) becomes used in a figurative sense. The analogy was developed as part of the language of political philosophy, and we can find it especially in the work of Plato.[7] From the Roman world, also, we have the famous story of Menenius Agrippa (494 BCE) about the stomach and the limbs of the body, recounted by the historian Livy (59 BCE–17 CE).[8] In later centuries, at the time of Paul, the idea was important to the Stoic philosophers.[9] In Paul's letters the idea is developed into his use of 'Body of Christ' as an ecclesiastical conception.

It is also clear that in classical antiquity the world as a whole, the universal cosmos, was seen as an organism, as a unified body with its limbs and organs, with an arrangement, harmony and sympathy for the whole. This idea is also to be found in Plato (cf. *Timaeus* 30b),[10] and later again in the philosophy of the Stoics.[11] People could imagine here that the cosmos is the body of a divine being, that divine beings

6. Cf. E. Schweizer, 'Griechentum', *TWNT*, VI, pp. 1025 (1.6)-42 (1.9).

7. Cf. the human body and the state in *Republic* 8.556e.

8. *Ab urbe condita libri* 2.32.9-12.

9. Cf. A. Demandt, *Metaphern für Geschichte: Sprachbilder und Gleichnisse im historisch-politischen Denken* (Munich: Beck, 1978), esp. pp. 20-25.

10. Here with body and soul.

11. Cf. Diogenes Laertius 7.138, to Chrysippus and Posidonius. See Ioannes ab Arnim, *Stoicorum Veterum Fragmenta*, II (Stuttgart: Teubner, 1979 [1903]), Fragm. 634, p. 192.

are members of this body or even its head. They supposed that the deity or the soul of the world (*Weltseele*), or the divine being as the soul of the world, penetrated the whole world, the universal cosmos, as an organism, working across it, steering, and controlling, just as the soul animates the human body with its limbs and organs. Human beings and the cosmos could therefore be conceived as analogous to each other, in a relation of micro- and macrocosmos, micro- and macroorganism.[12] We also find the idea that the world or the universe is actually created or constructed out of the body of the organs and limbs of a divine being.[13]

That leads us to the theory of cosmical monism in classical antiquity and to the related idea of a universal deity (*Allgott-Vorstellung*). The Stoic philosophers, especially, developed these conceptions in a cosmic direction. We must ask to what extent Paul took account of these ideas. It is very interesting that Paul in fact emphasized Christ's reign over the cosmos and especially the process of its complete realization, which is now continuing. But it is also interesting that he does not regard the whole world, the total universe, as the 'Body of Christ'. Even in Colossians and Ephesians we do not find this view expressed, although scholars have sometimes maintained that we do. I shall return to this particular point later. But I want here to make the point that one of my main theses in this paper is that the term 'Body of Christ' always refers, in Paul's letters and even in the Deuteropauline epistles to the Colossians and Ephesians, to the Christians and the church. It is an ecclesiastical not a cosmical phrase. Only in the tradition behind Colossians and maybe also behind Ephesians can we suppose such a cosmic language and cosmic ideas, and therefore a priority of Christ over the cosmic powers, in connection with a cosmic idea of the body with its limbs and organs, and the government of the 'head' of the 'body' in this context.

A further question is: do we find in classical antiquity an important role for the concept of the body and limbs and organs of a divine or heavenly figure who is in opposition to the bad powers and the anti-divine in the world? This would indicate a move from monism and pantheism to dualism.

12. Cf. here Schweizer, 'Griechentum', pp. 1029 (1.9-24), 1034 (1.8-14).
13. See here from the ancient Near East the famous epic *Enuma Eliš* (about Tiamat and Marduk and the creation), translated in *ANET*, pp. 60-72, 501-503 (esp. p. 67, Tablet IV, 128ff.).

In fact we can find indications of this,[14] particularly in the Gnostic traditions. But scholars dispute whether we can trace such ideas to the days of Paul or even earlier times. Generally scholars have objected to the view that we must find in a text or tradition the so-called Saviour- or salvation-myth in a developed form, if we wish to find the idea of the 'collection of the body' or the collection of the 'limbs and organs' by the 'head (of the body)' (that refers to the Saviour, Redeemer, 'salvator'). We do not find this earlier than in Manichaean texts, that means not earlier than the third century CE.[15] But still we find, perhaps in the Valentinian Gnostics and certainly in any case in the *Odes of Solomon* (cf. 17.14ff., 2nd century CE),[16] such ideas of a Redeemer or Saviour, who collects his 'limbs and organs', dispersed in the (evil) world, and who brings them back and joins them together, if need be as the 'head' of a 'body'.

Finally we should ask, especially in the context of our conference, what role the concept of Christ as messiah, grounded on the Jewish biblical tradition, plays here. The concept of the messiah leads to a dualism and to a collective and perhaps cosmic background and horizon. For the messiah will bring a special time of salvation, against the hostile powers. Can we, then, discover in the Jewish biblical conception of the messiah as it was known in New Testament times, particularly the times of Paul, a direct ground for the concept of the 'Body of Christ' as Paul uses it, with the sense of a body with its limbs and organs? Or, if this conception of the 'Body of Christ' cannot be so grounded, has it perhaps been influenced by a specifically Christian idea of the messiah, together with the formalized use of the title 'Christ' for Jesus? Is the special significance of the body ($\sigma\tilde{\omega}\mu\alpha$) in Paul's theology also important here, perhaps influenced or intensified by Paul's human experiences of his own body? Looking at the biblical Jewish traditions and sources, I cannot find direct proofs or examples to show that the concept of the messiah, especially the 'messiah ben David' or the 'messiah ben Levi', would be combined

14. But the Tiamat in the ancient Near Eastern epic *Enuma Eliš* belongs to evil.

15. Cf. W. Rudolph, *Die Gnosis* (UTB, 1577; Göttingen: Vandenhoeck & Ruprecht, 3rd edn, 1990), p. 141.

16. Cf. B. Murmelstein, 'Adam: Ein Beitrag zur Messiaslehre', *WZKM* 35 (1928), pp. 242-75; 36 (1929), pp. 51-86, esp. p. 268; K.L. Schmidt, 'ἐκκλησία', *TWNT*, III, pp. 502-39, 513 ll.24-26.

with a collective or cosmical 'body'-idea.[17]

But it is possible that there are in the context of the idea of the messiah two horizons or two fields of conception which are important. On the one hand, in the context of so-called 'national eschatology' the messiah could relate to the people of Israel or his tribes and to the dispersed people. From this could be developed the idea of a human collective as a 'body', with its limbs, and with the messiah as the 'head' of this body. We could then posit a link to the Pauline use of the concept of the body with limbs and organs to illustrate the constitution of the church and the Christian congregation. As I indicated above, however, I know of no Jewish biblical sources that directly support this hypothesis.

On the other hand, it is also possible that the concept of the messiah could have been understood in a cosmic context, with a cosmic significance and function. In this way the idea could have been linked to a cosmic 'body' idea, the messiah functioning perhaps as the 'head' of this body. Again, however, I do not know of any direct evidence for this, even taking into account ideas about the pre-existence of the messiah or of the participation of the messiah at the creation. Probably in Jewish antiquity such opinions connect more easily with so called hypostasy-speculations, with the *ḥokmâ*–Sophia tradition and their development on a biblical foundation. So here the example of the Hellenistic Jew Philo Alexandrinus would also be relevant, with his *logos–pneuma* conception, together with the reception of Platonic and Stoic ideas. I would also ask at this point about the relevance of the Torah. In scriptures such as Sirach, as is well known, the Torah is presented as having a special relation to *ḥokmâ* or Sophia; it has even been identified with *ḥokmâ* or Sophia.

To sum up, then, it seems to me that if we look at the concept of the messiah in the Jewish biblical tradition we can find possible links to

17. The discussion after my paper, especially with my Jewish colleagues, produced no new evidence at this point. This discussion pointed up for the Jewish horizon the understanding of 'Ebed' (in Second Isaiah) as the messiah and his relation to the people of God, for the history of religion the Egyptian Isis–Osiris legend (cf. the collection of the dispersed parts of the body of Osiris) and the Hittite Illuyanka-myth (cf. the heart and the eyes of the 'God of the Weather', lost and retrieved [*ANET*, pp. 125-26]). See here also the famous Greek myth of Dionysos (cf. Schweizer, 'Griechentum', p. 1035 [1.15-18]).

the concept of the body with its limbs and organs, but not direct evidence of the idea. As such possible links, I would suggest

1. the repatriation or collection of the dispersed tribes and of the elected by the messiah at the end of time[18]
2. pre-existence and astral-ideas in connection with the concept of the messiah;[19]
3. combinations of the concept of the messiah with the idea of the Son of Man as a heavenly Highness-figure,[20] with the Adam tradition, with the *ḥokmâ*–Sophia tradition, with the so-called mediating figure and hypostasy-speculations, generally in connection with the possible interchange of charges and functions in ancient Judaism;
4. statements about God and his hypostasies, penetrating the world, the creation, statements about God or his names as 'space' and so on.[21]

3. *Theses*

We now come to the following theses, which must be examined and argued.

Theses for the Concept of the 'Body of Christ'
The use of this motif in the New Testament particularly features the term 'Christ'. Can we relate this directly to the traditional Jewish concept of the messiah? It seems to me that we find, rather, developments of the messiah concept in early Christianity applied to Jesus of Nazareth, and we have then to consider whether the term 'Christ' has already come into usage as a *name*.

The 'Body of Christ' motif in the sense of the body with limbs and organs is used in the New Testament only in the so-called Pauline corpus. In the authentic epistles of Paul this motif only relates ecclesiastically to the Christian community or the church. This ecclesiastical

18. Cf. here W. Bousset and H. Gressmann, *Die Religion des Judentums im späthellenistischen Zeitalter* (Tübingen: Mohr, 4th edn, 1966), pp. 236-38.

19. Cf. in the New Testament Lk. 1.78-79.

20. See here the repatriation or collection in connection with the Son of Man idea in the New Testament, for example in Mk 13.26-27, Mt. 24.30-31. Cf. also *1 En.* 61.5.

21. Cf. Bousset and Gressmann, *Religion*, pp. 302-20, 342-57.

use is also found in the 'school of Paul', that is in the so-called
Deuteropauline epistles. But still it seems that in the background of the
Deuteropauline epistles, especially in the tradition behind Colossians
1, there appears the connection with a cosmic concept of the 'Body of
Christ'.[22] We need to consider whether Paul has created for himself
this motif as an ecclesiastical one, perhaps with various influences.
One influence could be his experience with his own body, in connection with the ancient tradition of analogy between the body with its
constituent parts and human collectives. Another influence could be
the development of the messiah idea and Christology in early
Christianity, grounded on the Jesus-events, the passion and death of
Jesus, his resurrection and exaltation, but also in connection with the
body of Jesus in the sacrament of the Holy Communion. We are, then,
faced here with multiple interpretive possibilities.

Among these we can also mention the following: the idea of Israel
as a vine in the Bible and Judaism; the language of the vine and the
branches as found in John 15; the conception of the so-called corporate personality, the idea of the ancestor who contains his descendants
within himself; generally, the Son of Man and Adam speculations.[23]

*General Aspects of the Relationship between Christ and the Cosmic
Powers*
The development of the concept of the messiah and Christology in
early Christianity, grounded there on the Jesus-events, in connection
with the passion and death of Jesus, his resurrection and exaltation,
did not bring to the concept of the Body of Christ a cosmic dimension.
This is true despite the fact that in Paul's theology the resurrected and
exalted Jesus is the clear lord of the powers and especially of the
cosmic powers. If we suppose a cosmic development in the background of the Deuteropauline epistles, it is not based primarily on the
resurrection and exaltation of Jesus and the power of Jesus by this, but

22. Cf. Schweizer, 'σῶμα', *EWNT*, III, p. 776: 'Doch tauchen kosmische Bezüge
erst in Kol und Eph auf, und Leib Christi ist immer die Gemeinde, nie die Welt'.

23. For this see for example Schweizer, 'σῶμα', *EWNT*, III, esp. pp. 775-79;
'σῶμα', *TWNT*, VII, p. 1064 (1.14)-79 (1.36); 'Die Kirche als Leib Christi in den
paulinischen Homologumena' (1961), in *Neotestamentica* (Zürich: Zwingli-Verlag,
1963), pp. 272-92; 'Die Kirche als Leib Christi in den paulinischen Antilegomena'
(1961), in *Neotestamentica*, pp. 293-316; 'The Church as the Missionary Body of
Christ' (1961), in *Neotestamentica*, pp. 317-29.

is primarily based on ideas of protology and theology of creation, up to the idea of pre-existence. I suppose that this follows the paths of the biblically rooted *ḥokmâ*, Sophia and hypostasy speculations applied to Jesus, perhaps in connection with the reception and treatment of wider ancient ideas of the cosmos, possibly monistic or pantheistic. Indeed Paul is familiar with such ideas of protology and pre-existence, in relation to the salvation-mediator and especially in relation to Jesus Christ as the mediator of creation. We can find this, for instance, in Phil. 2.5, Gal. 4.4 or, especially, 1 Cor. 8.6. But it is clear that Paul did not develop his Christology in his authentic epistles emphatically and deliberately in the direction of a creation-mediatorship. We can find such a development later in John 1 or Hebrews 1, for example, or in the older tradition behind Colossians 1.[24]

4. *Exegetical Observations, Arguments and Explanations*

In the following section I will trace our subject by more detailed exegetical investigations of the New Testament texts. I start with the authentic epistles of Paul, because they are the oldest literary proofs of our motif in the New Testament. But first I shall list the passages in the New Testament which are important and noteworthy as regards the motif of the 'Body of Christ' in the sense of the body with limbs and organs. These passages are: Rom. 12.6-8; 1 Cor. 6.15; 10.16-17(?); 12.12-31; Col. 1.18, 24; 2.10(?); 2.19(17-19); 3.15; Eph. 1.22-23; 2.16; 4.4, 12-16(25?); 5.23, 30; about 15 passages. Here we often find 'Christ' used as the christological term of highness or as a name, but sometimes also 'Son' and *soter*. In the following I will discuss only a small selection of these passages.

The Authentic Epistles of Paul
I shall begin with Romans. Particularly relevant here is Rom. 12.3-8:[25]

> In virtue of the gift that God in his grace has given me I say to everyone among you: do not be conceited or think too highly of yourself; but think

24. Cf. here also the relationship of these passages to 1 Cor. 8.6 or 2 Cor. 4.4.
25. Cf. here the commentaries on Romans; for example O. Michel, *Der Brief an die Römer* (MeyerK, 4; Göttingen: Vandenhoeck & Ruprecht, 14th edn, 1978); E. Käsemann, *An die Römer* (HNT, 8a; Tübingen: Mohr, 4th edn, 1980); U. Wilckens, *Der Brief an die Römer* (EKKNT, 6.3; Neukirchen–Vluyn: Neukirchener Verlag; Zürich: Benzinger Verlag, 2nd edn, 1989).

your way to a sober estimate based on the measure of faith that God has dealt to each of you. For just as in a single human body there are many limbs and organs, all with different functions, so all of us, united with Christ, form one body, serving individually as limbs and organs to one another. The gifts we possess differ as they are allotted to us by God's grace, and must be exercised accordingly: the gift of inspired utterance, for example, in proportion to a man's faith; or the gift of administration, in administration. A teacher should employ his gift in teaching, and one who has the gift of stirring speech should use it to stir his hearers. If you give to charity, give with all your heart; if you are a leader, exert yourself to lead; if you are helping others in distress, do it cheerfully.

First of all we realize from this passage the recourse Paul has, as already noted, to general human experience. Paul uses an analogy which relates general human experience to the idea of a human community as an organism with body, limbs, and organs, and the latter then connects with the 'Body of Christ' motif. But here in Romans 12 the expressions remain opalescent, if we look at the language relating to the 'Body of Christ' motif and its concrete and figurative aspects. Paul does not directly say: 'Body of Christ', but: 'so all of us, united with Christ, form one body, serving individually as limbs and organs to one another...' In this the idea of a human collective relates to the concept ἐν Χριστῷ, a well-known Pauline idea. At the same time it may show that Paul has simply used commonly known facts and ideas for Christian purposes.

This method of comparison, which refers to everyday life, further recalls the popular philosophy of the time, especially the so-called Stoic-Cynic Diatribe. In my opinion it is not surprising that Paul uses such a motif in his epistle to a Christian community which he did not know personally, which he had not founded. We can add that Christians in Rome certainly were sensitive to language comparing a human community with the organism of the body, especially if we remember again the famous tale of Menenius Agrippa about the rebellion of the limbs and organs against the stomach.[26]

Relations of power are addressed here in Romans 12 as relations within the Christian community itself, relating to God or Christ. We see the grace of God as might. Our motif of the Body of Christ is therefore set in the context of the gifts that God in his grace has given. And we may ask if such gifts of grace are also a kind of politics

---

26. See Livy, *Ab urbe condita libri* 2.32.

or theopolitics in the Christian community.

A second passage very important for our subject is 1 Cor. 12.12-27.[27] It belongs to the wider context of Pauline arguments for the spiritual gifts and gifts of grace in 1 Corinthians 12–14. Again, in 1 Corinthians 12 we see the recourse of Paul to general human experience, hence his use once again of the body with limbs and organs. When Paul concludes 'For Christ is like a single body with...', as in the Romans passage he does not explicitly use the term 'Body of Christ'. But then at the end in v. 27 he does use the term 'Body of Christ', and he relates it directly to the Christian community at Corinth. However, it is also possible that the relation of the concept of the body, limbs and organs to the Christ indicates a mythological background as in Romans. We should consider the arguments in scholarship for a pre-Gnostic development and the tendency to the Gnostic or pre-Gnostic Saviour-myth by the Pauline statements about Sophia in 1 Cor. 2.6ff. We should also remember the idea of the so-called corporate personality.

Finally in this passage the aspect of 'the same God', 'the same Lord', 'the same Spirit' is very interesting (cf. 12.4-6). Certainly here Paul tries to emphasize, by relating it to the motif of body, limbs and organs, the unity and superiority of the whole, considering the problems of the splits in the Corinthian community and the individualistic Pneumatics there. With this background he discusses the multitude and the splitting of the limbs and organs of the Body very extensively (cf. 12.14-26).[28] It also certainly relates to the Jewish biblical tradition of monotheistic confession to the one Lord or God (cf. Deut. 6.4) and generally to the wider background of the ancient εἷς θεός motif, especially in the religious and cultural melting pot of Corinth. In this melting pot particular religious and sociological differences are not important. Paul shows this by the motif of the one Body, and also by the one baptism and the one *pneuma* (cf. 12.12-13). And he says that especially the lower and weaker parts of the Body are remarkable (cf. 12.22-25).

27. Cf. the commentaries to 1 Cor., for example H. Lietzmann, *An die Korinther* (HNT, 9; Tübingen: Mohr, 5th edn, 1969); H. Conzelmann, *Der erste Brief an die Korinther* (MeyerK, 5; Göttingen: Vandenhoeck & Ruprecht, 12th edn, 1981).

28. Cf. here also the arguments of the limbs and organs which we can see in the tradition of the famous tale of Menenius Agrippa.

Another interesting and important passage here is 1 Cor. 10.16-17, especially in the context of 1 Corinthians 10–11 with its sacramental orientation. In 10.16-17 Paul discusses the Last Supper, Holy Communion and the communion with the Lord Jesus Christ against the communion with the demons. Paul writes this because the Christians of Corinth had problems with the 'food offered to an idol, offered in sacrifice'. And here Paul directly brings in the problem of powers in the world. At the same time he connects this with the 'Body of Christ' motif as an ecclesiastical idea.[29]

The Deuteropauline Epistles Colossians and Ephesians
In the Deuteropauline epistles of the New Testament, Ephesians and Colossians are important. They presuppose and take up the Pauline language. The motif of the Body of Christ is found in many places in these epistles.

Ecclesiastically we find a development from the works considered here authentically Pauline. The charges and functions have been differentiated, developed and established more extensively. We can see a deliberate terminological identification of 'Body of Christ' and the church. In connection with the organism ĭdea the functions and working of the 'limbs and organs' are further reflected upon. This leads to the notion of the superiority of Christ as the head of the body. These epistles talk about the growing of the organism, the growing to 'manhood', to the 'complete' ($\pi\lambda\acute{\eta}\rho\omega\mu\alpha$), the growing as 'building up', and so on. In Colossians the share of the Gentile Christians in the church as the 'Body of Christ' is important; this emphasizes the unity of the church of Jewish Christians and Gentile Christians. All this remains internal to the church. It does not shed much light on the problem of the cosmic powers and their relation to Christ or to the church as the 'Body of Christ'. At the most, then, we find here—as already seen in the authentic epistles of Paul—an opposition of church and cosmos or world. The title 'Christ' predominates. But is it used in the Deuteropauline epistles consciously as a messianic term or is it already becoming formalized as a name?

At this point it is important to ask if cosmology is important to the 'Body of Christ' concept in Colossians and Ephesians. To answer this question I will look briefly at a few passages which seem to me to be of significance. I start with Colossians.

---

29. Cf. here too 1 Cor. 6.15 (the problem of the intercourse with the prostitute).

The first passage to note is Col. 1.18.[30] It is part of a so-called Christ-hymn.[31] Col. 1.17-19 reads:

> And he exists before everything, and all things are held together in him. He is, moreover, the head of the body, the church. He is its origin, the first to return from the dead, to be in all things alone supreme...

There are good scholarly arguments to take Col. 1.15-20 to be a traditional Christ-song or hymn, which has been adapted, reworked and arranged by the author of the letter. The tradition in 1.18a would have read: 'He is the head of the Body', that is of the creatures, the cosmos. We would then have the concept of the Body being used here in connection with the idea of cosmic powers. But the author of Colossians then added 'the Church', and this changed the connotations of the term 'the Body' from being primarily cosmic to primarily ecclesiastic.[32] This seems to me a plausible account given what we know of the history of Colossians.

However, we do not find in this passage the title 'Christ'. We last find it before this passage in Col. 1.7 and then not until 1.24. We find in Col. 1.13 the title 'Son', but we do not find this title in the hymn itself. Only at the level of redaction does the traditional hymn relate to that title 'Son'. Instead of this we read in the hymn titles or terms such as 'image of...God', 'the primacy over all created things' or 'the first to return from the dead'. Therefore we could more correctly call the traditional hymn a mediator- or Saviour-hymn (*Mittelwesen-Erlöser-Lied*).

We can distinguish two parts of this so-called Christ-hymn, Col. 1.15-20, which on the whole are parallel or analogic. We find this pattern at the level of the tradition underlying Colossians.[33] And this is important for us. Here the first part, Col. 1.15-18a, is oriented to ideas of protology and theology of creation. In this part we find the cosmic statement about the Body and its head. By contrast the second part, in Col. 1.18b-20, is oriented to the endtime and eschatology. So

30. Cf. the commentaries on Colossians, for example E. Lohse, *Der Brief an die Kolosser und an Philemon* (MeyerK, 9.2; Göttingen: Vandenhoeck & Ruprecht, 15th edn, 1977); E. Schweizer, *Der Brief an die Kolosser* (EKKNT, 12; Neukirchen–Vluyn: Neukirchener-Verlag; Zürich: Benzinger Verlag, 3rd edn, 1989).

31 Many scholars have written about this passage. See especially Schweizer, *Brief an die Kolosser*, pp. 50-51.

32. Cf. for example Schweizer, *Brief an die Kolosser*, pp. 52-53, 69-70.

33. Cf. especially Schweizer, *Brief an die Kolosser*, pp. 56-59.

we find in the first part catchwords such as 'image of God, primacy over all created things, all things are held together in him', in the second part catchwords such as 'origin, the first to return from the dead, the complete came to dwell, to reconcile the whole universe to himself, making peace...' It is not clear how these two parts were generated in this way, because no direct logical link has been made between them, between the aspects of protology and theology of creation, and the endtime and eschatology. We can perhaps consider the catchwords 'primacy over...the first to...' to be the impulse to the parallelism.[34] The parallelism consists in a type of christological 'two governments' or 'two kingdoms' doctrine.

In this way the first part of the traditional Christ-hymn clearly tries to practise Christology against the background of monism and pantheism, against the background of the classical conception of the cosmos, and taking into account the integration of these ideas in a biblically rooted conception of creation. We may here also remember the tradition of the *ḥokmâ*–Sophia speculations in theological thinking about the creation in Early Judaism.[35] We may also refer to Philo's statements about Sophia and the *logos* as 'image' and 'beginning'.[36]

The author of Colossians having, by the addition in v. 18 of 'the church', transformed the cosmic conception of the 'Body' into an ecclesiastical one, we now find the collective concept of the body with limbs and organs, and this brings in the ancient idea of a political collective as a body with its various parts. In this way we might see Col. 1.18a as belonging to the second part of the hymn, which would put the dividing line between the two parts at the end of Col. 1.17. But Col. 1.18a does not link the two parts of the hymn by Christology, nor by the christological aspect of power. The cosmic idea of the power as 'head' of the 'body' has changed to an internal ecclesiastical relation, and the relation of Christ to the cosmic powers is no longer addressed here. The author of Colossians may possibly see a new,

34. In German *Erstgeborener*. Trying to connect the two parts by the idea of the *pleroma* does not work very well. Certainly, this idea is very important in Gnosticism and its development up to Manichaeism, especially in protological or cosmological and eschatological or soteriological contexts. But we find in Col. 1.19 a quite different orientation, founded on ideas of incarnation and theology of revelation.

35. Cf. here the development from Prov. to Sir. and Wis. (7.26!).

36. Cf. *Leg. All.* 1.43; *Conf. Ling.* 146-47; *Rer. Div. Haer.* 230-31.

superior framework for the connection of the two parts of the hymn
in Col. 1.15-20 in the statements in Col. 1.12-13 about 'the realm of
light' and 'the kingdom of his dear Son'. Moreover, it seems that the
author of Colossians has added the words 'to be in all things alone
supreme' in Col. 1.18c.[37] This phrase can also serve to connect and
hold together the two parts of the hymn through the view that the Son
is in all things supreme, whether in the area of theology of creation or
in the area of the endtime and eschatology.

A second passage to consider is Col. 2.10. Here we find the phrase:
'Every power and authority in the universe is subject to him as Head',
that is, to Christ. This clearly shows Christ as a ruler over the cosmic
powers. But here we find a linguistic usage already common in the
Hebrew and Aramaic traditions of the Bible and Judaism, and also in
Greek: that is, use of the term 'head' to mean 'chief, highest, supreme'
and so on.[38] We do not seem to have here the specific image of the
head of a body with various parts, as we find in Col. 2.10.

In Ephesians the statements of our motif have a stronger ecclesiastical
orientation, pointing us more consciously towards ideas of unity in the
church. Here I will look particularly at Eph. 1.22-23.[39] Here we read,
in the wider context of statements on the might of God and on Jesus as
universal deity and ruler through his resurrection and exaltation:

> ... the might which he exerted in Christ when he raised him from the
> dead, when he enthroned him at his right hand in the heavenly realms, far
> above all government and authority, all power and dominion, and any title
> of sovereignty that can be named, not only in this age but in the age to
> come. He put everything in subjection beneath his feet, and appointed him
> as supreme head to the church, which is his body and as such holds
> within it the fulness of him who himself receives the entire fulness of God
> (Eph. 1.20-23).

However, with regard to giving an exact and definite interpretation
the syntax is very difficult and complex. Here we find the dense and

37. It is notable here that Schweizer (*Brief an die Kolosser*, p. 52) does not cite
Col. 1.18c in discussing the parallelism-tradition of that hymn.

38. Cf. in this area Schweizer, *Brief an die Kolosser*, pp. 62, 69-70, 105, 109
(as '[Ober-]Haupt aller Macht und Gewalt'); Meuzelaar, *Leib*, p. 121.

39. See the commentaries on Ephesians; for example R. Schnackenburg, *Der
Brief an die Epheser* (EKKNT, 10; Neukirchen–Vluyn: Neukirchener Verlag; Zürich:
Benzinger Verlag, 1982); F. Mussner, *Der Brief an die Epheser* (ÖTK, 10; Gütersloh:
Gerd Mohn; Würzburg: Echter Verlag, 1982); J. Gnilka, *Der Epheserbrief*
(HTKNT, 10.2; Freiburg: Herder, 4th edn, 1990).

compressed style of language well known as typical of Ephesians. In 1.22a and 23b we have definite cosmic implications. In the first case the context is that of the well-known early Christian interpretation of the resurrection and exaltation of Jesus to a cosmic position of power, and the writer quotes Ps. 8.7 (cf. also the reference to Ps. 110.1 in Eph. 1.20). In the second case we have the tradition of the *pleroma*, the universal deity.

In 1.22b-23a we cannot give such a clearly cosmic interpretation, reading, 'and appointed him as supreme head to the church, which is his body...', or perhaps, 'and gave him as a head above all to the church...'[40] In this Ephesians passage the term 'head' is being used in two different ways: in the context of the metaphor of the body with head, limbs and organs, and more straightforwardly as a metaphor for 'highest', 'chief', 'supreme'. In v. 23 the two aspects or interpretations of v. 22b—cosmic and ecclesiastical—are separated, explicated and developed further.[41] The ecclesiastical aspect is expressed straightforwardly through the 'Body of Christ' motif: 'the church, which is his body'. Then a cosmic dimension to the church or a cosmic horizon for it is explicated: 'the church, which...as such holds within it the fulness of him who himself receives the entire fulness'. The fulness concentrated in the church, or the fulness that *is* the church, relates to him who himself 'fills all in all'. And here we find a link between the ecclesiastical conception of the body with its constituent parts and the cosmic tradition of the sovereign as 'head', as an all-penetrating, all-filling universal deity.

The Rest of the New Testament

In the rest of the New Testament we do not find the motif of the 'Body of Christ' used with reference to a collective. We do however find various problems relating to cosmic ideas. If we look at the aspect of power and Jesus Christ in the context of and in relation to the cosmic powers, we can of course find many relevant passages and different points of view in the New Testament writings. Some are mentioned or discussed above. Here it is important for us that, on the

40. The last version is my translation of the German version of this passage in the *Jerusalemer Bibel* (Freiburg: Herder, 15th edn, 1979): 'ihn selbst aber hat er seiner Kirche zum Haupt über alles gegeben...'

41. If we see in the ὑπὲρ πάντα in 1.22b only an internal, ecclesiastical aspect, then such reflections possibly fall away.

one hand, the New Testament uses the concepts of the Christ and the messiah in relation to the resurrection and exaltation of Jesus, therefore going beyond the 'end' for the earthly Jesus, his passion and death. In this way the 'Body of Christ' idea could have been developed in a cosmic and dynamic way, but in fact it is not.

On the other hand we should also take into account the importance in the New Testament of the power of the earthly Jesus throughout his passion and death, right up to the point of revelation of the messianic secret (especially emphasized in the Synoptic Gospels). Christological terms such as 'Son of Man' and the process from 'implicit Christology' to 'explicit Christology' could show the authority of Jesus, emphasized by christological terms of Highness and in the context of cosmic powers. Here even the 'body' of Jesus in the context of the tradition of the Holy Communion could build a bridge to the collective, ecclesiastical concept of the Body of Christ operative after Jesus' death.

A third point relates to the notions of protology and pre-existence. We see a movement from Jesus' heavenly position of power and pre-existence into his life as an earthly being (ἐν σαρκί, the Incarnate), and then from this earthly being back into heaven (cf. Jn 1; Phil. 2). The question is whether we can see a logical progression back from the resurrection and exaltation to the earthly Jesus and from this back to the idea of the pre-existing Son of God or *logos*, especially in respect to Jesus' might over the cosmic powers.

Everywhere in early Christianity Jesus as the Christ remains a person authorized by God, with a mandate by God, subordinate to God, but superior to the cosmic powers, to the powers in the world; there is always the tension between the power that Jesus actually has during his time on earth and the eschatological aspect of his power. This can be seen in all New Testament writings dealing with the dichotomy of the 'already' and the 'not yet', in its historical or eschatological aspect and at the same time in its anthropological, ecclesiastical and cosmic or universal aspects.

Finally, looking at the theme of our conference—politics and theopolitics—it seems to me that 1 Corinthians 15 is interesting and important here. Paul says in this passage that Christ was raised from the dead as 'the first fruit of the harvest of the dead' (v. 20) and has always been destined to reign, has been installed into government over the powers of the whole world. And we read here that Christ, at the end, when all things are subject to him, 'after abolishing every kind of domination, authority, and power', 'delivers up the kingdom to God the father'; 'then the Son himself will also be made subordinate to God who made all things subject to him, and thus God will be all in all' (1 Cor. 15.20-28). But we see in 1 Corinthians 15, and in Paul and the New Testament generally, the gradual process of the breaking down of the earthly powers; the powers of the world still appear to have authority, rivalling Christ Jesus and his sovereignty. As a Christian theologian I would particularly connect this breaking down of powers to the concept of the 'Body of Christ', referring both to the body of the crucified and raised Christ and to the exalted Christ, with its consequences for the 'body' of the Christians and for the subordination of the world powers (cf. here 1 Cor. 15 or Phil. 3.20-21). Also very relevant here is the concept of the body of Jesus in the context of the Holy Communion, the Last Supper, and the ecclesiastical conception of the 'Body of Christ' motif, the existence of the church in the world. In fact we can connect this idea of the breaking of the earthly powers with the whole metaphor, the hermeneutically opalescent relations within the language of the 'body' and its 'organs and limbs', especially within the language of the 'Body of Christ'.[42]

42. To do justice to the complexities of the metaphor and the language of the 'body', especially the 'Body of Christ', we would need a long linguistic and hermeneutic study, which I cannot undertake here. See, though, Demandt, *Metaphern.*

DAVID'S KINGSHIP—A PRECARIOUS EQUILIBRIUM

Frank H. Polak

The Problem

The tales of David and his sons in 2 Samuel (including 1 Kgs 1–2) do not allow an easy and unequivocal assessment of their meaning. On the one hand, these stories are extremely critical of the monarch; on the other hand, they present his rule as backed by a divine pledge. On the one hand, the narrator recounts a completely secular series of political events, as well as occurrences in the royal family; on the other hand he introduces divine guidance. Thus we note two apparent disparities: (1) the divergence between the political and the theological outlook, and (2) the contrast between opposition to the king and the defence of the Davidic dynasty.

Modern scholarship has tried to impose consistency by disentangling the opposed factors as if they were contradictory. This paper, in contrast, argues that these divergent points of view are interconnected, and result from the representation of David as a tragic king.

David: Weakness and Strength

The picture of David's behaviour is full of apparent contradictions. The ever-resourceful king is depicted as quite helpless vis-à-vis his sons' guiles. Both Amnon and Absalom succeed in fooling him, and Amnon even gets away with the rape of his half-sister, Tamar. As the matter of David's succession arises, he has to be prodded by Nathan and Bathsheba, for otherwise the issue would have been settled by Adonijah. On the other hand, the narrator indicates David's political acumen during Absalom's rebellion, in which he uses Hushai as his agent in his son's court for securing victory.

Might one suggest that David was always astute in matters of politics, but did not know how to overcome his weakness for his sons?

This explanation has been proposed by von Rad,[1] and is supported by the narrator's comment that David did not chastise Amnon after the rape of Tamar, out of love for his first-born (2 Sam. 13.22 [LXX]; 4QSamᵃ).[2] Moreover, Jonadab's ill-conceived advice to Amnon is based on the assumption that David will come and visit him in his illness (v. 5).[3] However, this explanation only fits David's disposition towards Amnon, and does not suit his attitude towards Absalom. Although the king refrained from persecuting his fratricidal son after his flight to Geshur (apparently a vassal kingdom of David), only Joab succeeded in convincing him to let him return from exile; even so, initially Absalom was not admitted into court (14.21-24). But still, the prince beguiled his father in his preparations for the coup d'état, as he did in his murderous trap for Amnon (15.2-9; 13.24-27). Only during the preparations for the decisive battle with the rebellious army did David show signs of weakness for Absalom, but by then it was too late (18.5; 19.1). Thus his attitude towards Absalom was wavering and irresolute, rather than weak because of love.

Politically, in contrast, David's behaviour is not as decisive as it might appear. The Israelite victory in the war against the Ammonites might be considered a success for David, but in fact this war was not decided by the king himself, but by Joab, whose courage and insight had already been established by the account of the war against the Aramaic coalition (10.10-12). The final capture of Ammon, therefore, is an ironic comment on David's responsibility, rather than an achievement on his part.[4]

---

1. G. von Rad, 'The Beginnings of Historical Writing in Ancient Israel', in *The Problem of the Hexateuch and Other Essays* (trans. E.W. Trueman Dicken; Edinburgh: Oliver & Boyd, 1966), pp. 166-204, esp. p. 182; R.N. Whybray, *The Succession Narrative: A Study of II Sam. 9–20 and I Kings 1 and 2* (SBT, 2.9; London: SCM Press, 1968), pp. 37-38; S. Bar-Efrat, *Narrative Art in the Bible* (JSOTSup, 70; Sheffield: JSOT Press, 1989), pp. 78, 81-85; J.P. Fokkelman, *Narrative Art and Poetry in the Books of Samuel. I. King David (II Sam. 9–20 & I Kings 1–2)* (Assen: Van Gorcum, 1981), pp. 112, 116, 263, 348-49.

2. This reading has been disregarded by Fokkelman, *David*, p. 112.

3. In her plea with Amnon, Tamar argues that David will allow him to marry her (2 Sam. 13.13), but this suggestion is probably motivated by the needs of the hour.

4. The ironic character of this passage has been perceived by M. Sternberg, *The Poetics of Biblical Narrative: Ideological Literature and the Drama of Reading* (Bloomington: Indiana University Press, 1985), pp. 196; hence irony balances the reconciliatory aspect, emphasized by Fokkelman, *David*, pp. 94-96.

Thus the problem of David's behaviour is not merely a matter of psychology. Well-known phraseological and thematic parallels between the Bathsheba tale and the Amnon narrative suggest that the king's failures issue from his sins in the affair of Bathsheba and Uriah.[5] Scholars speak of divine retribution, of a *gelālâ*, and even of 'negative karma'.[6]

5. J. Hempel, *Das Ethos des Alten Testaments* (BZAW, 67; Berlin: Töpelmann, 1938), p. 51; von Rad, 'Historical Writing', p. 196; J. Blenkinsopp, 'Theme and Motif in the Succession History and the Yahwist Corpus', in J.A. Emerton *et al.* (eds.), *Volume du Congrès International pour l'étude de l'Ancien Testament: Genève 1965* (VTSup, 15; Leiden: Brill, 1966), pp. 44-57, esp. p. 50. This is not a matter of similarity in motifs, but of structure: as Amnon matches David (the transgressor), so Tamar matches Bathsheba (the victim), and Absalom matches Uriah (the offended party); the parallel between David and Amnon, ultimately killed by Absalom, is a sign for the king. On parallel structure in narrative see: V. Chklovski, 'La Construction de la nouvelle et du roman', in T. Todorov (ed. and trans.), *Théorie de la littérature: textes des formalistes russes* (Paris: Seuil, 1965), pp. 170-96, esp. pp. 184-88; E. Lämmert, *Bauformen des Erzählens* (Stuttgart: Metzler, 1955), pp. 52-56; Y. Amit, 'The Use of Analogy in the Study of the Book of Judges', in M. Augustin und K.-D. Schunk (eds.), *'Wünschet Jerusalem Frieden': Collected Communications to the XIIth Congress of the IOSOT, Jerusalem 1986* (Frankfurt: Peter Lang, 1987), pp. 387-94. These data have not been sufficiently taken into account by C. Conroy, *Absalom, Absalom! Narrative and Language in 2 Sam. 13–20* (AnBib, 81; Rome: Biblical Institute Press, 1978), pp. 101-105; R.C. Bailey, *David in Love and War: The Pursuit of Power in 2 Samuel 10–12* (JSOTSup, 75; Sheffield: JSOT Press, 1990). The latter's argument that the extremely explicit representation of the inner life in ch. 13 is quite unlike the narrator's extreme reticence in ch. 11 is not decisive, since in both tales the narrator plays with the feelings of the characters. For the common wording see also Appendix 1. To the broad platform of analogies let me add one example: after the birth of Solomon the speech of judgment is complemented by an indication of God's affection for the young prince: יהוה אהבו וישלח ביד נתן הנביא ויקרא את שמו ידידיה בעבור יהוה (12.24-25). This note matches the explanation of David's forgiving attitude towards Amnon: כי אהבו כי בכורו הוא (13.22 LXX, 4QSamᵃ). This parallel–contrast posits David's weakness for his first-born against the divine preference for Solomon. On the parallels between the Bathsheba narrative and Nathan's parable see the important treatment by U. Simon, 'The Poor Man's Ewe-Lamb: An Example of a Juridical Parable', *Bib* 48 (1967), pp. 207-42.

6. On divine retribution see J.S. Ackerman, 'Knowing Good and Evil: A Literary Analysis of the Court History in 2 Samuel 9–20 and 1 Kings 1–2', *JBL* 109 (1990), pp. 41-64 (on the personal responsibility of David's sons see p. 51); von Rad, 'Historical Writing', pp. 195-96; M. Smith, 'The So-Called "Biography of

On the other hand, according to Würthwein, Veijola, Langlamet and their followers, this problem merely results from the tension between two strata in the David narratives: the ancient, realistic and anti-Davidic tales, and the more recent pro-Solomonic revision with its strong dynastic and theological orientation. To the latter stratum, the pro-Solomonic redaction (or DtrG), one assigns among other things the many passages alluding to David's awareness of his weaknesses, whereas the tale of his sins, as well as the story of the intrigues around Solomon's royal accession, are attributed to the ancient realistic narratives, largely composed from the point of view of the opposition to the Davidic dynasty.[7] Of late scholarship has become silent about these suggestions, no doubt because they cannot hold out in the confrontation with stylistic analysis, as carried out by Ridout, Bar-Efrat, Gunn, Conroy and Fokkelman.[8]

David" in the Books of Samuel and Kings, *HTR* 44 (1951), pp. 167-69; S. Bar-Efrat, 'The "Succession History" Reconsidered', in A. Rofé and Y. Zakovitch (eds.), *Isac Leo Seeligmann Volume: Essays on the Bible and the Ancient World* (Jerusalem: Rubinstein, 1983), I, pp. 185-211. On 'negative karma' see Fokkelman, *David*, pp. 159, 245, 414; on David's 'curse' see Hempel, *Ethos*, pp. 51-53 (speaking of 'objective guilt'); C.A. Carlsson, *David, the Chosen King: A Tradition-Historical Approach to the Second Book of Samuel* (Stockholm: Almqvist & Wiksell, 1964), pp. 24-25, 140-41, 161-63.

7. E. Würthwein, *Die Erzählung von der Thronfolge Davids—Theologische oder politische Geschichtsschreibung?* (Theologische Studien, 115; Zürich: Theologischer Verlag, 1974); T. Veijola, *Die ewige Dynastie: David und die Entstehung seiner Dynastie nach der deuteronomistischen Darstellung* (Suomalaisen Tiedeakatemian Toimituksia, B, 193; Helsinki: Suomalainen Tiedeakatemia, 1975); F. Langlamet, 'Pour ou contre Salomon? La rédaction prosalomonienne de 1 Rois 1–2, *RB* 83 (1976), pp. 321-79, 481-528; *idem*, 'David, fils de Jesse: une édition prédeuteronomiste de l'"Histoire de la succession"?', *RB* 89 (1982), pp. 5-47; see also Bailey, *David*. Würthwein's position has been criticized by F. Crüsemann, *Der Widerstand gegen das Königtum: Die anti-königlichen Texte des Alten Testamentes und der Kampf um den frühen israelitischen Staat* (WMANT, 49; Neukirchen–Vluyn: Neukirchener Verlag, 1978), pp. 183-85; H. Schnabl, *Die 'Thronfolgeerzählung Davids': Untersuchungen zur literarischen Eigenständigkeit, literarkritischen Abgrenzung und Intention von 2 Sam. 21,1-14; 9-20; 1 Kön 1–2* (Theorie und Forschung, 35; Regensburg: Roderer, 1988), pp. 127-28; D.M. Gunn, *The Story of King David: Genre and Interpretation* (JSOTSup, 6; Sheffield: JSOT Press, 1978), p. 116.

8. Bar-Efrat, *Narrative Art*; Gunn, *David*; Conroy, *Absalom*; Fokkelman, *David*; G.P. Ridout, 'Prose Compositional Techniques in the Succession Narrative (2 Sam. 7, 9-20, 1 Kings 1-2)' (PhD dissertation, University of California, 1971).

Hence, McCarter favours a different approach. In his opinion, the narrative in its final form has been created by the 'prophetic redaction', basing itself on an older tale, 'the Apology of Solomon' (underlying the tale of Solomon's accession). In a sense this apology constitutes the main narrative, but it made use of another ancient story, the account of Absalom's rebellion. The prophetic redaction included all this in an encompassing history, and composed the Bathsheba tale as a preface. McCarter argues that the apologetic character of the main narrative provides the explanation for the enigmatic picture of David's character: this kind of narrative aims at refuting attacks on the king, or at neutralizing them; hence, those elements alluding to criticism of the ruler do not represent the narrator himself, but reflect the anti-Davidic polemic, rebutted in the present narrative.[9]

In general, despite his severe criticism of Gunn, based on tendencies rather than on literary detail (F. Langlamet, 'La belle histoire du Roi David', *RB* 88 [1981], pp. 79-92), Langlamet's recension of Fokkelman, *David* ('L'histoire de la succession: structure et interprétation', *RB* 90 [1983], pp. 136-48) is rather sympathetic, although he tends to connect the literary design of the succession narrative to S^2, the latest stage of the comprehensive tale, before the revision by the pro-Solomonic redactor (S^3; Langlamet, 'Structure', p. 136). He bases his view on some blemishes in the concentric structure as proposed by Fokkelman (Langlamet, 'Structure', pp. 145-47). However, a structure of this type is not necessarily inherent in each and every narrative. On the other hand, Langlamet does not cope with Fokkelman's criticism of the criteria employed by Würthwein (Fokkelman, *David*, pp. 413 n. 1, 417-19).

For criticism of Fokkelman's approach as one-sidedly literary and psychological see H.-J. Stoebe, 'Überlegungen zur Exegese historischer Texte, dargestellt an den Samuelisbüchern', *TZ* 45 (1989), pp. 290-314. Stoebe correctly emphasizes that the present narrative centres on the tensions created by kingship as an institution, and answers the author's own doubts regarding David (pp. 310-11); however, he does not evaluate the literary means expressing this idea.

9. P.K. McCarter, Jr, *II Samuel* (AB, 9; Garden City, NY: Doubleday, 1984), pp. 7-16, esp. p. 16; *idem*, '"Plots, True or False": The Succession Narrative as Court Apologetic', *Int* 35 (1981), pp. 355-67; on the notion of court propaganda see Whybray, *Succession Narrative*, pp. 50-55, dating the narrative to the beginning of Solomon's reign. For some suggestions concerning the political constellation of this period see T. Ishida, 'Solomon's Succession to the Throne of David: A Political Analysis', in *idem* (ed.), *Studies in the Period of David and Solomon and Other Essays* (Tokyo: Yamakawa-Shuppansha, 1982), pp. 175-87. On royal apology as a genre see also H. Tadmor, 'Autobiographical Apology in the Royal Assyrian Literature', in H. Tadmor and M. Weinfeld (eds.), *History, Historiography and*

The Fundamental Tension

However, this view is also one-sided. The main point of our tale is not a certain tendency, nor the conflict of tendencies, but David's personal fate. Nowhere is this more obvious than in the well-known comment on Absalom's ill-fated decision to reject Ahitophel's advice: 'for the Lord had ordained to defeat the good counsel of Ahitophel to the intent that the Lord might bring evil upon Absalom' (2 Sam. 17.14).[10] This remark has been taken for an intrusion by the pro-Davidic redaction, as it implies David's victory over the rebellion. But the expression בעבור הביא יהוה אל אבשלום את הרעה ('to the intent that the Lord might bring evil over Absalom') carries far more weight than a merely 'pro-Davidic' comment. It is an anticipation of Absalom's death, and therefore first and foremost a narrative allusion to David's tragic loss of his son.

On the other hand, this notice attributes Absalom's decision to a divine dispensation in favour of David. Hence it has been considered a later addition, representative of the rationalistic, theological world-view, and thus belonging to the final stage in a long chain of religious evolution. The original narrative would seem to have been more realistic and free of theological reflection.[11] As a matter of fact, however, ancient Near Eastern literature does not preserve any example of

Interpretation (Jerusalem: Magnes, 1983), pp. 36-57; T. Ishida, '"Solomon who is greater than David": Solomon's Succession in the Light of the Inscription of Kilamuwa, King of *Y'dy*-Sam'al', in J.A. Emerton (ed.), *Congress Volume: Salamanca 1983* (VTSup, 36; Leiden: Brill, 1985), pp. 145-53.

10. Hence it is impossible to evaluate this comment as the real turning point of this narrative, as against L. Rost, *The Succession to the Throne of David* (trans. M.D. Rutter and D.M. Gunn; Historic Texts and Interpreters, 1; Sheffield: Almond Press, 1982), p. 100; von Rad, 'Historical Writing', pp. 199-200; Bar-Efrat, *Narrative Art*, pp. 27-28; F. Langlamet, 'Ahitofel et Houshai: Rédaction pro-salomonienne en 2 S 15–17?', in Y. Avishur and J. Blau (eds.), *Studies in Bible and the Ancient Near East, Presented to Samuel E. Loewenstamm* (Jerusalem: Rubinstein, 1978), II, pp. 57-90, esp. pp. 86-88. Langlamet ('Ahitofel', pp. 83, 87), though aware of Absalom's doom, relates it to the accession of Solomon. Whybray (*Succession Narrative*, pp. 62-64) calls attention to the similarity between this note and Prov. 19.21; however the neutral, gnomic tone of the proverb only highlights its fundamental difference from the comment of 2 Sam. 17.14.

11. Against Würthwein, 'Geschichtsschreibung', pp. 33-34, 42; Langlamet, 'Ahitofel', pp. 82-83, 88.

'realistic, non-theological' historiography.[12] In the account of Sethi's campaign against Yanoam and Beth Shean, the narrator expressly

12. See H. Seebass, *David, Saul und das Wesen des biblischen Glaubens* (Neukirchen–Vluyn: Neukirchener Verlag, 1980), p. 131; in his opinion the ancient tradition is throughout 'theonomous'; this view matches Lüthi's thesis that the ancient *Sage* is characterized by its vehemently 'numinous' character; see M. Lüthi, 'Märchen und Sage', in *Volksmärchen und Volkssage: Zwei Grundformen erzählender Dichtung* (Munich: Francke, 1961), pp. 22-48, esp. pp. 26-27; on the ancient Near Eastern world-view see B. Albrektson, *History and the Gods: An Essay on the Idea of Historical Events as Divine Manifestations in the Ancient Near East and in Israel* (ConBOT, 1; Lund: Gleerup, 1967); M. Weippert, 'Heiliger Krieg in Israel und Assyrien', *ZAW* 84 (1972), pp. 460-93. See also J.A. Soggin, 'Geschichte als Glaubensbekenntnis—Geschichte als Gegenstand Wissenschaftlicher Forschung: Zu einem Grundproblem der Geschichte Israels', in Rofé and Zakovitch (eds.), *Seeligmann Volume*, III, pp. 1-14, esp. p. 5. Old Akkadian inscriptions (as well as the inscription of Sargon's predecessor Lugalzaggesi) actually open with the invocation of the deity, as for example Naram-Sin's inscriptions, for which see R. Kutscher, *The Brockman Tablets at the University of Haifa* (Haifa: Haifa University Press, 1989), I, pp. 16ff.; II, pp. 14-19; P. Michalowsky, 'New Sources concerning the Reign of Naram-Sin', *JCS* 32 (1980), pp. 233-46, esp. pp. 234-35; B.R. Foster, 'The Siege of Armanum', *JANESCU* 14 (1982), pp. 27-36, esp. ii:29-iii:6: 'inu Dagan DI.KUD Naram-Suēn danim idīnūma Ri-DA-ᵈIM LUGAL Armanim qatīššu idinūma', that is: 'when Dagan the Judge gave a verdict in favor of strong Naram-Suen and delivered Ri-DA-ᵈIM, king of Armanum in his hands'. In the Idrimi pseudo-autobiography (for which see S. Smith, *The Statue of Idri-mi* [London: British School of Archeology in Ankara, 1949]; A.L. Oppenheim, *ANET*, pp. 557-58), the orientation on the divine is established by the reference to the omina token (1.28-29; Smith, *Statue*, p. 16) and the restoration of worship in Alalah, as recounted at the end of the event sequence (11.88-90; Smith, *Statue*, pp. 20-22). In the Babylonian Chronicle I, for which see A.K. Grayson, *Mesopotamian Chronicles* (TCS, 5; Locust Valley, NY: Augustin, 1975), pp. 70-87, the divine framework is not self-evident, but is firmly established by the many references to festivals, the fate of temples and so on, as for example col. i, 1.1*, 1.5; col. ii, 1.1′, 4′-5′; col. iii, 1.1-3; col. iv, i.17-18, 34-36. The historic retrospection in the preambles of the Hittite treaties cannot be adduced as evidence to the contrary, since the treaty itself is concluded in the presence of the divine witnesses. As to Egyptian historiography, the account of the conquest of Megiddo by Thutmose III (approximately 1467; *ANET*, pp. 234-38) mentions his courtiers' prayer: 'May thy father Amon... act' (p. 236), and utters 'praise to Amon [because of the victory] which he had given his son [this day]' (p. 237); similarly the inscriptions of Ramses III (1184–1153) recounting his wars against the peoples of the Sea (*ANET*, p. 263) and the Syrians (*ANET*, p. 260). In general, however, the king embodies the god on earth, and by consequence all his actions are considered divine; see S. Herrmann, 'Geschichtsbild

states that 'it is the strength of his father Amon that decreed him valor and victory'.[13] Although the biblical narrative is far more sophisticated, this remark belongs to the same class as the comment on Absalom. In particular, the verb צוה, 'ordained', implies divine rule by concrete speech, and is therefore far closer to the mythic world-view than to Aristotle's conception of first mover and intermediate causation.[14] Like the Aristotelian analysis this world-view implies a distinction between concrete real-world events and abstract divine rule. But this idea is not expressed by the explicit distinction between various levels of causality, but by the recognition of divine 'decree' on the one hand and human action on the other hand. Nowhere does the narrator indicate his view of the effective connection between these different kinds of 'events'. Thus, on the one hand his account seems rather abstract; on the other hand, it remains open to interpretation in magical and mythic terms.[15]

---

und Gotteserkenntnis: Zum Problem altorientalischen und alttestamentlichen Geschichtsdenkens' in Rofé and Zakovitch (eds.), *Seeligmann Volume*, III, pp. 15-38, esp. pp. 23-26 (for the scholarly discussion see p. 22 nn. 18-19); W. Brede Kristensen, 'De Ark van Jahwe (1933)', in *Godsdiensten in de oude wereld* (Utrecht: Spectrum, 1966), pp. 167-200, esp. pp. 171-73; G. van der Leeuw, *De godsdienst van het oude Aegypte* (The Hague: Servire, 1944), pp. 111-20. Hence many inscriptions represent the king's actions in battle as manifestations of divine valour; for example Thutmose III (*ANET*, p. 236); Raamses II (1229–1213; *ANET*, pp. 255, 256; his divisions are named after Amon, Re, Ptah and Seth).

For the dates given see K.A. Kitchen, 'The Basics of Egyptian Chronology in Relation to the Bronze Age', in *High, Middle, or Low: Acts of an International Colloquium on Absolute Chronology* (Göteborg: Aström, 1987), pp. 37-55, esp. p. 52.

13. *ANET*, p. 253 (1294–1279 according to Kitchen, 'Chronology').

14. Rost (*Succession*, pp. 108-109) speaks of *causae secundae*; see M. Maimonides, *Guide for the Perplexed* (trans. M. Friedlaender; London: Routledge, 1919), pp. 102-103 (Book I, ch. 69), pp. 249-50 (Book II, ch. 48). See also I.L. Seeligmann, 'Menschliches Heldentum und göttliche Hilfe', *TZ* 19 (1963), pp. 385-411, esp. pp. 385-91; R. Rendtorff, 'Geschichte und Wort im Alten Testament', *EvT* 22 (1962), pp. 621-49, esp. p. 633; Amit, 'The Dual Causality Principle and its Effects on Biblical Literature', *VT* 37 (1987), pp. 385-400, esp. pp. 399-400. The ancient origin of this idea is proven by the ancient law of the asylum (Exod. 21.13; 'but God caused it to come in hand').

15. L. Dürr, *Die Wertung des göttlichen Wortes im Alten Testament und im antiken Orient* (MVAG, 42; Leipzig: Hinrichs, 1938), pp. 51-68. Albrektson

A similar ambiguity may be noted in the narrative comment on the relation between Abimelech and the Shechem patricians: 'God sent a spirit of mutiny' (רוח רעה) between them (Judg. 9.22). Behind the psychological dimensions of this note, one still discerns its connections with the lying spirit dispatched to fool Ahab (1 Kgs 22.20-23). On the one hand God 'has put a lying spirit in the mouth of all these, your prophets' (v. 23), but on the other hand 'the spirit' in the heavenly court has volunteered to 'go forth and be a lying spirit in the mouth of all his prophets' (v. 22). Significantly, the historian's comment on the split of the monarchy refrains from concrete terms, such as 'ordaining', 'sending' or 'going', but asserts that 'there was a סבה from God in order to establish His word that He spoke by the mouth of Ahijah' (1 Kgs 12.15). In the notion of סבה מעם יהוה (even if rendered as 'a turning point from before God', not unlike the quasi-local use of מן קדם in the targumim) one detects a certain similarity to Aristotelian abstraction, quite unlike the comments in the books of Samuel and Judges.

Thus, the world-view implied by the notice on the divine dispensation against Absalom is not necessarily late, and does not prove this comment to be a late addition. On the contrary, its tragic content clearly links it to the ancient story itself.

More than that, even the narrative reconstruction, as entailed by the proposals of Würthwein and followers, seems slightly flawed. In their opinion, the pericope of Absalom's council meeting (16.21–17.14) originally included only Ahitophel's advice, as he urged immediate pursuit of David (17.1-3); Hushai learned of this plan and, by the services of Ahimaaz and Jonathan, immediately informed David. Thus the king succeeded in escaping (17.15a, 16-22).[16] On the face of it,

(*History and the Gods*, pp. 55-58) quotes many of the most important examples for the use of *zikrum*, *gibītum* and the verb *gabûm* in Akkadian literature, from Old Babylonian (Epilogue of Codex Hammurapi; Ištar Hymn) to neo-Assyrian and neo-Babylonian. However, the distinction between 'announcing by oracle' (as for example in neo-Assyrian texts) and 'magical decree' (as for example in the Epilogue of Codex Hammurapi), although acknowledged (*History and the Gods*, p. 58), is not sufficiently radical, as the former always denotes immediate, concrete causation (inspection of the liver), whereas the latter indicates indirect and unspecified causation. On the problematic mechanism of intervention see also W.G. Lambert, 'History and the Gods: A Review Article', *Or* 39 (1970), pp. 170-77, esp. pp. 171-72.

16. Würthwein, 'Geschichtsschreibung', pp. 40-41; S.A. Cook, 'Notes on the Composition of 2 Samuel', *AJSL (Hebraica)* 16 (1899–1900), pp. 145-77, esp. pp. 146-49.

this analysis has much to recommend it. One might get the impression that Absalom actually followed Ahithophel's advice and attacked David with no delay. That is why he could already cross the Jordan at the time David took refuge at Mahanaim (17.24). Had Absalom really followed Hushai's suggestion of a general conscription (17.11), all this would have taken much more time. Nevertheless, Würthwein's position is untenable. The delicate question of tempo is hardly decisive.[17] On the other hand, Hushai's counsel is essential for the continuation of our narrative, since only he advised Absalom to take a personal part in the campaign against David (17.11).[18] Ahithophel, in contrast, wanted to deal with David by himself (17.1, 3). If he had had his way, Absalom would not have participated in battle and thus would not have been killed. Hushai's counsel, then, is a vital link in a tragic series of events.

What is more, the contrast between these counsels also pertains to the characterization of David. Whereas Ahithophel represents the king in his actual weakness, 'weary and weak handed', and his loneliness ('and all the people that are with him shall flee, and I will smite the king alone', 17.2), Hushai describes him as the great warrior he was in the past: 'your father is a mighty man, and they that are with him are valiant men' (17.10). The narrator posits David's strength and grace as against his weakness and sins.[19]

This contrast dominates the ensuing narratives of David and his sons. Centring on David's status before God, they present the history of his life in its tragic tension between these poles.[20] The first and

17. Gunn, *David*, p. 116.

18. 2 Sam. 17.11b; ופניך הלכים בקרב; LXX (Kaige) reads בקרבם, which seems original (cf. Exod. 33.3, 5; Jer. 46.21). For פניך as an indication of personal presence see Ibn Ezra on Exod. 33.13, 14; and also Isa. 63.9 LXX.

19. On this tension see F.H. Polak, 'The Succession Narrative of David (2 Samuel 7, 9-20; 1 Kings 1-2): Integration and Continuity' (MA thesis, Hebrew University of Jerusalem, 1974), pp. 49-50, 168-74; Stoebe, 'Exegese', p. 311. On the tension between the tragic sense of life and religious optimism see T.C. Vriezen, 'De overwinning van het tragische levensgevoel in Israel', in *Kernmomenten der antieke beschaving en haar moderne beleving* (Mededelingen en Verhandelingen van het VoorAziatisch-Egyptisch genootschap 'Ex Oriente Lux', 8; Leiden: Brill, 1947), pp. 33-48.

20. See M.A. Beek, *David en Absalom, een hebreeuwse tragedie in proza? Rede uitgesproken ter gelegenheid van de 340e dies natalis van de Universiteit van Amsterdam* (Amsterdam, 1972); G. von Rad, *Old Testament Theology. I. The*

foremost manifestation of this view occurs in the two prophecies that stand at the head of the court narrative. In the dynastic oracle David's kingship exemplifies divine grace: his successes are due to divine succour; after his death kingship will pass to his son, who will also be granted divine auspices (7.8-16). This promise comes true with Solomon's royal accession, as affirmed by Benaiah's blessings and David's prayer of thanks (1 Kgs 1.37, 47-48).[21] The divine grant, conveyed by Nathan, is countered by the same prophet's speech of judgment, announcing David's punishment for his adultery and murder (12.7-12). The fundamental relation between these diametrically opposed prophecies is concretized by their wording. David was promised that if his son were to sin, he would suffer punishment, but 'My Mercy shall not depart from him, as I took it from Saul whom I removed before you' (7.15). This statement is echoed by the prophetic threat that 'the sword shall never depart from your house' (12.10). The contrast between these proclamations, both uttered by Nathan, is

Theology of Israel's Historical Traditions (trans. D.M.G. Stalker; Edinburgh: Oliver & Boyd, 1962), pp. 316-17. On the 'place before the divine' in tragedy see K. Reinhardt, *Sophokles* (Frankfurt: Klostermann, 4th edn, 1976), pp. 9-10, 169. The tension between greatness and doom, rather than Aristotle's 'some flaw', is the basic feature of tragedy; see H.D.F. Kitto, *Form and Meaning in Drama: A Study of Six Greek Plays and of Hamlet* (repr.; London: Methuen, 1960), pp. 232-35; see also J.M. Bremer, *Hamartia: Tragic Error in the Poetics of Aristotle and in Greek Tragedy* (Amsterdam: Hakkert, 1969), pp. 87-95, 132-56, 195-96; K. Reinhardt, 'Die Sinneskrise bei Euripides', in *Tradition und Geist: Gesammelte Essays zur Dichtung* (Göttingen; Vandenhoeck & Ruprecht, 1961), pp. 227-56.

21. Veijola (*Dynastie*, pp. 16-18) identifies the spoken reports of 1 Kgs 1.30, 35-37, 46-48 as secondary intrusions, since they deviate from the narrative account or the previous dialogue (vv. 17, 38-39, 32-34 respectively); in v. 38 he finds the direct continuation of v. 34. However, he does not take into account the analyses of the event–report/announcement–event sequences offered by W. Baumgartner, 'Ein Kapitel vom Hebräischen Erzählungsstil', in H. Schmidt (ed.), *Eucharisterion: Studien zur Religion und Literatur des Alten und Neuen Testaments H. Gunkel Dargebracht* (FRLANT, 37; Göttingen: Vandenhoeck & Ruprecht, 1923), pp. 145-57; M. Weiss, 'Weiteres über die Bauformen des Erzählens in der Bibel', *Bib* 46 (1965), pp. 181-206. According to their findings, further substantiated by Sternberg, *Poetics*, pp. 375-427, deviation is frequent and functional in biblical narrative. For functional deviation in ancient Near Eastern epic and royal inscription see F.H. Polak, 'Some Aspects of Literary Design in the Ancient Near Eastern Epic', *Tel Aviv*, forthcoming. On 2 Sam. 7 see Appendix 2.

even more obvious in Hebrew, as the same sounds are used for both:[22]

| The threat: | (12.10) ועתה לא תסור חרב מביתך עד־עולם |
| The promise: | (7.15) וחסדי לא יסור   ממנו |

This similarity is not a matter of chance. Punishment by the sword
is a result of David's sin, as expressed in the accusation מדוע בזית את
דבר ה, in obvious contrast with the חסד of the dynastic oracle. Thus,
sound similarity accompanies and strengthens the contrast between
grace and doom. What is more, the verse preceding the promise concerning David's successor contains an explicit threat of chastisement
'with the rod of men and with stripes of the children of men' (7.14);
although David is not directly addressed, this threat cannot but antici-
pate his suffering because of Amnon and Absalom. Because of David's
sins with Bathsheba and against Uriah, the divine pledge is countered
by a threat.

This general idea is buttressed by other similarities, such as the
mention of Saul, alluded to in promise (7.15) as well as in denunciation (12.8). In both prophecies one meets the verbs קום and שכב. David
is promised that his son will inherit kingship: והיה כי ימלאו ימיך ושכבת
את אבתיך והקימתי את זרעך אחריך (7.12; for והיה cf. LXX 1 Chron. 17.11;
see Appendix 2).

In Nathan's speech of judgment this promise turns into a threat,
once again concerning David's offspring: ...הנני מקים עליך רעה מביתך
ושכב עם נשיך לעיני השמש הזאת (12.11). Of course, this use of שכב is a
reverberation of the Bathsheba narrative (11.4, 10-11; note also the
use of קום: 11.2).[23] The contrast between the divine grace to David and
his transgressions is also expressed by the terms 'good' and 'bad'.
David speaks of the promise conveyed by Nathan as הטובה הזאת (7.28).
On the other hand, the prophetic reproach mentions the 'evil deed'
committed by David (12.9: הרע); he will be punished by 'an evil' out
of his own house (12.11: רעה). These details, motifs and keywords
enhance and deepen the intricate tension between promise and threat,
grace and doom.

These elements also strengthen the connection between the judgment
speech and the tales of Amnon and Absalom. The keyword 'evil'

22. Carlsson (*Chosen King*, p. 157) remarks on the similarity in phraseology
but does not elaborate.
23. This similarity is only one item in a comprehensive framework of common
lexemes, as shown in Appendix 1.

recurs not only in Tamar's characterization of her brother's offence (13.16 LXX; cf. v. 22), but also in the tale of the rebellion, the most obvious instance being David's fear that his son 'will bring down evil upon us' (15.4).[24] Additionally one notes the opposition between 'bad' and 'good'. Shimei vilifies David with 'you are in your own evil' (16.8), but David hopes that 'the Lord will requite me good for his cursing of me' (v. 12; see below). And once again, Ahithophel's 'good counsel' is defeated in order 'to bring evil upon Absalom' (17.14). Thus the prophetic threat foreshadows Absalom's rebellion. This is not merely another instance of the prophecy–fulfilment scheme, so common in the books of Kings. The prophecy does not present an unequivocal announcement of some sure and well-defined future event. It contains veiled threats, sufficiently clear for suggesting a perspective, but not so transparent that one may know what is going to happen. Only after the narration of the event itself can the reader attain full comprehension of the prophetic anticipation. The intrinsic connection between foreshadowing and event constitutes a narrative framework,[25] which is not the result of redactional interference.

24. Note the permanent change in meaning of רעה, denoting 'rebellion' (12.10; cf. W.L. Moran, 'A Note on the Treaty Terminology of the Sefire Stelas', *JNES* 22 [1965], pp. 173-76, especially his reference to Sef I C 19-20), 'outrage' (13.16), 'misfortune' (15.8) and so on. Even though 'evil' is a common word, it certainly can be said to accompany the narrative, to clarify its structure, and to elucidate its meaning; hence it is a keyword.

25. See Lämmert, *Bauformen*, pp. 139-43, 175-92. From the literary point of view, the function of the prophetic anticipation relates to unity and perspective of the literary construction; it dictates our perception of the narrative plot. This point of view is fundamentally different from the theological outlook, for which prophecy is the self-fulfilling announcement of future occurrences (see G. von Rad, 'The Deuteronomic Theology of History in I and II Kings', in *The Problem of the Hexateuch*, pp. 205-21). However, von Rad shows that the prophecy 'gives to the phenomena of history a purpose and a meaning, so binding together into a single whole in the eyes of God its manifold and diverse elements' ('Deuteronomic Theology', p. 221). This is exactly the function of anticipation in narrative. On the relation between prophecy and narrative see also I.L. Seeligmann, 'Die Auffassung von der Prophetie in der deuteronomistischen und chronistischen Geschichts-schreibung (mit einem Exkurs über das Buch Jeremia)', in J.A. Emerton (ed.), *Studies in the Historical Books of the Old Testament* (VTSup, 30; Leiden: Brill, 1978), pp. 254-84, esp. pp. 258-61; R. Rendtorff, 'Geschichte', pp. 624-25, 634; and of late especially H. Weippert, 'Geschichten und Geschichte: Verheissung und Erfüllung im deuteronomistischen Geschichtswerk', in J.A. Emerton (ed.),

The prophet utters three threats, which steadily become more and more specific. At first he speaks of his house in general: 'the sword shall never depart from your house' (12.10). The sequel affects the king himself: 'an evil out of your own house' (v. 11a; note the ominous epipher מביתך). The last threat alludes to a specific event: 'your wives' will be taken 'before your eyes' by 'your neighbour' who is to 'lie with your wives in the sight of this sun' (v. 11bc). This series of threats is rounded off by a reassertion of divine punishment (v. 12). This is a dramatic amplification of the first part of the prophecy, built as a climax of $k^e l\bar{a}l$ and $p^e r\bar{a}t$ (the troops of the general and the particular). In the opening of this pericope one notes the conspicuous use of 'evil' (רעה); in its closure we meet the verbs 'did' and 'do' (אעשה, עשׂיה). These vocables echo Nathan's first prophecy: 'to do that which is evil in my sight' (לעשׂות הרע בעיני, v. 9; *kethib*: בעינו), and of the conclusion of the Bathsheba tale: 'But the thing that David had done was evil in the sight of the Lord' (וירע הדבר אשׁר עשׂה דוד בעיני יהוה, 11.27b).[26]

On another level, Nathan's prophecy obviously alludes to Ahithophel's suggestion that Absalom should prove his rebellion to be final and irreversible by having intercourse with David's harem-wives (16.21-22). This scene seems strange in its context, since the sequel recounts how Ahithophel urges speedy action (17.1-3). How is this reconcilable with Absalom's having sex with David's women? Besides, how are we to understand the course of events? Did Absalom enter the harem at the very same time the council was being held?[27] Actually,

Congress Volume: Leuven 1989 (VTSup, 43; Leiden: Brill, 1991), pp. 116-31; on patriarchal narrative see L.A. Turner, *Announcements of Plot in Genesis* (JSOTSup, 96; Sheffield: JSOT Press, 1990).

26. These indications of unity disprove the common view that 12.11-12 constitute a later addition; see for example K. Seybold, *Das Davidische Königtum im Zeugnis der Propheten* (FRLANT, 107; Göttingen: Vandenhoeck & Ruprecht, 1972), pp. 45-50; W. Dietrich, *Propheten und Geschichte: Eine Redaktions-geschichtliche Untersuchung zum deuteronomistischen Geschichtswerk* (FRLANT, 108; Göttingen: Vandenhoeck & Ruprecht, 1972), pp. 127-32. As to phraseology: וירע הדבר בעיני (11.27b) is not Deuteronomistic; it harks back to 11.25 (אל ירע בעיניך את הדבר הזה); a similar sequence occurs in the tale of Ishmael's expulsion (Gen. 21.10: וירע הדבר אל ירע בעיניך על הנער ועל אמתך; v. 12; מאד בעיני אברהם על אודת בנו).

27. Cook, 'Composition', p. 164; Würthwein, *Geschichtsschreibung*, pp. 36-40; F. Langlamet, 'Absalom et les concubines de son père: Recherches sur II Sam., XVI, 21-22', *RB* 84 (1977), pp. 161-209.

however, these questions are not to the point. The fact that the implementation of Ahithophel's advice is recounted immediately after his speech is in keeping with the order–execution scheme, thanks to which the narrator can allow himself a small leap into the future.[28] This trope, though rare, is paralleled by other passages, and does not entail any difficulties. Moreover, in Ahithophel's advice, Absalom has nothing to do with the pursuit after David. As noted above, Ahithophel wants to deal with the king himself (17.1, 3), and does not leave room for any activity on Absalom's part, apart from his harem performance. Apparently, this division of the tasks is to forestall any possibility of a reconciliation between the king and his son.

The harem scene, then, deepens the relationship of the rebellion tale with the prophetic reproach and the Bathsheba tale. The analogy with David's adultery is only too well known: the violation of his concubines, paralleling his violation of Uriah's wife, is another indication of divine judgment ('poetic justice').[29] It is a significant detail that these concubines had been left behind at the time David fled to the Gilead, just as Bathsheba was left in Jerusalem when Uriah went to participate in the siege of Rabbath Ammon (15.16).

What is more, an obvious connection exists between the Bathsheba tale and the pericope of Absalom's death. Fokkelman has highlighted the parallel in the messenger scenes after Uriah's death and after the killing of Absalom. In both cases Joab is responsible for the instructions to the messenger, and in both cases he is fully aware of the delicacy of the message.[30] One is reminded of David's servants who do not find the courage to inform the king of the death of the infant, 'lest he will do harm', to wit, to the bringer of the bad news (12.18).[31]

28. Cf. Esth. 8.1-2, and see Lämmert, *Bauformen*, pp. 150-53, 163-75; he even adduces examples from medieval narrative poetry (p. 165).

29. Blenkinsopp, 'Theme', p. 50. However, unlike the analogy between the Bathsheba tale and the Amnon–Tamar narrative, this parallel is only an episodic reminder of the general structure. Fokkelman (*David*, p. 210) adds the function of the roof, reminding one of the roof where David was standing when he saw Bathsheba.

30. Simon, 'Ewe-Lamb', p. 237; similarly Fokkelman, *David*, pp. 245-46, 263-64.

31. On the importance of this scene and its parallels with the Uriah episode, see Simon, 'Ewe-Lamb', pp. 239-40; Fokkelman, *David*, pp. 91-93.

Moreover, in both narratives Joab expresses disapproval of David's actions, implicitly in the Uriah narrative, explicitly in the tale of the rebellion. The main point, however, concerns the relation between Joab and Uriah. Unlike the MT and LXX, the Samuel Scroll from Qumran has Uriah introduced as וש[נ]א כלי יואב (11.2), a detail also mentioned by Flavius Josephus (*Ant.* 7.7.1 §131).[32] The content of this surplus is highly untypical of explanatory glosses,[33] and therefore the longer reading seems original. It implies an extremely involved introduction, which presents Bathsheba in her relation to Eliam, and to Uriah, who is related to Joab. Such long introductions, though rare, are attested in biblical narrative, for example in the narrative on the appearance of Rebecca (Gen. 24.15). In the book of Samuel one notes the introduction of Ahijah the priest in the tale of Jonathan's heroism (1 Sam. 14.3). Actually both these introductions exhibit the same structure, also shared by the longer version of the introduction of Uriah. Opening with the name of the main character, they continue to indicate other persons to whom he or she is connected, in order to close with a character of special relevance:

32. See E.C. Ulrich, *The Qumran Text of Samuel and Josephus* (HSM, 19; Missoula, MT: Scholars Press, 1978), p. 73; McCarter, *II Samuel, ad loc.*

33. The fact that this reading has not been transmitted by the LXX is not evidence for its secondary character in 4QSam[a], since this portion must be attributed to the Kaige revision, which was quite close to proto-MT. On the other hand, the character of this gloss is quite unlike that of obvious exegetic additions in this scroll, for which see F. Foresti, 'Osservazioni su alcune varianti di 4QSam[a] rispetto al TM', *RivB* 29 (1981), pp. 45-56; A. Rofé, 'The Nomistic Correctures in Biblical Manuscripts and its Occurrence in 4QSam[a]', *RevQ* 14 (1989), pp. 247-54. On the relationship between 4QSam[a] and LXX see F.H. Polak, 'Statistics and Textual Filiation: The Case of 4QSam[a]/LXX (With a Note on the Text of the Pentateuch)', in G.T. Brook and B. Lindars (eds.), *Septuagint, Scrolls and Cognate Writings: The Proceedings of the Manchester Symposium on the Septuagint and its Relations to the Dead Sea Scrolls and Other Writings (Manchester, 1990)* (SBLSCS, 33; Atlanta: Scholars Press, 1992).

name	*other characters*	*important character*
Rebecca came out, who	was born to Bethuel,	
	the son of Milcah,	the wife of Nahor,
		Abraham's brother
Ahijah, the son of	Ahitub, Ichabod's	
	brother, the son of	
	Pinchas,	the son of Eli, the priest
		of the Lord in Shiloh
(additional detail:)		carrying the ephod.[34]
Bathsheba,		
the daughter of	Eliam, the wife of	
	Uriah the Hittite	(armourbearer to Joab).

The introductions of Elqanah and Kish both extend over four generations, and are even continued in the next verse, stating the names of
additional members of the family. On the other hand, in later narrative this form is not attested. The expository pericopes in the tales of
Ruth and Esther exhibit a different structure; the introduction of
Zephaniah as the great-grandson of Hezekiah looks similar, but is not
embedded in narrative (Zeph. 1.1); the genealogy of Zelaphad (Num.
27.1; cf. 36.1) fits the book of Numbers, but cannot be compared to
our case, as it presents a straightforward ascent to the father of the
tribe. Hence the attribution of the extended introduction of Uriah to a
later copyist or reviser would go against the grain. On the other hand,
it could easily have been omitted, since the introduction of Bathsheba
is quite elaborate even without it. Of course, the mention of Joab in
the introduction of the man who is to be killed by his co-operation
with the king (cf. 13.1-2) exhibits the bitter irony characteristic of
this narrative. More importantly, it creates a deep psychological
tension, as Joab inevitably was quite close to the man he had to kill by
the king's order. This tension adds another dimension to Joab's
sarcastic message after Uriah was killed.

The Qumran reading also sheds new light on the tale of Absalom's
death. First of all, one notes the structural opposition: Uriah, Joab's
armourbearer, must die by the express order of David; Absalom,
David's son, is killed by Joab, against David's express interdiction.

---

34. The importance of the additional detail for closing off the introductory
exposition and building up the complication (1 Sam. 9.1: איש ימיני גבור חיל; 17.14;
1.1 בן צוף אפרתי) has not been sufficiently perceived by W. Richter, *Traditionsge-
schichtliche Untersuchungen zum Richterbuch* (BBB, 18; Bonn: Peter Hanstein,
1964), pp. 12-13.

The latter scene, then, is the counterpart of the former one. Moreover, after hitting Absalom with three arrow-heads (שלחים),[35] Joab has him killed by ten of his armourbearers. Among the many other reminiscences one must mention the 'roof of the gate' on which the spy stood in order to inform the king of any news (18.24). This roof is an echo of the roof on which David was walking when he espied Bathsheba (11.2).[36] Another intriguing detail is the mention of the wall (18.24: אל גג השער אל החומה), reminding us of the wall from which Uriah was hit (מעל החומה, 11.24), as was Abimelech (11.21; this sound constellation is similar to המלחמה, vv. 7, 15-20, 25). The town gate appears in the pericope of Uriah's death in the heroic attempt to use the counter-attack for forcing a way into the town (11.23). All these features enhance and deepen the intricate connection between these two tales. Absalom's death is an act of divine retribution for the murder of Uriah.

David: A Tragic Consciousness

The idea that David's suffering is a punishment for his sins is also expressed, in a very subtle way, by some comments of the king himself. As Ebiathar and Zadok bring up the Ark in order to accompany David in his flight, David has them return: 'if I shall find favour in the eyes of the Lord, He will bring me back, and show me both it, and His habitation. But if He says thus: I have no delight in thee; here I am, let Him do to me as seemeth good unto Him' (15.25-26).[37] Thus, David is conscious of his dependence on God. He is aware of the rupture between them, and is not certain whether he is destined for doom or for grace. Significantly, David's doubts are expressed in relation to the Ark; this symbol of divine presence was also mentioned by Uriah in his rejection of David's suggestion to go home to his wife, as 'The

35. 18.14: MT שבטים; LXX-Luc. βέλη, apparently = שלחים, as suggested by this equivalence in Joel 2.8.

36. For the mention of this roof in 12.11 see note 29.

37. Würthwein (*Geschichtsschreibung*, pp. 43) would consider 15.24-26, 29 a redactional intrusion, as only vv. 27-28 are firmly entrenched in the narrative. However, the only way to find fault with this pericope is to assume that a narrative character does not utter evaluations of his position or anticipations of his future, as against all evidence; see Lämmert, *Bauformen*, pp. 175-79; Weiss, 'Bauformen', and cf. 1 Sam. 3.18; 2 Sam. 10.12 (the very same wording), as well as 'The Plague-Prayers of Muršiliš' (*ANET*, pp. 394-96), esp. pericopes 6-10, p. 395.

Ark and Israel and Judah abide in booths (בסכות)' (11.11). Thus, in the present scene, David is shown to know that he is not worthy of the presence of the Ark. This newly won moral consciousness contrasts sharply with his bluntness in the Uriah episode.

By the same token, at the appearance of Shimei, who is not afraid of cursing him and casting stones at his party (16.8-12), David avows that 'my son, who came forth of my body, is seeking my life; how much more this Benjaminite now' (v. 11).[38] Significantly, this episode adds allusions to the king's guilt. Shimei curses him as 'the man of blood, and the man of ruin'; 'and see, you art in your own evil, for you are a man of blood' (16.7-8). No doubt the reference to the fate of Saul and his house is highly meaningful to this member of Saul's family (v. 8a). Nevertheless, one should not overlook the connotations of David's sin as a 'man of blood'. Shimei's mention of 'your evil' is an echo of Nathan's speech of judgment, which chastises David for his doing that which is evil in the Lord's sight (12.9) and announces 'an evil against you out of your own house' (v. 12). Hence David's mention of 'my son' is the counterpart of Shimei's denunciation of 'your evil', for both motifs are connected in Nathan's prophecy. The sequel of David's avowal deals with the divine side of the matter: 'leave him alone and let him curse, for the Lord has bidden him'. David's recognition of the divine nemesis suggests an increasing moral awareness. On the other hand the king also expresses hope for a turn for the better: אולי יראה יהוה בעוני (v. 12; *qere* בעיני). David, then, is conscious of sin and punishment, but by virtue of his

---

38. Würthwein (*Geschichtsschreibung*, pp. 43-44) attributes this entire episode to a redactional intrusion, because of its lack of realism, as against the well-known realistic attitude of the ancient David narratives. This argument is buttressed by reference to the doubling of ויאמר, indicating duplication of sources (16.10, 11). However, the latter indication is quite doubtful since this doubling of the *inquit* is quite customary in biblical narrative and is of stylistic value, as shown by M. Shiloah, 'ויאמר...ויאמר', in *Q Sefer Korngrin* (Tel Aviv: Niv & The Society for Bible Research, 1964), pp. 251-76; J. Wellhausen, *Der Text der Bücher Samuelis* (Göttingen: Vandenhoeck & Ruprecht, 1871), p. 107, on 1 Sam. 17.37, quoted approvingly by S.R. Driver, *Notes on the Hebrew Text and the Topography of the Books of Samuel* (London: Oxford University Press, 2nd edn, 1913), p. 145. Secondly, realism is too general an impression to serve as grounds for critical judgment. In our case, however, the narrator may have shunned some vital details, for instance the mention of the people accompanying Shimei (19.18), or David's awareness of the political importance of this Benjaminite (1 Kgs 2.8-9).

138   *Politics and Theopolitics*

suffering he is allowed to entertain hopes for the future.[39]

Apparently, this constellation provides the explanation for the strange alternation of weakness and strength in the way David copes with the vicissitudes of his fate. The picture of David as a weak king, easily beguiled by his sons, is dependent on his sins against Bathsheba and Uriah. Slowly purified by his suffering, he recovers his human feelings bit by bit, at first in his mourning over Amnon (13.36-37), and afterwards in his renewed acceptance of Absalom, who returns to Jerusalem (14.1, 24, 23-24). But this recovery is partial only, and has no impact on his position before God. And yet, at the outbreak of Absalom's uprising he is allowed to escape, and the new signs of his awareness of his dependency on divine succour and guidance (15.25-26, 31; 16.10-12) render him worthy of regaining his kingdom. David is given a reprieve, but has to atone for his sins by ever-increasing punishment until he retains his moral awareness.

The high point of this process is the moment David is informed of both his victory and Absalom's death (18.32–19.1). Only at this moment does he become fully conscious of his guilt. That is the meaning of his reaction to Absalom's death: מי יתן מותי אני תחתיך—a very far cry from Nathan's assurance גם יהוה העביר חטאתך לא תמות (12.13), and very much unlike David's laconic behaviour after the death of the baby Bathsheba bore to him (12.22),[40] or his public weeping after Amnon was killed, during which he does not utter a word (31.31-36).[41] The moment of his victory, then, is also the climax of his suffering. Only Absalom's death purges him sufficiently to justify his rescue from utter ruin; only now does he attain full understanding of his responsibility.

---

39. W. Brueggemann ('On Trust and Freedom: A Study of Faith in the Succession Narrative', *Int* 26 [1972], pp. 3-19, esp. pp. 13-19) correctly points to the optimistic side of these remarks, in contrast to Würthwein's comments on his 'resignation'; David's deep humility has been commented upon by Fokkelman, *David*, pp. 186-89, 201.

40. See Fokkelman, *David*, p. 263-64, as against Simon, 'Ewe-Lamb', pp. 240-41, who finds in 12.16-23 a complete change of heart.

41. The issue is not David's expiation by suffering in itself but his consciousness. On his growing awareness see also J. Rosenberg, '1 and 2 Samuel', in R. Alter and F. Kermode (eds.), *The Literary Guide to the Bible* (Cambridge, MA: Harvard University Press, 1987), pp. 122-45, esp. 136.

Tension and Equilibrium

Thus, David's tragedy is not conditioned by his personality, but relates to his status before God. His weakness is connected to his guilt, his acumen to his consciousness of having sinned; suffering is a precondition for his ultimate success. In the end, the equilibrium between grace and doom is positive, but precarious.

However, even though precarious, the outcome *is* positive. This is the point of the tales of Bathsheba and of Solomon's succession to the throne. The Bathsheba narrative prefigures the tale of Absalom's uprising, as in the end David is saved at the cost of the life of his son (12.14). Although David's belated confession and his remorse over the dying infant are not convincing enough to forestall further suffering, he is allowed to return to his wife, now recognized as lawful,[42] and to beget another son, Solomon (12.22-25), whom 'the Lord loved' (12.24),[43] a transparent indication of his accession to the throne, as well as an interesting allusion to the dynastic promise: 'I shall be to him as a father and he will be to Me as a son' (7.14). Hence, in contrast to the general tenor of the Bathsheba narrative, this comment buttresses the positive side of the David narrative.

The tale of Solomon's succession to the throne also exhibits a precarious equilibrium. Even though the ultimate outcome is good, and David may pronounce a blessing over his success (1 Kgs 1.47, reminiscent of 7.12, 16), it is still heavily flawed: it results from complicated intrigues within the court, in which even the prophet is involved; Adonijah is to pay with his life, as is Joab. Furthermore, the reference to David's former pledge of making Solomon his heir to the

---

42. On the positive implications of 12.24a see Simon, 'Ewe-Lamb', p. 35; Fokkelman, *David*, pp. 91-93.

43. Rost, *Succession*, p. 99; being loved by the deity is a frequent royal epithet in ancient Near Eastern texts, as evidenced by M.J. Seux, *Épithètes royales akkadiennes et sumeriennes* (Paris: Letouzey & Ané, 1957), pp. 19, 65-66 (*dādu*), pp. 237-38 (*râmu*), pp. 163-64 (*migru*); W.W. Hallo, *Early Mesopotamian Royal Titles: A Philologic and Historical Analysis* (AOS, 43; New Haven: American Oriental Society, 1957), pp. 137-41. Note the parallel between chs. 11 and 12, as both open with the indication of a crime (11.2-5; 12.1-4), continue with confrontation, death (11.6-16; 12.5-18), the announcement of death and the reaction thereto (11.17-26; 12.19-23), and the birth of a son (11.27a; 12.24a), in order to close with a note of censure (11.27b) or approval (12.24b-25).

throne is only partly confirmed by the account of his birth. Even the
role of Nathan, not very much the prophet in this narrative, seems
problematic. Thus, the Davidic dynasty is shown to suffer from inherent weakness. Only by divine grace is it allowed to escape extinction:
David has atoned for his sins.

The tragic, but positive, view of David's kingship is complemented
by the assessment of Saul's rule, whose history has been described by
the very same historian who dealt with David and his sons. A long
sequence of utterances abundantly clarifies the importance of the
doom of Saul and his house: 6.21-22, 7.15, 12.8, 16.8-12. Moreover,
Meribaal is a kind of antipode to David, with his alleged false hopes of
receiving the kingship (16.3), the confiscation of his estate (16.4), his
utter dependency on the king (9.13), and his final resignation to the
loss of half his estate (19.28-31). So is Shimei: he has forfeited his
life, but is forgiven by David, at least for a while (19.20-24); 1 Kgs
2.8, 36-46). Saul's demise, then, serves to typify David's suffering. In
this connection we must mention the parallel between David's flight
from Absalom and his flight from Saul, as exemplified by the appearance of Ittai of Gath (15.19-22; cf. 1 Sam. 27.1-6; 29.3-4, 6-7), the
appearance of Ziba (2 Sam. 16.1-4), and the vilifications by Shimei
(16.5-8), who depicts Absalom's rebellion as a nemesis for the death
of Saul's people, and thus mentions both David's enemies in the same
breath (v. 8). Abishai's insistence on killing the villain (16.9-10;
19.22-23) is anticipated by his proposal to kill Saul (1 Sam. 26.8-9).
Extremely significant is the arrival of the priests, Abiathar and Zadok,
who wish to accompany David while carrying the Ark (15.24), even
as Abiathar took refuge with David while carrying the ephod (1 Sam.
22.20-23; 23.6). Hushai seems to allude to the period of David's exile
in the Judaean desert (17.8-10; cf. 1 Sam. 22.1-2; 26.5-12; 24.4).[44] In
particular, one notes obvious parallels between the performance of
Abigail, who seeks to prevent the destruction of Nabal's household
and inadvertently warns David not to kill Saul (1 Sam. 25.25-26, 28-
31; 26.10-12),[45] and the wise woman from Tekoa who intervenes for

44. See Polak, 'Continuity', pp. 61-63; Bar-Efrat, *Narrative Art*, p. 237.
45. For the recognition that Nabal serves as a type for Saul see H.J. Stoebe, *Das
Erste Buch Samuelis* (KAT, 8.1; Gütersloh: Gerd Mohn, 1973), p. 458; R. Polzin,
Samuel and the Deuteronomist: A Literary Study of the Deuteronomic History. II.
1 Samuel (San Francisco: Harper & Row, 1989), p. 206; J.D. Levenson, 'I Samuel
25 as Literature and as History', *CBQ* 40 (1978), pp. 11-28, esp. pp. 23-24;

Absalom, and thus unwittingly contributes to his death. This analogy is all the more forceful as it is matched by the parallel contrast between Abigail and Bathsheba, whose husband is killed by order of David whereas Nabal's death is brought about by God (1 Sam. 25.37-38).[46]

What is more, David's cause is furthered by his refraining from killing Nabal, whereas his sins against Bathsheba and Uriah almost cause his ruin. This intricate network of connections, allusions, correspondences and contrasts, both in plot structure and in wording, strongly suggest that we are dealing with one cohesive text rather than with a redactional concoction and revision of various pre-existing tales. This history has been created by a prophetic narrator, rather than a prophetic redactor.

This narrator probes the place of the human king before his divine overlord, and evokes the tragic tension between pledge and doom, between divine grace and human failure. The tragic dimensions of failure are exemplified by the tales of Saul. The David narratives indicate the ultimate equilibrium, as the outcome is precarious but still positive.

Thus far this interpretation of the David narratives. However, we must raise the question whether these tales are no more than an individual creation concerning an individual king. The importance of the period described, as well as David's position in history, suggests a more general outlook. From the point of view of political theology the tension between grace and doom embodies a fundamental antithesis.[47] The pledge to David represents the divine legitimation of royal authority; the punishment represents the king's responsibility for the use and abuse of his power. In the human world this antithesis has no real solution: even though David may succeed, the equilibrium is not perfect, and the final outcome still contains conflicts and

J.P. Fokkelman, *Narrative Art and Poetry in the Books of Samuel*. II. *The Crossing Fates (I Sam. 13–21 & II Sam. 1)* (Assen: Van Gorcum, 1986), pp. 504-505, 538. The wording of 26.10 reminds one not only of Saul's death in battle, but also of 25.38. 25.26 obliquely confirms the comparison: the reference to David's persecutors fits Saul (26.18) rather than Nabal (25.29).

46. The wording does not contain any immediate indications of this contrast–parallel; still, 2 Sam. 14.16 recalls 1 Sam. 26.19; 2 Sam. 26.20 echoes 1 Sam. 29.9; both these narratives are closely related to the Abigail tale.

47. See Christofer Frey's article in this volume.

tensions. In biblical thought, the synthesis is provided only by the messianic idea. In this sense, utopianism constitutes a necessary component of religious thought.

Appendix 1: Plot Structure and Cohesion in 2 Samuel 7–13

In chs. 7–13 of 2 Samuel one notes an intricate transition structure, based on wording and plot structure alike. All these tales are concerned with one generalized theme, the succession to the throne. This theme, obvious in the dynastic promise (as well as in 6.21-23), recurs in the Meribaal narrative, which deals with the inheritance of the last descendant of Saul (9.4, 7, 9, 12). It returns in the opening scenes of the Ammonitic war narrative, which recounts the death of Nahash and the accession of his son, Hanun (10.1-2); the Bathsheba tale points to Solomon (12.24-25), and includes threats to David's realm (12.10-12). The central characters in the Amnon tale are David's sons and heirs-in-waiting, Absalom and Amnon.

On the other hand, the relation between these tales is dominated by analogy and contrast, inducing a gradual transition from grace to doom and punishment. The divine *hesed* to David and his house (7.14-15; הטובה, 7.28) is matched by David's *hesed* to Meribaal (9.1, 3, 7), expressly styled a חסד אלהים (v. 3). By the same token David wishes to act with *hesed* towards Hanun, since his father was always loyal to him, but Hanun rejects David's overtures and repays him with ignomy (vv. 3-5). This rebellious behaviour is matched by David's violation of the divine commands in the Bathsheba affair; the connection is laid by the introduction in 11.1; Rabbath Ammon is the scene of Uriah's death; from the point of view of *leitmotifs* one might note the similarity between וישכרו (10.6) and וישכרהו (11.13), both used for treacherous behaviour; the town gate of Rabbath Ammon figures in both narratives (10.8; 11.23; note the Ammonitic sortie in 10.8; 11.17, 23). David's punishment of Ammon prefigures the divine punishment of David. The Amnon narrative matches both David's adultery and the murder of Uriah.[48]

These central themes are enhanced and concretized by a complete series of common keywords, which recur in these pericopes.[49]

---

48. Parts of this structure have been described by Fokkelman, *David*, pp. 43, 49, disregarding, however, ch. 7.

49. Wording (*discourse*) deepens and enhances plot structure (*histoire*) by creating a general semantic platform; see also F.H. Polak, 'Literary Study and "Higher Criticism" according to the Tale of David's Beginning', in *Proceedings of the Ninth World Congress of Jewish Studies, Division A: Period of the Bible* (Jerusalem: World Union of Jewish Studies, 1986), pp. 27-32; S. Chatman, *Story and Discourse: Narrative Structure in Fiction and Film* (Ithaca, NY: Cornell University Press, 1978), pp. 19-26, 43.

lexeme/ unit with synonym/ antonym	2 Sam. 7	9	10	11	12	13.1-22
חסד	15, 15 28 הטובה ברך 29, 29, 29	1, 3, 7	נבאשו 26	- 27 וירע	9, 10 בזה נאץ 14 רעה 9, 11, 18	12 נבלה 16 רעה
ישב	1, 2, 5, 6, 18	מושב 12 13	5	1, 11, 12	3	20
כסא/שלחן	13, 16 כסא ממלכתך	7, 10, 11, 13 שלחן נמלך	-	-	-	-
בית	1, 2, 5, 6, 7, 11, 13, 15, 26, 27, 29	1, 2, 3, 4, 5, 9	6	2, 4, 8, 9, 10, 11, 13, 27	8, 10, 11, 15, 17, 20	8, 20
שכב	12	-	-	משכב 2	3, 11, 16, 24	5, 8, 11, 14
שלח	-	5	2, 3, 5, 6, 7, 15	1, 3, 4, 5, 6, 12, 14, 18, 22, 27	1, 25, 27	7, 16, 17
אכל	7, 11 רעה	7, 10, 11, 13	-	11, 13, 25	3, 20, 21	ברה 9, 11; 6, 7, 10
נתן	PN 2, 3, 4, 8 לקח	5 לקח 9	10	15 הבו 16 4 לקח	8, 11 PN 1, 5, 7, 13, 13, 15 לקח 4, 4, 10, 11, 30	11 ותגש 8, 9, 10, 19

Appendix 2: The Dynastic Promise in 2 Samuel 7

The 'dynastic oracle' of 2 Samuel 7 is mostly attributed to the Deuteronomistic redactor, who welded different ancient traditions into one whole (DtrG);[50] McCarter[51] finds traces of both Dtr and the prophetic redaction. But is this approach correct? This question must be clarified according to a number of different criteria.

First, one may ask whether this oracle is as disintegrated as critics tend to believe. True, this oracle encompasses a variety of different motifs that might occur separately: temple building, David's rise to kingship and the dynastic promise. The

50. See Veijola, *Dynastie*, pp. 72-77.
51. *II Samuel*, pp. 7-8.

question is, however, in which way these motifs are combined. Is this combination superficial, or is it rooted in the wording itself? In the former case one might consider the combination secondary, but in the latter case this conclusion would appear to be mistaken: in this case the combination of these motifs is conditioned by their wording; thus, whoever welded them together would also be responsible for their formulation. In the first case one is concerned with the redactorial combination of pre-existing units; in the latter case we are dealing with a narrator handling different motifs as his own matter. Hence it is important to note, with Wellhausen,[52] that the keyword בית (בנה/עשה) occurs in three passages: the divine refusal to allow David to build a temple (האתה תבנה לי בית לשבתי, v. 5), the promise to found a Davidic dynasty (בית יעשה לך יהוה), and the promise that David's son and successor will be allowed to build a temple (הוא יבנה בית לשמי, v. 13; 1 Chron. 17.12, הוא יבנה־לי בית; LXX Sam = הוא יבנה לי בית לשמי, doublet). This keyword indicates the structural connection between the motifs: the promise that the temple will be built by David's son at once resolves the tension evoked by the divine refusal of v. 4, and embodies the combination of these motifs, Solomon being David's successor and as such representing the dynastic idea. In this respect, the connection between these motifs seems authentic; it is hardly dependent on redactorial intervention. What is more, the combination of these motifs is not unnatural. In innumerable ancient Near Eastern inscriptions the king bases his merits before the deity on his contribution to divine worship in general, and to temple building or rebuilding in particular. So also the Phoenician building inscriptions from Byblus;[53] this connection is obvious in Ps. 132.1-5, 11, 13, and also stands in the background of the juxtaposition of 2 Samuel 6 and 7.[54]

This principle is implicitly rejected in our wording of the dynastic promise, not given in recompense for David's endeavours, but as an additional divine grace (unlike Ps. 132.1-5). Moreover, this idea is also embodied by the divine retrospection on David's kingship, representing all his victories as acts of divine grace to David and Israel (vv. 8-11), culminating in the dynastic promise (as already noted by R. David Kimchi).[55] From the point of view of wording, many scholars detect a rough transition in v. 11, והגיד לך; however, W. Nowack[56] proposes to read ואגדלך (with LXX 1 Chron. 17.10, as against the MT ואגד לך). This text-critical

52. *Text*, p. 171 note; see Ridout, 'Prose Techniques', pp. 175-77, 183.

53. *KAI*, 4.3-7; 6.2-3; 7.3-4, all from the tenth century BCE.

54. See also H. Gese, 'Davidsbund und Zionserwählung', *ZTK* 61 (1964), pp. 10-26, esp. pp. 14-19; R. de Vaux, 'Jerusalem et les prophètes', *RB* 73 (1966), pp. 481-509, esp. pp. 483-84; T.E. Fretheim, 'Ps. 132: A Form-Critical Study', *JBL* 86 (1967), pp. 289-300.

55. On the position occupied by these motifs in the royal grant, see P. Calderone, 'Oraculum dynasticum et foedus regale', *VD* 45 (1967), pp. 91-96; C.F. Fensham, 'Covenant, Promise and Expectation in the Bible', *TZ* 23 (1967), pp. 305-22, esp. pp. 308-17; and in particular M. Weinfeld, 'The Covenant of Grant in the Old Testament and in the Ancient Near East', *JAOS* 90 (1970), pp. 184-203.

56. *Die Bücher Samuelis* (HKAT, 1.4.2; Göttingen: Vandenhoeck & Ruprecht, 1902), pp. 177-78. See also I.L. Seeligmann, 'Indications of Editorial Alteration and Adaptation in the Massoretic Text and the Septuagint', *VT* 11 (1961), pp. 201-21, esp. p. 208.

decision is confirmed by the parallel in v. 9; for the importance of the 'greatness' motif (also Gen. 12.2) see Weinfeld.[57]

From a literary point of view this unit closes the story of David's rise as a retrospective summary (vv. 8-11);[58] on the other hand it anticipates the succession narrative. From a historical point of view, this text quite probably alludes to conservative opposition against the idea of temple building.[59] Of course, a conservative opposition of this kind should not be confounded with the rationalistic attitude of the Deuteronomic school.[60]

Hence the dynastic promise is firmly embedded in its own literary and historical context. To be sure, the charter of the Davidic dynasty is of primary importance for the Deuteronomistic redaction of the book of Kings. But are there objective indications of a Dtr redaction? Veijola[61] finds such indication in the doubling of והכינתי את ממלכתו (v. 12b) and וכננתי את כסא ממלכתו עד עולם (v. 13b), with interchange of *hiphil* and *polel*. Of course, this might be a case of epanalepsis, but it might also be a matter of parallelism, not unexpected in *gehobener Rede*; thus it would demonstrate the originality of v. 13a, rather than rendering it suspect. In vv. 1 and 11 Veijola[62] detects the Deuteronomic מנוחה formula. However, v. 1 is no more than a preparation for v. 11; the latter verse differs from the normal Deuteronomistic formula in that its immediate context actually deals with defeated mortal enemies: vv. 9-11: והניחתי לך מכל איביך (matching v. 9, ואכרתה את כל איביך מפניך). Of course, v. 1 is based on the account of David's victories in his battles against the Philistines (5.17-25, immediately continued in 6.1: only after his conquest of Beth Shemesh and its surroundings was it possible to bring up the Ark). Hence, in this unit the מנוחה formula follows organically from the context and is not dependent on Dtr phraseology; on the contrary, it might well constitute the source of the Deuteronomic formula.[63] In v. 13a לשמי is not necessarily authentic; as it is not represented in the variant in 1 Chron. 17.12, it probably constitutes a scribal amplification, inspired by the frequent Dtr formula, as suggested by Gese[64] and Seeligmann.[65]

The ideology of this chapter is not quite Deuteronomistic. The idea of an unconditional promise (7.11-15) is foreign to this school. In Psalm 132 the promise is made conditional (vv. 11-12). The way the dynastic promise is treated by the Deuteronomistic redaction of the book of Kings is characteristic: the prophecy is

57. 'Covenant of Grant', pp. 200-201.
58. As shown by A. Weiser, 'Die Legitimation des Konigs David', *VT* 16 (1966), pp. 325-54.
59. See A. Weiser, 'Die Tempelbaukrise unter David', *ZAW* 77 (1965), pp. 153-68.
60. For which see M. Weinfeld, *Deuteronomy and the Deuteronomic School* (London: Oxford University Press, 1972), pp. 191-207.
61. *Dynastie*, p. 72.
62. *Dynastie*, pp. 72-73.
63. See I.L. Seeligmann, 'From Historical Reality to Historiosophic Conceptualization in the Bible' (Hebrew), *Peraqim* 2 (1972), pp. 273-313, esp. pp. 285-86.
64. 'Davidsbund', p. 23.
65. 'Historiosophic Conceptualization', p. 302 n. 61.

quoted *in extenso* in Solomon's prayer (1 Kgs 8.15-26), its application to Solomon is made explicit (vv. 19-21), the promise conditional (v. 25b). This change is further authorized by the divine response to Solomon's prayer (9.4-7).

The problematic absence of conditionality is not remedied by the possibility of attributing divine threats against the dynasty to DtrN.[66] Conditionality is one of the main tendencies of Deuteronomium, since it embodies the covenant formulae of curse and blessing as well as wisdom admonitions.[67] Secondly, those pericopes in which the redaction of the book of Kings alludes to the unconditional promise differ from 2 Sam. 7.14-15; the image used is not that of adoption (7.14), but of an eternal 'light' (or rather 'rule'; 1 Kgs 11.36; 15.4; 2 Kgs 8.19). Since the latter passages all adhere to this one stereotypic formula, the difference from Nathan's prophecy is significant; so is the mention of punishment in 2 Sam. 7.14b.[68] Some central concepts of this verse are not expressed in Dtr language: והוכחתיו represents a root not used in Deuteronomistic texts; the root of בהעותו is used only in the exilic addition to Solomon's prayer (1 Kgs 8.47).[69]

Extremely meaningful is the allusion to Saul in 7.15; the death of Shimei is the last event relating to the house of Saul mentioned in the book of Kings; further parts of this book do not even allude to Saul, including the account of the schism in the monarchy. That is to say, for the authors of the David tales anything associated with Saul is of vital importance, whereas for the redaction of the book of Kings (as well as for the poets of Pss. 89.25, 28; 132) this is a matter of the most distant past, not even fit to serve as a typical figure for the sinful king. For the same reasons one must reject the attribution of these pericopes to the prophetic editor.

The distance of this prophecy from the Deuteronomistic redactions has been admitted by R.D. Nelson.[70] In his opinion, however, the conditional promise concerns Solomon only; in Dtr thought the threat implied was fulfilled by the secession of the ten tribes, the unconditional promise being related to the rule over Judaea;[71] because of this idea, and out of respect for the ancient tradition, the redactor retained the promises of 7.11-16.[72] However, in the dynastic oracle itself such interpretation, if correct, would necessarily entail the collapse of David's kingdom (7.14). Hence the Deuteronomistic use of this promise would be based on reinterpretation.

Moreover, Nelson fails to take into account the fact that Psalm 132 represents both promise and condition. Secondly, we must distinguish between positive conditions (promise of an eternal dynasty, if certain criteria are met, as in Ps. 132.12; 1 Kgs

66. See R. Smend, *Das Entstehen des Alten Testaments* (Stuttgart: Kohlhammer, 1978), pp. 114-15.

67. See Weinfeld, *Deuteronomy*, pp. 116-46, 307-19.

68. See Weinfeld, 'Covenant of Grant', pp. 193-94.

69. See E. Talstra, *Het gebed van Salomo: Synchronie en diachronie in de kompositie van I Kon. 8, 14-61* (Amsterdam: VU Uitgeverij, 1987), pp. 100-101, 180-85, 234-35.

70. *The Double Redaction of the Deuteronomistic History* (JSOTSup, 18; Sheffield: JSOT Press, 1981), pp. 99-101.

71. *Double Redaction*, pp. 101-104.

72. *Double Redaction*, p. 108.

9.4-5), and negative conditions, threatening annihilation of the dynasty, if certain criteria are not met (1 Kgs 9.6-9). Positive conditions do not necessarily presuppose the collapse of Judaea. On the other hand, negative conditions as such have existed before the exile; for definite, positive proof of a seventh-century date for Deut. 28.15-68 see R.N. Frankena[73] and Weinfeld.[74] These data should be taken into account for the critical assessment of certain elements in the Josiah narrative (2 Kgs 22.11-13, not to be attributed to the late expansion of the Huldah prophecy in vv. 16ab-18a, as shown by Dietrich[75]).

In short, the argument for the secondary (either Deuteronomistic or prophetic) redaction of the dynastic oracle is basically flawed. This promise is an integral part of the David narrative.

---

73. 'The Vassal Treaties of Esarhaddon and the Dating of Deuteronomy', *OTS* 14 (1965), pp. 122-54.

74. *Deuteronomy*, pp. 116-29.

75. *Propheten*, pp. 55-56; see also Nelson, *Double Redaction*, pp. 76-79.

THE 'LAW' AND THE NOAHIDES

Nahum Rakover

The Source of the Obligation of the Seven Noahide Commandments

Jewish tradition traces back to the Bible the obligation of all humankind to establish a judicial system, even before the Jewish people were so commanded. The Sages found the main source of this obligation in the command to Adam in Gen. 2.16—'And the Lord God commanded the man, saying: "Of every tree of the garden thou maye: : eat, but of the tree of knowledge of good and evil, thou shalt not eat"'—and in what is said about Abraham in Gen. 18.19: 'For I have known him to the end that he may command his children and his household...that they may keep the way of the Lord to do righteousness and justice'.

The Sages called the obligation to establish a court system 'the commandment of "law"', as one of the commandments given to all humankind. The *Tosefta* states that 'the children of Noah were given seven commandments concerning law, idolatry, blasphemy, adultery, bloodshed and robbery. Just as Israel is commanded to institute courts of law...so the children of Noah were commanded to institute courts' (*t. 'Abod. Zar.* 9.4). This statement is substantially repeated in *Sanh.* 56a-b, with the addition that R. Yohanan points out the similarity of phrase (*vayetzav* and *yetzaveh*: 'G–D commanded' and 'He [Abraham—the father of all nations] will command') in the above verses from Genesis.

It has been emphasized that the first commandment in human history—not to eat from the tree of knowledge—is the source for the obligation to sustain a compelling judicial system. It would, however, appear that the biblical source is not the basis for the commandment but merely a peg on which to hang it, as R. Yehudah Halevi writes in his *Kuzari* (3.23).[1]

---

1. Translation of H. Hirschfeld; New York, 1964.

Maimonides also observes that these commandments are a tradition transmitted to Moses at Sinai: 'Adam was commanded about six things: idolatry, blasphemy, bloodshed, adultery, robbery and law. Although all are of Sinaitic tradition and are intelligible to reason, it appears generally that scripture commanded them all!'[2] It will be noted that Maimonides adds to tradition the element of reason, and the general sense of statements in the Torah. In the last century a leading scholar, R. Me'ir Dan Plotzky, wrote that 'these remarks are obscure, and I do not know what the Master intended by them. I have given them much thought but without success'.[3] Maimonides, parallel to tradition, reason and biblical inference, ordains that the person who observes the Seven Commandments out of intellectual conviction is not one of the righteous but one of humanity's 'wise men' (the phrase 'a wise man' is found in MS although not in our printed text), but one who 'has accepted them and acts accordingly because they were commanded by the Holy One blessed be He in the Torah and, as Moses tells us, were given to the children of Noah, he is one of the righteous of mankind and has a portion in the world to come' (*Laws of Kings and Wars* 8.11).

The Content of 'Law'

In what ways are the Noahides obligated? Are they required to observe the laws of the Jews, or are they simply required to enact their own laws? If the laws of the Jews must be observed, are they to be interpreted as the Sages interpreted them in the Oral Law, or are the Noahides bound only by what is actually written in the Torah? If their obligations are not based upon the laws of the Jews, is humankind free to legislate as it wishes, or are there any governing principles?

According to Maimonides, 'A gentile who occupies himself with the Torah is liable to the death penalty. He should only occupy himself with the Seven Noahide Commandments' (*Laws of Kings and Wars* 10.9). This statement may be variously understood as meaning either that Gentiles are bound by the Seven Commandments in all their details, like Jews, and may study these details, or that they may study them but are not bound by them.

---

2. *Laws of Kings and Wars* 7.1, in *The Code of Maimonides* (Yale Judaica Series; New Haven, CT: Yale University Press, 1949).

3. *Hemdat Yisrael, Kuntres Ner Mitzvah* (repr.; New York, 1965), p. 86a.

Politics and Theopolitics

Naḥmanides, in his critique of Maimonides, says with regard to the people of Shechem: 'but He commanded them about theft, fraud, extortion, wages, bailees, rape, seduction, torts, lender and debtor, sale and so on, like the Jews were commanded',[4] and Shechem was killed for transgressing some of these laws. This statement need not, however, be taken to imply that the situation of the Gentiles was exactly the same as that of the Jews, only that it was similar.

Rema makes a novel departure in his noted responsum on the issue of the infringement of the copyright held by Maharam of Padua by the publication by a Gentile of Mishneh Torah.[5] According to Rema, the question of the identity of the laws is disputed by R. Yohanan and R. Yitzhak in *Sanh.* 56b (as noted above). The former finds in the biblical sources a similarity of terms, which enables the Noahides to prescribe their own laws. R. Yitzhak finds the similarity of the term 'God' with that appearing in the law relating to bailees— 'And the master shall be brought unto *elohim*' (that is, God, a judge [Exod. 22.7])—which was said at Sinai to assert that Noahide law is the same as Jewish law. It appears, Rema claims,

> that the [Talmud] had no need to explain the difference between R. Yohanan and R. Yitzhak, since it is clear as daylight: R. Yohanan thinks that the Noahides are only commanded to observe their customary law and give equitable judgment, but not in the manner of the Jews whose laws were given to them by Moses at Sinai; whereas R. Yitzhak... thinks that the Noahide Laws are those which the Jews were commanded at Sinai.

Rema adduces proof that the decided law is according to R. Yitzhak—that the Noahides were commanded to obey generally and in their particulars all the laws of the Jews. However, Netziv of Volozhin is critical of this conclusion: 'All would agree', he says, 'that the Noahides were not given the details of the laws, but were only commanded to appoint judges as they saw necessary'.[6] He adds that taking the law into one's own hands is forbidden to the Noahides. It is also the opinion of Hazon Ish that Jewish law does not apply to the Noahides, who are only obliged to act humanely and establish good government and just law.[7]

4. Naḥmanides, *Perush haRamban Al haTorah* (ed. Chavel; Jerusalem, 1959), on Gen. 34.13.
5. *She'alot uTeshuuot Rema* 10, in *Resp. Rema* (New York, 1954).
6. *Ha'amek She'elah* 2.3 (Jerusalem, 1955).
7. *Hazon Ish* (Benei Berak, 1966).

Noahide Law as Natural Law

We might understand Noahide law as a specific type of natural human law. The Talmud in *Sanh.* 57b tells us:

> R. Yaakov b. Aha found it written in the Book of Aggada of the school of Rav that a Noahide is punished on the ruling of one judge, on the evidence of one witness and without forewarning, on the evidence of a male, not a female, and even if the witness is a relative. In the opinion of R. Ishmael, even for the killing of an embryo.

It should be noted that the rules of procedure and evidence mentioned are taken to be rules of natural human law. The laws of the Torah which apply to Jews introduce certain restrictions not essential under natural law, such as that proceedings must be conducted before a bench of three judges, and in penal cases a bench of twenty-three, and that judgment must be given on the evidence of two witnesses.

Laws Based on Equity

If Jewish law is not identical with Noahide law, what should the latter comprise? Does the determination that a rule is a legal norm comply with the obligation to follow laws, or are there further requirements as to the contents of that rule?

From what was said about Abraham concerning righteousness and justice, we may infer that there is a connection between law and justice. The verse is quoted in the Talmud in association with the verse about Adam. I have already indicated that the latter is not the legal basis for the obligation of the Noahides to follow laws, but is quoted as part of an explanation, a quasi-*asmakhta*.[8] Nevertheless, the observations of Rema, cited above, show that Noahide law must be equitable, since in explaining the view of R. Yohanan who derives the obligation from the command to Adam, Rema lays down that the Noahides are only commanded to observe customary law and give equitable judgment. The commandment to law is not really concerned with *prescribing* regulations but with *implementing* just and equitable law.

This idea is a dominant theme of many Sages when dealing with the content of the commandment to follow laws. For instance, R. Shelomoh

8.   *Asmakhta* refers to a type of textual support in which the verse signifies something already known by oral tradition.

Helma writes: 'The commandment of "law" necessarily means the appointment of judges to uphold proper law and guard the oppressed from the oppressor. Judges must study all the laws relating to oppression and violence and apply them'.[9]

The Parallel of Noahide Law and the Law of the King

Following upon the view that Noahide law is natural human law, an interesting parallel is found between that law and the powers of the king, which are also seen as upholding natural human law.

R. Me'ir Dan Plotzky seeks to base certain powers of the king on this parallel; for instance on the rule permitting judgment on the evidence of a single witness (*Hemdat Yisrael, Kuntres Ner Mitzvah,* Commandment 248) he writes that two forms of government exist, the natural, which is Noahide, and that of the Torah given to the Jews. Thus a Noahide is sentenced by a single judge, on the evidence of one witness, notwithstanding the rule of the Torah, which requires three judges and two witnesses. The rule of the king is natural human law government as explained in the Bible: 'And thou shalt say: I will set a king over me, like all the nations that are around me' (Deut. 17.14). Hence laws of the king are derived from the same source as Noahide law. Moreover, Plotzky seeks to restrict the authority of the king's law to matters that concern Noahide law only. 'It seems', he writes, 'that the laws of the King obtain in regard only to the Seven Noahide Commandments which are intended for the public good'.

Reciprocally, it is possible to learn about Noahide law from what is contained in state law. *Sefer HaHinukh,* Commandment 192, observes that Noahides are punished on their own confession, which scholars find surprising, but Plotzky says that the same would seem to follow from what Maimonides has to say in *Laws concerning the Sanhedrin* 8 about David's killing of the Amalekite, who had killed King Saul. King Saul, after a military disaster, was near death and asked a young man to slay him. The lad acceded to the dying king's request and then sought out David to report Saul's death to him. Thus, David knew of the incident only from the young man's own report. However, Maimonides does not justify David's action on the basis of the lad's being a descendant of Noah, but explains, rather, that this was an

9.   *Mirkevet haMishneh* to *Laws of Kings and Wars* 9.14, in *Mirkevet haMishneh,* V (Jerusalem, 1956).

emergency measure (*hora'at sha'ah*). From here, it must be concluded that in Maimonides' opinion the death penalty may *not* be imposed on a descendant of Noah as a result of his own testimony.

R. Meir Simhah of Dvinsk (3.10) also expresses surprise that Maimonides held that under the law of the king a person may be punished on the evidence of a single witness.[10] And he suggests that it is only under the law of the Sanhedrin that two witnesses are required, whereas under the laws of the king, which are concerned with furthering public good, the rule is as it is in Noahide law, that is, to apply customary practice.

The Effect of the Obligation to Follow Laws on the Validity of Acts of Non-Jewish Courts in the Light of the Rule that 'the law of the King is the Law'

Just as there is a relationship between Noahide law and laws of the king, the obligation to follow laws is also important in the legal relations of Jew and non-Jew by virtue of the general rule that the law of the host state has legal effect. In view of the Noahide obligation to set up a judicial system, the question of the jurisdiction of Gentile courts over Jews arises. The *She'iltot* of R. Aha expresses the view that this jurisdiction extends only to non-Jews and not to Jews, who are commanded to maintain a judicial system of their own and are forbidden to litigate in non-Jewish courts.[11]

The *She'iltot* commences with a discussion of the duty to settle disputes judicially and not to assert one's rights by violent action. This is in accord with R. Shimon b. Gamliel's dictum that the world is preserved by truth, by judgment and by peace (*m. Ab.* 1.18). The first man, Adam, had in Gen. 2.16 already been commanded to apply the law, as construed by R. Yohanan, above. For non-Jews that means that disputes should be judicially resolved by their own law, whereas Jews are governed by the laws of the Torah and may not resort to non-Jewish courts even when the applicable law is the same as Jewish law.

But how can all this be reconciled with the rule that state law prevails? If the obligation to maintain a judicial system is imposed by the Torah, a duty to submit to Gentile jurisdiction should apply equally

---

10. *Or Same'ah* to *Laws of Kings and Wars* 3.10 (New York, 1946).
11. *She'iltot R. Aha Gaon* (ed. Mirsky; Jerusalem, 1959), p. 23a.

to Jews, but that might entail a displacement of laws particularly affecting Jews.

Rashbatz deals with another aspect of the problem in his well-known writing on the appointment of Ribash as a state judge.[12] He seeks to show that such an appointment is of no effect under the Halakhah in spite of the rule that state law prevails, since that rule applies only to customary state practice, 'and it is known that the appointment of a Judge by the state to try cases between Jews is entirely unusual, and therefore to initiate such a practice is ineffective' under Jewish law. At this point Rashbatz adds a new dimension: the appointment of judges is a religious matter lying outside state law and not involving the rule about the prevalence of state law. He also notes that Rashba was of like opinion.

The last reference is to the well-known responsum of Rashba dealing with a case of succession in which a man claimed return of a dowry from his son-in-law after the latter's wife had died.[13] Although under Jewish law a husband inherits his wife's property, the father-in-law argued that it was otherwise under non-Jewish law. Rashba had forcefully rejected reliance on the rule that the law of the state prevails since that would mean the uprooting of the whole Torah and nothing would remain of the learning that had accumulated on the matter over the centuries.

Explicit Differences between Noahide and Jewish Law

We can now deal with some matters in which Noahide law differs from Jewish law. I have quoted above the passage from *Sanh.* 57b to the effect that under Noahide law punishment may be ordered by a single judge, on the evidence of a single witness, and without fore-warning. A number of questions arise. First, may we conclude that these Noahide rules rest on the assumption that Noahide law is essentially the same as Jewish law, and only differs in this respect? Not necessarily. Even if Noahide law is altogether different, and not subject to Jewish law, the Noahides may not be free to make rules as they desire and go so far as not punishing a person on the evidence of the one witness; or perhaps they are free to do even that, and bound only to require some other degree of evidence, such as circumstantial evidence.

12. R. Shimon ben Tzemah Duran, *Tashbetz* 1.158-62 (Lemberg, 1891).
13. *She'elot eteshuvot* 6.152, in *Resp. Rashba*, VI (New York, 1958).

As regards circumstantial evidence under Noahide law, *Minhat Hinnukh* (Commandment 82) expresses some doubt. On the one hand, since a person can be convicted on the evidence of witnesses who are not qualified, or of only one witness, there is nothing to exclude circumstantial evidence. On the other hand, on the view that such evidence is excluded because of the possibility of error, the same should apply to the Noahides. That is to say, even though circumstantial evidence is excluded for Jews not on the basis of scriptural decree but on the grounds of reason, as explained by Maimonides in *Sefer HaMitzvot*, the same applies to the Noahides.

Me'iri to *Sanh.* 56b[14] thinks that the Noahides do not punish on the evidence of witnesses disqualified under the Torah, but *Sefer HaHinnukh* (Commandments 26 and 192) thinks that they will punish even on a confession and possibly, therefore, also on circumstantial evidence. R. Meir Arik, in analysing Maimonides' ruling regarding confessions (*Laws Concerning the Sanhedrin* 18.6) suggests that David's slaying of the Amalekite was not because the latter was a Noahide but because it was a matter of emergency;[15] and that Maimonides actually thought that the Noahides do not convict on a confession, for the reason that the person may be insane, and, so to speak, be ready to commit suicide by confessing to something he or she had not done. Here once more we have a rule that rests on logical reasoning, applying to the Noahides.

Me'iri to *Sanh.* 56b, it may be noted, goes further, stating that under Noahide law the evidence of a criminal, disqualified from giving testimony under the Torah, is not sufficient for conviction, which is another example of the application among the Noahides of a rule that is not explicitly laid down but is logically inferred.

Hazon Ish raises an interesting question about the position of Noahides who do not strictly observe the Seven Noahide Commandments but follow civil and penal law (*b. Qam.* 10.15). Are such people disqualified from acting as witnesses or judges? Hazon Ish does not think so. They are not disqualified from acting as judges or witnesses, since they are clearly strict about the other obligations and regard robbery, murder and false testimony as serious matters.

An interesting suggestion is made by R. Shelomoh Yehudah

14. R. Menahem haMe'iri, *Beit haBehirah* on tractate *Sanhedrin* (ed. A. Sofer; Frankfurt am Main, 1930).

15. *Hiddushei R. Me'ir Arik* to *Sefer haHinnukh* 192.

Tabak[16] in construing the verse 'At the hand of every living thing will I require it' (Gen. 9.5), from which he infers that credibility attaches to a single witness, but imports the requirement that the witness be properly examined to show that he is telling the truth (see *B. Meṣ.* 28b) regarding the restoration of lost property). To that end one credible witness is sufficient. He then raises the possibility that the single witness must be the judge himself for otherwise one person might 'devour' his fellow. Here again we can see how the limits of Noahide jurisdiction are determined on grounds of reason.

Are Jews Bound to Enforce a Noahide Commandment?

Is the Noahide obligation to follow laws linked with any obligation falling upon Jews? A link may arise in a number of situations: the appointment of judges for non-Jews, the punishment of non-Jews for not appointing judges or their punishment for offences they have committed.

Maimonides is explicit that there is a duty to appoint judges, to try resident aliens in accordance with Noahide law, so that the world is not destroyed (*Laws of Kings and Wars* 10.11). As regards those who are not resident aliens, one must examine how Maimonides defines the commandment to follow laws (*Laws of Kings and Wars* 1). First he lays down that 'they are obliged to install Judges and Magistrates'. Then, by way of illustration, he refers to a Noahide who transgressed one of the Seven Commandments and 'was killed by the sword'. Does that mean that a Jewish court has the duty to pass sentence, or is at liberty to do so, or is that the duty of the Noahides themselves?

Maimonides goes on to say 'And for this reason all the people of Shechem were liable to be slain', which seemingly means that the children of Israel were duty bound to kill them. *Sefer HaHinnukh* (Commandment 192) states: 'It is a principle that as long as they are under our rule *we* must apply the law to them in all matters that mankind was commanded'.

Nahmanides understands Maimonides to mean that Jews are obliged to try Noahides. In his commentary to Gen. 34.13, dealing with the acts of Shimon and Levi regarding the people of Shechem, he writes: 'Many have asked: how the righteous sons of Yaakov could spill

16. *Erekh Shai* to *Sanh.* 576 (Israel, 1974).

blood', and he quotes Maimonides as above, but adding 'this does not seem to be correct to my mind', since it involves the assumption of an obligation to punish the people of Shechem. Nahmanides' approach is entirely different. Contrary to Maimonides, he holds that the commandment to follow laws does not mean only to install judges but also to enforce the laws about robbery and fraud, which itself involves the appointment of judges. The duty to appoint judges must be distinguished from the duty of a judge to give judgment in a particular matter. However, in certain cases where a Jewish judge must give judgment, a Noahide judge is free not to do so. Accordingly, the fact that the people of Shechem refrained from sending a prince of theirs to trial constituted no offence on their part.

Furthermore, says Nahmanides, even for those offences for which the people of Shechem were liable, idolatry and adultery, the children of Israel had no jurisdiction, but since the people of Shechem were wicked people, the children of Israel wished to take revenge upon them, and killed the king and all those under his rule, an act which Yaakov said had put him in danger (see Gen. 34.30-31). Accordingly Nahmanides' view is that as long as the Noahides did no evil to Jews, the latter might not punish them.

Hatam Sofer suggests that Maimonides and Nahmanides do not differ over the Noahides' being commanded in matters of civil law, but on the question whether this obligation comes under the commandment to follow laws or the question of robbery.[17] As for Nahmanides' critique that the Noahides are not punishable for non-observance of a positive commandment, Hatam Sofer observes that although not punishable by court they are nevertheless guilty, and thus Shimon and Levi were not at fault in killing the people of Shechem.

Conflict of Laws

We have seen that a Noahide court has no jurisdiction to try Jews. Only a Jewish court can do that. When both parties are Noahides and desire to have judgment given in accordance with Jewish law, a Jewish court, according to Maimonides, may try the case and will try the case according to the Jewish law (*Laws of Kings and Wars* 10.12); but if they disagree as to the applicable law, Noahide law alone may be

17. *She'eloth Teshuvot Hatam Sofer* 6.14, in *Resp. Hatam Sofer*, VI (New York, 1958).

applied. As to the evidence on which the court may rely, Hazon Ish at
b. Qam. 10.16 takes the view that the witnesses must be Jews. Hazon
Ish is here dealing with penal law and is concerned with evidence
acceptable under Jewish law and the protection of resident aliens who
can only be condemned on the testimony of competent witnesses. In
civil law, also, he argues that Jewish law is the applicable law,
following R. Asher son of R. Yehi'el (Piskei HaRoš, b. Qam. 1.19).
Hazon Ish goes on to discuss the question whether in a Jewish court
the evidence of a single Jewish witness is sufficient, as it is in Noahide
law, and appears to conclude that it is not. He cites Sefer HaHinnukh
(Commandments 192 and 195) on the necessity of two witnesses.
Some later authorities, dealing with Sefer HaHinnukh, consider this
requirement to be a scribal error since it seems contrary to the rule in
the Talmud and in Maimonides.

Conclusion

I have discussed in this paper one of the fundamental issues of human
society; I have attempted to review and clarify a number of questions
on the Jewish attitude towards the obligation of maintaining a legal
system. We have seen that this obligation is incumbent upon all people
and that it dates back as far as Abraham, who was expected to command his children to do righteousness and justice, and Adam, who was
prohibited from eating of the tree of knowledge. In the words of Rav
Kook, the late Chief Rabbi of Eretz Yisrael:

> Law is the concern of all humanity, as we were commanded (Avot 3:2),
> 'Pray for the welfare of the state', for it is the state that establishes law in
> the land, 'The king by justice establishes the land' (Proverbs 29:2). And
> all of this is equally true of Gentile governments, for the Noahides were
> also commanded concerning dinim.[18]

The Noahides' commandment of dinim establishes a point of commonality between the Jewish people and the other nations, on the most
fundamental level of social existence, and I have examined here a
number of views on the extent of this commonality and points of
divergence.

Several interesting questions arise with regard to possible conflicts
of legal systems, in questions of jurisdiction, both jurisdiction of non-

18. Tehumin 7 (1986), 1.275.

Jewish courts over Jews and jurisdiction of Jewish courts over non-Jews, and with regard to the body of law used to adjudicate such cases. It appears that the most important aspect of the commandment of *dinim* is the commandment itself, as it emerges from the various sources: the obligation of establishing the rule of law, of natural equity and of justice.

THE BIBLICAL AND CLASSICAL TRADITIONS OF 'JUST WAR'

Henning Graf Reventlow

The problem of 'just war' has a long tradition in Western thinking. We might say that it has been a peculiarly Occidental concern; only comparatively recently, under the impact of Western thinking, has it become important in other civilizations, for instance in connection with international contracts, in the League of Nations and the UN. Its importance does not need to be emphasized, as the many conflicts exploding in wars in diverse parts of the globe keep the discussion running about the right to make war and rights in warfare. Power, right and ethics are catchwords that come to mind when we remember the Nuremberg trials, but also in connection with the monument planned for 'Bomber' Harris in his native country.

Where are the roots of this topic to be sought? The title of my paper mentions two origins: biblical and classical heritage. The two cannot, however, be neatly separated; the relations between them are far too complicated. The impact of the Bible and the impact of antiquity affect one another and are mixed with one another in the history of Christianity in a special way. This relation could be shown in very different fields, but the topic of 'just war' is exemplary for illustrating a development which moved, under the banner of Christianity, but also always under the impact of classic antiquity, in the direction of modern Western thinking.

I

It is not surprising that the problem of 'just war' did not exist as a problem in the early church of the first three centuries. Early Christianity was for a long period a small and unimportant minority in the Roman Empire and often suffered severe persecution. Taking part in military service for this empire—which required an oath of allegiance to the emperor venerated as a god—was theoretically out of the question for Christians and also mainly so in practice, because the majority of them belonged to the lower classes in the towns which had no right to the service. In spite of this there were actually individual Christians serving in the Roman forces. Tomb-inscriptions and indirect hints in the writings of Tertullian and others show that Christian soldiers did enrol.

The situation changed with Constantine the Great. In the person of Constantine (306–337) and his (one Julian Apostata excepted) Christian successors the empire was represented by a Christian as ruler, and its defence against the barbarians who pressed from all sides against its borders could be valued as a Christian task. The situation was the more complicated as the Germanic tribes which lived close to the borders and partly already inside the borders of the empire were Christians themselves, but Arians, who accorded Jesus Christ merely human status. Arianism had for a while adherents even in the ruling dynasty. The defence of faith was therefore for Catholic Christians partly a defence against heresy. From this situation one has to understand the position of Ambrose, Bishop of Milan (339–397), then the most important chair besides or even including Rome. Milan was in this period the city of governmental residence, after the importance of Rome had declined more and more. Ambrose composed a book around 379 for the emperor Gratian, *On Christian Faith* (*De fide Christiana*). In it he encouraged the catholic emperor to wage war against the Visigoths who, shortly before, in a battle close to Adrianopel (Edirne) had dealt to his predecessor, the Arian Valens, a deadly blow. 'Go ahead, protected by the broad shield of faith, in your hand the sword of spirit. Go ahead to the victory that has been promised in earlier times and prophesied in divine oracles!' Ambrose refers to the prophecy about the mythic enemy Gog from Magog in Ezekiel 38–39: 'Gog is this Gothian whom we have already seen marching out, on whom a coming victory is promised…' The defeat of Valens has been caused by his Arian heresy: 'It has become clear enough that those who hurt the faith could not be secure'. The forthcoming fight planned by the catholic ruler, on the other hand, is a just war: 'There can be no doubt, holy emperor, that we, who have started the combat because of the perfidy of the strangers, will have the support of catholic faith, which is alive in you'.[1]

1. Ambrose, *De fide Christiana libri tres* 2.16, in *PL*, XVI, pp. 587-90. Some of the texts cited in the following are also contained in an English reader, A. Marrin

From just these few quotations we can see the double motivation that underlies the Christian opinion about a just war: on one side a war is justified whenever the cause of the enemy is regarded as unjustified—this is the case above all when the enemy is regarded as heretic—while on the other side it must be possible to find a justification in the Bible. To see a war directly prophesied in the Bible, as Ambrose does in this case, is just one of the possibilities. Another method is to take as a model biblical wars and heroes. Ambrose also founds personal bravery on biblical models: he mentions Joshua, who defeated five kings in one battle and was so valued by God as to have his request fulfilled that the sun stand still during the battle against the Amorites (Josh. 10.5ff.), Gideon's battle against the Midianites with troops of three hundred warriors (Judg. 7), the bravery of Jonathan in his fight against the Philistines (1 Sam. 14) and the victories of the Maccabees (1 Macc. 2.35ff.).[2]

A war has to be just to be undertaken; David's wars were just, because he consulted God before starting any battle (see for example 2 Sam. 5.19-20); also in his struggle against Goliath he scorned weapons and relied exclusively upon God's help (1 Sam. 17.45).[3] The *jus in bellum* (as the later law of nations termed it) being founded in the Bible in this way, for a good Roman citizen and Christian it was obligatory to observe the *jus in bello* in dealing with the adversary. When the place and time of the battle were agreed upon, one could not prevent it. Adversaries who caused greater damage deserved a fiercer revenge. Therefore Moses, after the victory over the Midianites, gave orders to kill the Midianite women also (Num. 31.17), because they had seduced Israel to the service of idols at Baal-Peor (Num. 25).[4] On the other hand David honoured with a dinner the commander-in-chief of his adversary Išbaal, Abner, during his visit to Hebron (2 Sam. 3.20ff.).[5] Contracts are to be concluded without deceit and to last. Joshua acted thus towards the Gibeonites (Josh. 9), although the Gibeonites used a trick in order to get a treaty protection. Nevertheless the Israelites kept to the treaty even when the deceit was

---

(ed.), *War and the Christian Conscience: From Augustine to Martin Luther King, Jr* (Chicago, 1971).

2. Ambrose, *De officiis ministrorum* 1.40.81.
3. *De officiis ministrorum* 1.35.75.
4. *De officiis ministrorum* 1.29.63.
5. *De officiis ministrorum* 2.7.112.

detected, but Joshua punished the Gibeonites by putting them in a serving position.

Ambrose was the governor of a Roman province when he was unexpectedly elected bishop. He possessed a classical culture from his origins and education, and a detailed knowledge of the Bible from his task as a preacher. So he could regard *fides Romana* and *fides catholica*, faith in the State and Catholic faith, as one and the same thing. He believed that, when their unity was broken, the world would end.

A similar pattern of education was followed by the most famous teacher of the church in the Occident, Augustine (354–430), since 395–96 Bishop of Hippo in North Africa. He was trained as a rhetorician and for a while was engaged as a teacher of rhetorics before he was, after several years as an adherent of an Oriental Christian dualistic sect, the Manichees, converted to the Catholic faith by Ambrose's sermons. Even though he developed more than any other theologian the depths of Paul's understanding of sin and grace, he could never disclaim the classical roots of his thinking. Nonetheless, like Ambrose, Augustine was intimately acquainted with the Bible by his activity as a bishop; before he entered his office he had spent a long time in an intense study of the Bible.

We possess a whole series of remarks on the question of the just war from the pen of Augustine. Because of the important influence that he exerted in this field on later developments, he is generally regarded as the founder of the Christian position regarding the just war in antiquity and the Middle Ages.[6]

In his book against the bishop of the Manichees, Faustus (*Contra Faustum*), which he wrote shortly after his accession in Hippo in 396–97, we find his first detailed reference to the wars reported in the Old Testament. The Manichees rejected the Old Testament, as did other Gnostic sects,[7] with moral and rationalistic arguments. One of the

6. See for example P. Ramsay, *War and the Christian Conscience* (Durham, NC: Duke University Press, 1961), pp. 15ff.; F.H. Russell, *The Just War in the Middle Ages* (Cambridge, 1975), pp. 16ff.; J. Rief, *'Bellum' im Denken und den Gedanken Augustins: Beiträge zur Friedensethik* (Barsbüttel, 1990). It seems to me, however, that Rief, with his apologetic interest and from his lexicographical approach (cf. p. 41) does not sufficiently distinguish between the metaphoric and the literal use of the term 'war' in Augustine. There is an enormous amount of literature on Augustine.

7. The best known is Marcion (first half of the second century). See H. Graf

accusations was directed against the war-narratives contained in the Old Testament. In the series of Faustus's complaints against the moral conduct of the patriarchs, kings and prophets, which Augustine lists,[8] one finds the remark against Moses, 'that he conducted war, that he ordered many cruel things and performed them'[9]—an accusation that can be understood against the background of the strict pacifism of the Manichees.

Augustine answers in detail. A programmatic sentence can be cited: 'It is essential for what reasons and what originator people undertake wars which shall be carried on'.[10] This remark is to be connected with another one: 'It is most important if something is allowed out of human greediness or rashness, or if divine order is obeyed'.[11] Moses' wars are not to be condemned,

> because, as he obeyed divine orders, he did not ravage, but was obedient, and also God, when he ordered that, did not ravage, but paid back what deserved the ones deserving it and frightened the ones deserving it. What, therefore, is reproached regarding war? Perhaps, that men die, who have to die at sometime anyway? In order that people will be tamed to live in peace now? Finding fault with that is the matter of cowards, not of the pious. The greed to harm, cruelty in revenge, a spirit unreconciled and not reconcilable, wildness in rebellion, the desire to rule... these are things to be rightly reproached in connection with wars...[12]

Augustine speaks here about the Bible, but the principles which he adduces derive largely, as we shall see, from antiquity. To this heritage also belongs the rule, introduced as 'natural order', that the authority and the decision to undertake a war lies with the ruler, whereas the soldiers owe the service to obey the warlike commands to the general peace and welfare.[13]

In the following context Augustine adds his answers to the objections taken from the New Testament, which are adduced against the

Reventlow, *Epochen der Bibelauslegung*, I (Munich: Beck, 1990), pp. 132-50.

8.   Formally the book *Contra Faustum* is a dialogue, but the standpoint of the Manichees is always reproduced in the form of a summary, whereas Augustine develops his own opinion at much greater length.

9.   Augustine, *Contra Faustum* 22.5, in CSEL, XXV, p. 595.

10. *Contra Faustum* 22.75 (CSEL, XXV, p. 673).

11. *Contra Faustum* 22.74 (CSEL, XXV, p. 671).

12. *Contra Faustum* 22.78 (CSEL, XXV, p. 678).

13. *Contra Faustum* 22.75 (CSEL, XXV, p. 673).

participation of Christians in war. It seems they are still virulent also in the Catholic church. To them belongs the order of Jesus in the Sermon on the Mount (Mt. 5.39), not to resist the evil. To this Augustine remarks, the order is meant 'not in the body, but in the heart' and is related to the future otherworldly life.[14] The office of a soldier has in any case been acknowledged by John the Baptist as well as by Jesus himself as legitimate. John did not say to members of the armed forces, when they came to be baptized: 'Throw away your weapons, desert from the army', but only: 'Do no violence or wrong to anybody, be content with your pay' (Lk. 3.14). In saying 'Give the emperor what belongs to the emperor' (Mt. 22.21) Jesus was aware that wars were financed from this money. He also praised the faith of the captain of Capernaum who came to him on behalf of his servant (Mt. 8.9-10).[15] The apparent contradiction between Jesus' admonition to the disciples to buy a sword (Lk. 22.36)[16] and his reaction when Peter cut off the ear of the servant of the High Priest (Lk. 22.51) is explained by Augustine with reference first to the changed circumstances, and secondly because Peter acted spontaneously without command.[17]

Augustine is also concerned with the concept of just war in his monumental work *City of God* (*De civitate Dei*), in which he contrasts the worldly state (*civitas terrena*) and the kingdom of god (*civitas Dei*). The work is also written in order to refute the claim against the Christians that they were guilty of the capture and pillage of Rome by the Gothians under Alarich in the year 410, an event that shocked the world. In the first five books of the *City of God* Augustine takes the empire of earlier centuries to task. The wars waged by it were guided by the 'desire to rule'.[18] This greed for power also characterized the wars waged under the veneration of false gods throughout the history of Rome, from the capture of Troy onwards, both civil wars and wars against foreign states.[19] Augustine describes all the suffering and cruelty of these wars: 'Hunger, illness, war, pillage, captivity,

14. *Contra Faustum* 22.76 (CSEL, XXV, p. 674).

15. *Contra Faustum* 22.74 (CSEL, XXV, pp. 672-73).

16. Augustine understands the command literally, not metaphorically as it was intended.

17. *Contra Faustum* 22.77 (CSEL, XXV, p. 677).

18. Augustine, *De civitate Dei* 1 (Preface), in CChr, XLVII, p. 1.

19. *De civitate Dei* 3 (CChr, XLVII, pp. 65-98).

slaughter',[20] all in contrast to what Virgil formulated as the proud ideal of the Romans: 'To spare the subjected and to fight against the proud'.[21] The fate of Rome under Alarich shows that through Christianity, which was now spreading through Rome, a change had been brought about, for now the barbarians respected the numerous churches and spared all who sought shelter in them.[22]

Wars under Christian command are something different, as Augustine shows with the example of the warfare of the Catholic emperor Theodosius.[23] Theodosius reinstated the expelled co-regent Valentinian II after his victory won by divine help over the usurper Maximus; he did not allow anybody to take private revenge after the war, and he did private penitence when a massacre was committed in Thessalonica[24] against his intentions.

Nevertheless it is not the large size of the Roman Empire as such that is problematic for 'good people'. Augustine can imagine as an ideal situation the existence of a large number of small states living in peace with one another. But the necessity to wage wars was a result of the wickedness of the neighbours; the Roman Empire would have stayed small, 'if the rest and justice ruling with the neighbours would not have caused by any unjustice the necessity to wage war against them'.[25] Wars in this sense are a necessity;[26] but it would be a better fortune to have good neighbours.

Augustine also claims that all wars have peace as their aim. In a long chapter[27] he argues that it is a part of human nature (and the nature of beasts) that the aim of combatants in war is always somehow to reach peace for themselves. On all levels of living together this peace is grounded on an order given by nature, which is an 'institution

20. *De civitate Dei* 3 (CChr, XLVII, p. 65).

21. 'Parcere subjectis et debellare superbos'; Virgil, *Aeneid* 6.853, cited by Augustine in the Preface to *De civitate Dei*.

22. Augustine, *De civitate Dei*, 1.1 (CChr, XLVII, pp. 1-2).

23. Theodosius I (the Great), Augustus since 379, since 392 the only ruler. See Augustine, *De civitate Dei* 5.15 (CChr, XLVII, pp. 161-62).

24. In the year 390; cf. Ambrose, *De officiis ministrorum*.

25. Augustine, *De civitate Dei* 4.15 (CChr, XLVII, p. 111).

26. Cf. also epistle 189.6, 'To have peace demands the will, war the necessity, in order that God may make us free from the necessity and preserve us in peace' (CSEL, LVII, p. 135).

27. Augustine, *De civitate Dei* 19.12 (CChr, XLVIII, pp. 675-78).

assigning to equal and unequal things each its place'.[28] All conflicts, even small ones, are waged to restore this order or to reorganize it according to the ideas of the warring factions, so there is no war that is not waged on behalf of peace. On the other hand Augustine very well knows that a complete 'rest of order' cannot be expected in this world. The possibility that the good people might be defeated in the just war and the bad ones win is not discounted by him. This would then be an instrument of correction, causing humility, in God's hand.

It is also important here to look at Augustine's references to the Old Testament. In his commentary on the Pentateuch[29]—which despite its title includes the books of Joshua and Judges—he delivers in connection with his exegesis of Josh. 8.2, where God commands Joshua to lay an ambush, a definition of the just war: 'Normally those wars are called just wars, by which injustice is punished, in cases when a tribe or a citizenship fails to punish injustice done by its own people, or to restore what had been seized without having a claim on it'. The ambush itself is not unjust, if it takes place in a just war. It only depends if the one waging war had the right to do it. 'But also the manner of war without doubt is just, which God commanded, with whom there is no unjustice and who knows what has to happen to anybody. In this war commander, army and even the people are to be regarded not so much as originators of the war, but as servants who execute it'.[30]

Augustine had for a long time kept to the opinion that wars by the sword are exclusively the matter of the worldly state. Christians taking part in wars please God by serving the end of worldly peace.[31] Later he arrived at the judgment that warlike force could also be used

28. Augustine, *De civitate Dei* 19.13 (CChr, XLVIII, p. 679).

29. *Quaestionum in Heptateuchum liberi* 7 (CChr, XXXIII; CSEL, XXVIII, pp. 1-506).

30. *Quaestionum im Heptateuchum* 6.10 (CChr, XXXIII, pp. 318-19; CSEL, XXVIII, pp. 428-29).

31. This is also the topic of the letter 189 to the officer Bonifatius, section 4 (CSEL, LVII, pp. 133-34) where Augustine writes: 'Don't believe that nobody could please God who fights with weapons of war'. As examples he mentions David, the captain of Capernaum (Mt. 8.8-10; Lk. 7.6-9) and Cornelius (Acts 10.1-8, 30-33). However, he regards the spiritual war without weapons as more valuable (cf. epistle 189.5). In realizing, however, that the body of the soldier is also a gift of God, one comes to the conclusion that one must not act against God: 'Where confidence has been promised, it has also to be kept towards the enemy against whom a war is waged' (epistle 189.6 [CSEL, LVII, p. 135]).

against heretics, when all peaceful means had been fruitless. According to his principle mentioned above also here it depends by whom and to what aims a war is waged. In a letter[32] he speaks about the difference between the suppression of the Israelites by Pharaoh and the slaughter of three thousand Israelites by the Levites on Moses' command after the episode of the golden calf in Exod. 32.26-28. The difference lies in the motivation: 'Pharaoh suppressed the people by hard compulsory labor'; Moses hurt the same people by severe punishments, when they acted as idolaters. They did similar things, but they did not intend to be of use in a similar way. The one was inflated by the greed of power, the other inflamed by love'.[33]

II

I have considered the arguments of Augustine in an especially detailed way because his theory of just war, although further developed by later theologians, above all Thomas Aquinas,[34] formed the basis for the theory of war in the whole Christian Middle Ages. The next step would be to ask to what extent Augustine's remarks can be shown to be grounded in classical antiquity and to what extent biblically grounded. It is in fact fairly clear that Augustine's basic theories are, despite his biblical claims, mainly derived from classical ideas. This is true despite his polemics against the ancient pantheon, his critical attitude towards the pagan history of the Roman Empire and the theological orientation visible in the central role he gives to the term 'love'. But it is evident that all theologians are affected by the common intellectual conditions of their time and culture. Through his training as a rhetorician and his education—which included classical philosophy and literature—Augustine became an expert in the realm of thought.

The idea of the just war had a long history in classical, especially Roman, tradition. We first encounter the term in Aristotle. He regarded a war as just if it served as an instrument for the enslavement of non-Greeks, who as barbarians deserved this, or to prevent Greeks themselves being subjected or enslaved. Best known is his utterance in which Aristotle calls the war 'in a certain way an art of

32. Epistle 93 (CSEL, XXXIV, pp. 445-96).
33. Epistle 93.6 (CSEL, XXXIV, pp. 450-51).
34. See below.

acquisition', 'which has to be used not only against beasts, but also against such people, who, by nature destined to be ruled upon, are not willing to be ruled upon. For such a war is just'.[35] A war waged by gentle, brave soldiers serves the aims of peace, glory and strength.[36] Only if the war becomes an end in itself is the city waging the war destined to fall.[37]

In Roman tradition the theme of the just war goes back as far as the period of the kings.[38] Originally there was a particular cultic ceremony: the board of the Fetiales,[39] a special group of priests, convened and debated the violation of a treaty by a foreign people, a treaty they had made with Rome. Peace was regarded as a system of juridical relations regulated by contracts between the tribes of Italy. When the Fetiales discovered a violation, one of their number was sent as ambassador to the foreign capital; there he announced publicly in a solemn ceremony to the foreign state the claim of Rome to reparation of the damage caused. Only if this claim was not accepted after a fixed time could war be declared by the senate, again according to a report by the Fetiales. This war was then a 'just war'. Jupiter and Janus were called on as witnesses, so that the war also had a sacral character.[40] When later the Fetiales lost their importance the juridical valuation of war remained valid. Of course reality did not always conform to theory; we can read in Livius and Polybius how—while formally maintaining the rules of 'just war'—one could find ways to wage wars of conquest, which resulted in the enormous extension of the Roman

35. Aristotle, *Politics* 1.1256b 23-26.

36. See also *Politics* 1.1255a 3–1255b 3; 1255b 37-40; 7.1333a 30-36; 1333b 37–1334 a 16; *De Rhetorica ad Alexandrum* 1425a 10-16; *Nicomachean Ethics* 10. 11777b 6-15.

37. *Politics* 7.11334 6-9.

38. See: C. Philippson, *The International Law and Custom of Ancient Greece and Rome*, II (2 vols.; London, 1911), chs. XXII–XXVI, pp. 166ff.; E. Seckel, *Über Krieg und Recht in Rom* (Berlin, 1915); A. Heuss, 'Die völkerrechtlichen Grundlagen der römischen Außenpolitik in republikanischer Zeit', *Klio* sup. 31 (1933); M. Gelzer, 'Römische Politik bei Fabius Pictor', *Hermes* 68 (1933), pp. 129-66; repr. in V. Pöschl (ed.), *Römische Geschichtsschreibung* (Wege der Forschung, 90; Darmstadt: Wissenschaftliche Buchgesellschaft, 1969), pp. 77-129; A. Nussbaum, 'Just War—A Legal Concept', *Michigan Law Review* 42 (1943), pp. 453-79.

39. Cf. Philippson, *International Law*, II, ch. XXVI, pp. 315ff.

40. A report about the measures taken is in Livius, I, 32, 6ff.

Empire.[41] On the basis of these traditions of public law Cicero developed his ideas on just war, which were transmitted to Augustine and the whole Middle Ages. Cicero refers expressly to the right of the Fetiales, declaring, 'One can learn from it, that no war is just if it is not waged either to regain something lost or is declared and substantiated in advance'.[42] The phrase *rebus repetitis*, 'to regain something lost', is a technical term that can include damage to bodies or things.[43] Vice versa one can say: 'Those are unjust wars which are waged without reason. For besides the reason to revenge themselves or to repulse the adversaries no war can be waged';[44] 'No war can be waged by the most excellent state except for loyalty or welfare [of the state]'.[45]

III

When we compare the utterances of Ambrose and Augustine on 'just war', we see that Roman theories of sacral right have found an echo in the thoughts of Augustine. For Ambrose the direct reference to biblical models is characteristic. But neither is reference to the Bible completely absent in Augustine. Holy Scripture remains the decisive reference for Christian theology. Both aspects should play an important role in the future of the church. They contain different valuations of war: in Roman tradition the 'just' war is the decisive measure, whereas the reference to the Bible has the 'holy' war in view, which means the war intended and directed by God. This view prevailed in the Middle Ages in the programme of the crusades, whereas the juridical valuation which, as we saw, originally also had sacral roots, was rationalized by arguments taken from the law of nature.

IV

How were Ambrose and many later Christian theologians justified in referring directly to the Old Testament for the idea of holy or just war? The results of modern historical criticism are not in favour of

41. Details in Gelzer, 'Römische Politik'.
42. Cicero, *De officiis* 1.11.36.
43. Cf. Philippson, *International Law*, I, p. 327.
44. Cicero, *De re publica* 3.23.35.
45. Cicero, *De re publica* 3.23.34.

the earlier opinions based upon a pre-critical view of the Bible.[46] One
has to judge in a much more subtle way.

A first look at the Bible seems to confirm the view that in an early
period of Israelite history there did exist an institution which we could
call 'holy war'—although the term does not appear in the Bible. At
some places 'wars of YHWH' are mentioned (1 Sam. 18.17; 25.28;
Num. 21.14; cf. Sir. 46.3). G. von Rad, in his classic study *The Holy
War in Ancient Israel*,[47] detected in a series of texts, especially from
the books of Judges–2 Samuel, but also in Deuteronomy, a scheme of
several steps in which such wars are described, especially from the
early periods of Israelite history. The steps mentioned are: the levy
by blowing the horn (Judg. 6.34-35) or by sending around the pieces
of a body by messengers (Judg. 19.29ff.; 1 Sam. 11.7ff.). The array
assembled in the camp receives the name 'people of YHWH' (Judg.
5.11-13; 20.2). This army has to obey severe ritual directions and is
revered as holy (cf. for example Josh. 3.5; Deut. 23.10-14). The
leader of the host proclaims sureness of victory: 'YHWH has given the
enemy [enemies] into your hands' (Josh. 6.2-16; 22.24, for example).
God himself (or the Ark) marches in front of the army (cf. Deut.
20.4). He is the one who acts alone; the enemies of Israel are his
enemies (Judg. 5.31; 1 Sam. 30.26). So the number of the warriors
on the side of Israel is not important (cf. Judg. 7.2ff.; 1 Sam. 14.6).
Rather the courage vanishes from the enemies automatically
(Exod. 15.14-16); a 'terror of God' comes over them, so that they
kill one another in panic or flee without stopping (Exod. 23.27;
Deut. 7.23). The booty is 'banned', that is, dedicated to YHWH.

Thus von Rad's description. More recently, however, more and
more doubts have arisen as to the historical accuracy of these descriptions. Remarkably enough, most relevant texts belong to more recent
sources, above all to the Deuteronomistic history, which seems to have
originated in the exilic period. Here older traditions were reworked
and ideologized, events were raised to a superior level theologically
and interpreted as God's combat for Israel; so the texts we have may
well give an exaggerated view of the importance of the warlike
character. It has long been demonstrated that a conquest by war as is

46. An overview and extensive list of secondary literature are to be found in
J.A. Soggin, 'Krieg II. Altes Testament', *TRE* 20 (1990), pp. 19-25.
47. Göttingen: Vandenhoeck & Ruprecht; Zürich: Evangelischer Verlag Zollikon,
1951.

described in the first half of the book of Joshua never took place in that way.[48] In other texts too the character of the source must be checked. For instance the passage Exod. 32.26-28, the chapter on the golden calf (which mirrors the much later quarrel with the sanctuary of Bethel from the standpoint of Jerusalem) is a rather late addition. But just this short narrative, which reports that Moses ordered the Levites to execute a bloody punishment on their own people, was often used as justification for similar proceedings against heretics and adherents of other religions.[49] Many of the texts which tell about holy wars in the early period can be understood from the situation in which they originated: the small remnant community that had been preserved after the end of the state of Judah and the period of the exile maintained its faith in God even in the circumstances of an arduous restoration under politically and economically oppressed conditions by rewriting a glorious history in a legendary way. At that time the possibility of ensuring survival by the sword was quite out of the question, since Judah was now part of the Persian provincial system. The future one could imagine—going back to ancient Jebusite traditions about the shelter which God's presence in the temple would guarantee for city and sanctuary (cf. Pss. 46; 48)—as a time of peace in which the foreign peoples would no longer assault Judah and Jerusalem (cf. Zech. 14.2), but would peacefully come there for receiving the Torah (Isa. 2.2-3//Mic. 4.1-3). Then they would turn their swords to ploughshares—an eschatological expectation which should not be, as it often is, understood as a political programme.

On the whole, the Old Testament cannot be usurped for an ideology which legitimates aggression as willed by God. If the help of God in wars is postulated as a motif in the interpretation of Israel's salvation history, the protection of Israel against an always hostile and often too powerful environment is the central background. That such a small minority as the Jewish community could maintain itself through all the ups and downs of history was explained as the result of the wonderful help of its God.

48. See M. Noth, *Das Buch Josua* (HAT, 1.7; Tübingen: Mohr, 2nd edn, 1953); cf. also J.A. Soggin, *Josué* (CAT; Neuchâtel: Delachaux & Niestlé, 1970).
49. Cf. M. Walzer, 'Exodus 32 and the Theory of the Holy War', *HTR* 61 (1968), pp. 1-14.

V

In conclusion I want to look at a few of the more important later developments of the idea of just war.

The first person to be mentioned is Thomas Aquinas (1125–1274). In his most important theological work, the *Summa theologica*,[50] one chapter[51] is dedicated to questions of war. The position of this chapter is interesting: it is arranged, in a context treating Christian love,[52] among the sins which principally are an obstacle to love, such as hate, envy, discord and quarrel.[53]

The argument is laid out in the traditional academic style, with the thesis at the head of the section. The thesis, based on Scripture (for instance on Mt. 26.52, 'Everyone who takes up the sword shall perish by the sword'), is that it is always sinful to wage war, and doing so is in contravention of the law of Mt. 5.39 not to resist one who does evil. But the thesis is then refuted in a detailed way. In numerous quotations Aquinas is going back to Augustine, who has an unrestricted authority for him in this area. Basic rules in the first article are: (1) only a prince, no private individual, has the right to wage war; (2) a just cause is required (the guilt of the enemy)—war is justified for instance for *commune bonum* (the common good, an Aristotelian term); (3) good intentions are needed (no cruelty). Finally, Aquinas claims, just wars serve peace.

The following articles forbid to clergymen and bishops the right of taking part in the fight (article 2),[54] confirm the opinion of Augustine that ambushes are allowed in war (article 3) and decide positively that battle is also allowed on holy days (article 4). There are also dispersed

50. Although there are remarks on the subject of the just war in few other works of Aquinas I will consider only the one main work.

51. 'De Bello', *Summa theologica* 2.2, qu. 40. On the topic see also H. Gmür, *Thomas von Aquino und der Krieg* (repr.; Hildesheim: Olms, 1971 [1933]); J. Tooke, *The Just War in Aquinas and Grotius* (London: SPCK, 1965), pp. 21ff.; Russell, *The Just War*, pp. 258ff.

52. Qu. XXIII-XLVI.

53. Qu. XXXIV-XLIII.

54. There is a double argument. 1. Philosophical: as two occupations cannot be undertaken at the same time, the more important for 'the welfare of the human community' must be preferred (appealing to Aristotle, *Politics* 1.1). 2. Cultic: because the priests administer the sacrament, they are not allowed to shed blood.

throughout the work further remarks relating to war. A prince has the right and the duty to kill evildoers, which is not allowed to private men.[55] The office of the soldier is needed to defend the service of God and public welfare (with a reference to Ps. 80.4), but is also justified for the protection of the poor and oppressed.[56] For this task above all bravery is needed.[57] In his use of 'bravery' as a central idea Aquinas follows Aristotle, whom he considers along with Augustine the most important philosopher with regard to ethical argument over theological issues. In this way under new auspices the combination of antiquity and Christianity is renewed in a form fitting to the views of the time. It is important to note that the Bible does play an important role for Thomas Aquinas in providing support for arguments, even if many of the biblical quotations he uses have been inherited from Augustine.

The hispanic scholastics Vittoria, Molina, Soto and Suarez and a hundred years later Hugo Grotius established the theory of 'just war' on a completely new basis. It now became part of the secular law of nations, founded on the 'law of nature'. The transition, however, did not happen all at once; one still finds in the work of Franciscus de Vittoria[58] the traditional biblical quotations and reference to the authority of Augustine and Thomas Aquinas. His lecture on 'The Law of War' (*de jure belli*) became notwithstanding the basis of a new approach, because he allowed the law of nature a prominent place in his argumentation. 'The law of the gospel does not interdict anything that is allowed according to the law of nature', he formulates, expressly referring to Aquinas,[59] and he adds the complementary rule: 'Whatever therefore is allowed according to the law of nature and written law, is likewise allowed according to the law of gospel'.[60] He also presents a clear review of the traditional arguments relating to the *jus ad bellum* (the right to war) and the *jus in bello* (the right in

55. Qu. LXIV.
56. Qu. CLXXXVIII, art. 3.
57. Qu. CXXIII.
58. His lectures 'De Indis recenter inventis et de jure belli Hispanorum in Barbaros' are now easily accessible in the Latin–German edition of W. Schätzel (Tübingen, 1952). On the topic see J.T. Johnson, *Just War Tradition and the Restraint of War* (Princeton, NJ, 1981), pp. 174ff.
59. *Summa theologica* 1.2.
60. In Schätzel's edition, pp. 120-23.

war), in which he considers the treatment of enemies, their cities and the civil population (which must not be killed). So his utterances became the basis of a new approach, grounded on the secular idea of the law of nature, which left Christian thinking largely behind.

In thinking on or debating the problems of war Christians and Jews can look back to what is laid down in the Bible, although from this source no easy solution is to be expected. Biblical sayings and arguments are as much as any others products of their times, and need to be re-evaluated according to our situation. The ancient heritage is, however, less and less helpful, for we recognize more and more the conflict between what the Roman tradition says relating to a juridical justification of war and God's will for peace as shown in the Bible. This does not mean, however, that radical pacifism is the fitting solution. This would contrast with the reality of the fallen world, which is characterized now as before by wars. Pacifism, as a form of idealism, is likewise strange to the Bible. The Bible does not expect peace, as Kant did,[61] to come from human reason, but from God's acting at the end of time. For this intermediate period, then, the *jus in bello* will remain helpful in preventing human wickedness giving vent to its cruel instincts. We still need law as protection so long as love has not yet taken its place.

In a stimulating paper, H.E. von Waldow[62] has shown that the biblical narratives about the premonarchic wars are to be understood as wars based upon decisions of God in a fallen world. Genesis 1–10 shows that the created world is no longer the good one willed by God, but is in a state of corruption. In this fallen world God himself is at work in the wars as the one who decides about the result and the victory. But war is sin, a sign of the fallen world and one of the proverbial plagues, 'sword, hunger and pestilence'. So God's acting in wars can only be a means to prevent a bad situation worsening. From a biblical standpoint there cannot really be such a thing as a 'just war'.

61. I. Kant, *Zum ewigen Frieden* (1795), in *Kants Werke: Textedition*, VIII (Berlin: de Gruyter, 1968), pp. 341-86.

62. H.E. von Waldow, 'The Concept of War in the Old Testament', *HBT* 6 (1984), pp. 27-48.

ISAIAH'S AND MICAH'S APPROACHES TO POLICY AND HISTORY

B. Uffenheimer

The concept of theopolitics was introduced by Buber when describing the original Hebrew idea of monotheism as an attempt to establish a society ruled exclusively by the living king. Today it seems commonplace in biblical research that the political views of the classical prophets of the seventh and eighth centuries BCE were a combination of pragmatism and utopian elements, the latter being based on the ancient tradition of divine kingship and the idea of the Davidic kingdom as reflected in popular fantasy.

This paper attempts to outline the mutual influences of pragmatism and the theopolitical tradition in forging the approaches of the prophets of the eighth century BCE to the existential problems facing the kingdoms of Judah and Israel. In other words, I shall try to analyse the conflicting views of Isaiah and Micah, who were living in the heyday of the Assyrian imperialism. In further papers I shall deal with the confrontation of their views with those of Jeremiah, who was haunted from the very beginning of his career by the premonition of the impending catastrophe finally brought about by the Babylonians.[1]

The political and eschatological viewpoints of the above prophets were formed in the light of the momentous decisions that confronted the kings of Judah in their days, when the land came under the sphere of influence of the Assyrian, and later of the Babylonian, empire. The religious and moral problems that these prophets had to face were the theological and moral justification of the rise of these empires of evil, which had such a deep impact on the fate of Israel. Another question they dealt with was how to respond to imperialistic aggression.

---

1. See my papers, 'Jeremiah and the "False Prophets"' (Hebrew), in *Neiger Memorial Volume* (Jerusalem, 1959), pp. 96-111; 'The Historical Outlook of Jeremiah', *Immanuel* 4 (1974), pp. 9-17; 'Jeremiah's Fluctuating Attitudes and Approaches to History' (Hebrew), in *Baruch Kurzweil Memorial Volume* (Bar Ilan University Press; New York: Schocken Books, 1975), pp. 49-61.

I

I shall begin with Isaiah. Two events stand out in his book: the first is the aggression against Judah by an Ephraimite–Aramean coalition, probably in 734; the second, the siege of Jerusalem by Sennacherib in 701.

The events of 734 are reported in Isa. 7.3; 2 Kgs 15.37, 16; 2 Chronicles 28, and the contemporary Assyrian sources, namely the annals of Tiglath-Pileser III and the eponym chronicle. According to the above Hebrew sources, Isaiah 7 in particular, the joint forces of Ephraim and Aram invaded Judah from the north and closed in on Jerusalem. Their intention was to depose King Ahaz, in all likelihood because of his refusal to join their anti-Assyrian coalition;[2] they wanted to replace him with a certain Ben-Tabeel, who is completely unknown to us.[3]

In his annals, Tiglath-Pileser III boasts of having conquered the whole Phoenician coast as far as the border of Egypt.[4] The details of these events cannot be restored with certainty, for the Assyrian sources are badly mutilated. But this is the historical setting of the above-mentioned war, which occurred in all probability in 734, for the Assyrian eponym chronicle reports a campaign to Philistine in 734, and towards Damascus in 733 and 732. According to Isa. 7.1-2 Ahaz was intimidated by this aggression, while the source mentioned in 2 Kgs 16.7ff. reports that he sent a 'bribe', an enormous gift or tribute, to Tiglath-Pileser, and begged for his assistance. This appeal

---

2.   This suggestion has been adopted by J. Bright, *A History of Israel* (London: SCM Press, 1990), pp. 271-72; M. Noth, *Geschichte*, pp. 222ff.; and H. Donner, in J.H. Hayes and J.M. Miller (eds.), *Israelite and Judaean History* (OTL; London: SCM Press; Philadelphia: Westminster Press, 1977), pp. 421-41. B. Oded, in *CBQ* 34 (1972), pp. 153-65, however, challenged this conception, arguing that it was Judah's expansion into Gilead during the days of Uzziah and Yotham which prompted Pekah the Gileadite to join forces with Rezzin in order to undermine Judah's weakening supremacy; see also M. Cogan and H. Tadmor, 'II Kings', in AB (Garden City, NY: Doubleday, 1988), p. 191. In my opinion, this may have been a secondary cause, but the chief motivation was doubtless the above-mentioned one.

3.   On the identity of Tab'el (properly Bêt Tab'el), Ben Tabeel, see Albright, *BASOR* 140 (1955), pp. 34-35, and B. Mazar, *IEJ* 7 (1957), pp. 236-37. But these are mere speculations.

4.   See *ANET*, pp. 282-83.

was tantamount to political submission, as may be gathered from the phrase 'I am your servant and your son' (2 Kgs 16.7), reminiscent of the submissive style of the Assyrian vassal treaties. Indeed, this unfortunate step of Ahaz was far from being the result of rational balanced political considerations, but rather a sign of confusion, fear and consternation.

It seems that Isaiah's dramatic appearance before Ahaz described in this chapter preceded the above act of submission to the Assyrian conqueror. Apparently the prophet attempted at the last moment to prevent the king from taking this dangerous step, calling him to 'Be firm and calm' (Isa. 7.4). Moreover, he encouraged him to withstand the invaders by ridiculing them as 'those two smoking stubs of firebrand' (Isa. 7.4). Hereby Isaiah also expressed his strong opposition to those who had advised the king to join the above coalition (8.6, 12), for in his view much of this advice was based on a completely inaccurate assessment of the real balance of power between the Assyrian empire and the above coalition of petty rulers. In this context he also warned the intimidated king about not trusting in God, saying אם לא תאמינו כי לא תאמנו (v. 9).[5] In order to understand this phrase properly it should be emphasized that the semantic range of the verb האמין is not limited to human mental conditions, as Western translations such as 'to believe', 'glauben' or 'croire' may suggest. On the contrary, the root אמן also implies endurance and physical strength in phrases like ויהי ידיו אמונה ('his hands remained steady' [Exod. 17.12]), and ונאמנים וחלים רעים ('evil and lasting plagues' [Deut. 28.59; cf. also Isa. 22.23, 25; 28.16]). In the *niphal* it also occurs in the sense of 'to persist', 'to last', and even 'to fulfil' (for example 1 Chron. 17.23, 24; 2 Chron. 1.9).

Consequently, אם לא תאמינו is not used here as a transitive verb, in the sense of believing in some object, person or God (as in 2 Chron. 20.20, האמינו ביהוה אלהיכם ותאמנו והאמינו בנביאיו) but intransitively, in the sense of being steadfast, trusting or firm, without reference to any object (compare Isa. 28.16: he that is strong [המאמין] shall not make haste). So the translation of the above slogan would be: 'if you are not steadfast you shall not stand firm'. The preceding call (v. 4), 'fear not, neither be fainthearted', reminds us of the exhortation to the armies

5. Cf. R. Smend, 'Zur Geschichte von האמין', in G.W. Anderson and P.A.H. de Boer (eds.), *Hebräische Wortforschung: Festschrift für W. Baumgartner* (VTSup, 14; Leiden: Brill, 1967), pp. 284-90; H. Wildberger, 'Erwägungen zu האמין', in Anderson and de Boer (eds.), *Hebräische Wortforschung*, pp. 372-86.

about to go into battle (Deut. 20.8), and words of encouragement to Abraham (Gen. 15.1), both of which are close to the Deuteronomic formula (for example Deut. 1.21; Josh. 8.1). There are also ancient Near Eastern parallels to this usage, which aim at providing encouragement to people in times of war and travail.[6] Many years later Isaiah further expanded his demand in the words 'For thus said my lord God, the Holy One of Israel: In stillness and rest you shall be saved; in quietness and in trust shall be your strength' (בשובה ונחת תושעון בהשקט ובבטחה תהיה גבורתכם [Isa. 30.15]).[7]

The demand in Isa. 7.4, 9 was addressed to Ahaz when he was filled with fear of an enemy who turned out to be nothing more than a straw man. But when the prophet wanted him to ask for a sign, Ahaz avoided the issue (vv. 10ff.), for in all probability he had already made up his mind to appeal to the Assyrian king for aid. Hence he had already forfeited his freedom of action and spiritual fortitude to accept the consequences of a clear prophetic sign. As pointed out above, it seems that at that moment the delegation to Tiglath-Pileser III was already on its way. The meaning of the name Immanuel ('God with us'), and the verse 'None but the Lord of Hosts shall you account holy; give reverence to Him, hold Him alone in awe' (Isa. 8.13), round off the prophet's theopolitical outlook, which had taken final shape by that time, that is, during the Ephraimite–Aramean siege of Jerusalem in 734. His former vision of the divine king seated upon a high and exalted throne (Isa. 6) is rendered here in terms of practical political behaviour.

The full political consequences of this approach were proclaimed by the prophet about thirty years later in 701, during the reign of Hezekiah, when Sennacherib laid siege to Jerusalem.[8] The above slogan of stillness and rest, quietness and trust then became the

6. I. Nougayrol, *Le palais royal d'Ugarit IV: Mission de Ras-Shamra* (ed. F.A. Schaeffer; Paris, 1959), IX, Text 17.132, pp. 32-35; *idem*, ZAW 62 (1957), p. 265. Šupiluliuma King of Ḫatti encourages Niqmd King of Ugarit in the above letter to be steadfast and not fainthearted towards his enemies: 'You, Niqmd, do not be afraid' (lû tapalaḫšunu).

7. The RSV has 'In returning', but the *parallelismus membrorum* בשובה/בהשקט would suggest the derivation of the word from the stem ישב, i.e. 'in sitting quietly', בישבה שקטה, as Rashi and D. Kimchi contended.

8. For an analysis of that situation see Noth, *Geschichte*, pp. 230ff., and Bright, *History*, pp. 261-69.

byword for the rejection of any reliance upon military might or foreign powers. It reflects Isaiah's opposition to Hezekiah's pursuit of Egypt, whose aim was to obtain political and military backing for his planned rebellion against Assyria. The prophet's words in chs. 30–31 are formulated in sharply antithetical terms: 'who set out to go down to Egypt without asking Me, to seek out refuge with Pharaoh, to seek shelter under the protection of Egypt' (30.2); 'For the Egyptians are men, not God, and their horses are flesh, not spirit. And when the Lord stretches out his arm, the helper shall trip and the helped one shall fall, and both shall perish together' (31.3). Here Isaiah formulates his principal opposition to the official policy, which dated back to King Solomon, and was carried out by the Omeride kings of Israel, by Uzziah and Hezekiah of Judah. The practical implication of this reliance upon God alone is the removal of Judah as fully as possible from the complications of involvement in international politics.

The activist aspect of this approach became evident throughout the crisis of 701, when Isaiah strongly opposed the idea of capitulation to the Assyrian king. He maintained his conviction that the king of Assyria must be resisted to the very end. In his words of encouragement to Hezekiah (Isa. 37.22-35; cf. 2 Kgs 19.20-34), which include sharp condemnation of the Rabshakeh's words, Isaiah expands upon the historical outlook implied in ch. 10, whose date seems to be close to 734, when the Assyrian imperialism began to threaten the security of the small nations. Here he develops the theory of 'the rod of God's anger', based upon the assumption that Israel is at the centre of world history, so that the rise of the Assyrian conquerors is meaningful only if viewed in terms of the history of Israel, in which Sennacherib was sent by God to punish his sinful nation. Sennacherib's arrogance in ascribing the Assyrian king's victory to his own might and wisdom blinds him to the true state of affairs—namely, that he is a passive instrument of God's vengeance upon Israel. He will be punished for this, and led to his destruction like a bull led by hook and bit (Isa. 37.29). At that moment in world history, 701 BCE, Judah's spiritual centrality will have concrete political and military significance: 'I will protect and save this city for thy sake, and for the sake of thy servant David' (37.35). From this viewpoint the faithful courageous military opposition of Judah to Assyrian aggression is the only way to bring about a radical change in world history. Then the Assyrian conquerors will become the victims of their own madness, their hubris, which had induced them to claim superhuman powers and to stand up against the only One who is superb (Isa. 6).[9]

Isaiah's confidence in divine intervention in favour of Judah is based on the tradition of the sanctity of the Temple Mount being the dwelling place of the Lord, an idea expressed many times in ancient Psalm literature.[10] The expected fall of Sennacherib at the gates of Jerusalem will be the proof of the absolute supremacy of the Lord and of the vanity of Sennacherib's claims. Thus, in ch. 37, the obscure visions of the terrors of the 'Day of the Lord', found in chs. 2–3, are applied in concrete fashion to the Assyrian invasion. Isa. 37.26-27 implies that these events are the realization of an ancient decree, the chapter concluding with words of comfort to the remnants of the House of Judah (37.31). Just as in chs. 10–11 the emergence of a shoot from the stick of Jesse is related to the fall of Assyria, so too in ch. 37 the taking root of the remnant of the Davidic house is connected with the disasters which will befall the king of Assyria.[11]

Because of its theological significance, let us briefly dwell on the close relationship between chs. 10 and 11. In 10.18-19 the devastation of Judah by the Assyrian armies is described as the destruction of the forest and the fruitful land. The remnant of the trees of his forest will be so few that a child could write them down (v. 19). Again, when speaking of the Assyrian defeat Isaiah uses the same simile as in vv. 33-34:

> Behold, the Lord, the Lord of Hosts will lop off the boughs with terrifying power; the great in height will be hewn down, and the lofty will be brought low. He will cut down the thickets of the forest with an axe, and Lebanon with its majestic trees will fall.

Against this picture of the hewing off of the crowns of trees and the cutting down of the thickets of the forest, ch. 11 opens with the emergence of a shoot from the stump of Jesse and a twig from his stock. Thus it becomes evident that ch. 11 is the immediate continuation of

9. Cf. my paper 'Isaiah 6 and its Rabbinic Exegesis' (Hebrew), in B. Uffenheimer (ed.), *Ha-Mikra ve-Toldot Yisrael (J. Liver Memorial Volume)* (Tel Aviv: Tel Aviv University Faculty of Humanities, 1971), pp. 15-50, esp. p. 39.

10. Cf. my paper 'The Religious Experience of the Psalmists and the Prophetic Mind', *Immanuel* 21 (1987), pp. 7-27.

11. For the latest critical analysis of Isa. 36–39 with full bibliography see H. Wildberger, *Jesaja* (BKAT, 10; Neukirchen–Vluyn: Neukirchener Verlag, 1978), pp. 1369-1508.

ch. 10, that both chapters are conceived by the final redaction as one single prophecy, contending that the ideal Davidic king of righteousness and peace will rise immediately after the expected fall of Assyria. This king will not rule the country by force, but by the spirit of the Lord which will rest upon him. The principle of peace and righteousness which will rule inter-human relationships after the abolition of evil will also dominate the realm of nature, where force and aggression will give way to sociability and conviviality.[12]

The centrality of Jerusalem and Zion in world history, which is briefly mentioned in 37.32, is the major motif of the vision in 2.1-4. One should bear in mind that this is the only prophecy which can be termed eschatological, its fulfilment being postponed until the remote future, as may be understood from the opening formula, 'It shall come to pass in later days' (2.2).

The range of this prophecy is universal, while the framework of 11.1-9 is the land of Israel exclusively. All nations will flow to the mountain of the Lord seeking his word and his arbitration in their quarrels. Thus the very cause of all wars will disappear, and peace will be the hallmark of human history. This utopian picture of the last stage of human history reflecting the utter contrast to the events of Isaiah's generation seems to have taken shape during the siege by the Assyrian army, which was composed of units from many nations. The eschatological aim of human history will be the antithesis of that situation: all nations will accept the rule of the divine king. In other words, the utopia of divine kingship will be the common concrete religious and social basis of all nations. The time of this great event and the historical conditions that will bring it about are beyond the horizon of this prophecy. On the other hand, the prophet is convinced that the fall of Assyria, the re-establishment of the Davidic kingdom and the restoration of the remnant of the house of Judah are imminent. They are seen as growing organically out of the events of the prophet's own time.

An interesting problem is the role assigned to human beings in bringing about these revolutionary changes which are the precondition of the predicted redemption. According to Isaiah, there is no room

12. As to the historical problems of ch. 10 see Wildberger, *Jesaja*, pp. 390-435. His conception is quite different from the above one. Owing to a lack of precise historical details, however, every historical analysis of these chapters remains only tentative in character.

for human activism: God's outstretched hand alone acts in history (10.5).

Thus, Isaiah's unique historical-philosophical outlook precludes any demand that could be interpreted as human initiative. Moreover, the boastful conquerors who claimed superhuman powers turned out, in Isaiah's view, to be but unconscious tools in the hand of God, the real master of history. On the other hand, Isaiah was far from any quietistic flight from reality. In his view the only authentic activism is strength of spirit and quiet anticipation, while relying on the Holy One of Israel, in whose hands lies the only initiative in world history. The concrete political military meaning of this approach, however, is the duty to resist the imperialist aggressor without fear, until the Lord's intervention becomes evident.

We may summarize as follows the major points so far made.

1. Regarding the problem of theodicy in world history, Isaiah contends that the rise of the Assyrian empire of evil is to be explained only in terms of the relationship between God and his sinful people. Assyria has been called upon in order to punish Israel. But because of his unprecedented aggressiveness and hubris the Assyrian ruler and his army will be destroyed and exterminated before the gates of Jerusalem. This will be the worldwide proof of God's exclusive rule in history.

2. After the fall of the empire of evil, the Davidic kingdom will be restored. The future king, who will rise immediately after the fall of Assyria, will impose the principles of righteousness and mercy by the strength of the divine spirit which will rest upon him. Even all of nature will change its character, for brutality and force will be replaced by conviviality and peaceful relations between the strong and the weak.

3. Isaiah's pragmatic advice to the king of Judah was resistance to the aggressor, be it a coalition of petty rulers (734), or the Assyrian superpower (701). On the other hand, he warned of any political or military initiative, including any coalition with foreign powers. Such political behaviour was a sign of spiritual strength and reliance on God, who is the only initiator in world history. In other words, active reliance on God's intervention was the main theme of Isaiah's demands from the kings of Judah.

4. The only eschatological prophecy is Isa. 2.1-5, its range being universal regarding Jerusalem and Zion as the future worldwide

centre of monotheism. But while the restoration of the Davidic kingdom will immediately follow the fall of Assyria, the fulfilment of this
prophecy is beyond the prophet's historical horizon.[13]

II

It was Isaiah's prophetic contemporary, Micah the Morashthite,[14] who
challenged this approach. While it is true that he borrowed from
Isaiah the vision of eternal peace at the end of the days (Mic. 4.1-5),
which implies that Zion and Jerusalem are at the watershed of human
history, it is here that the similarity ends.[15] Indeed, the verse that he
added to Isaiah's prophecy, 'Though all the peoples walk each in the
name of its gods, we will walk in the name of the Lord our God forever and ever' (4.5), indicates that he did not agree with the former's
assumption concerning the future acceptance of monotheism by the
other nations. Furthermore, his image of the ideal king, that of the

13. For a detailed analysis of this prophecy cf. Wildberger, *Jesaja, ad loc.*
14. See the following commentaries: K. Marti, *Das Dodekapropheten* (KHC, 13;
Tübingen: Mohr, 1904); J.P.M. Smith, W.H. Ward and J.A. Bewer, *Micah,
Zephaniah, Nahum, Habbakkuk, Obadiah and Joel* (ICC; Edinburgh: T. & T. Clark,
1911); W. Nowack, *Die Kleinen Propheten* (HKAT, 3.4; Göttingen: Vandenhoeck
& Ruprecht, 3rd edn, 1922); E. Sellin, *Die zwölf Propheten* (KAT, 12.1; Leipzig:
Deichert, 3rd edn, 1929); R.E. Wolfe, 'The Book of Micah: Introduction and
Exegesis' (*IB*, 6; Nashville: Abingdon Press, 1956); A. Weiser, *Das Buch der
zwölf Kleinen Propheten* (ATD, 24.1; Göttingen: Vandenhoeck & Ruprecht, 3rd
edn, 1959); J.L. Mays, *Micah: A Commentary* (OTL; London: SCM Press;
Philadelphia: Westminster Press, 1980). Cf. also the following studies: W. Beyerlin,
Die Kulttraditionen Israels in der Verkündigung des Propheten Micha (FRLANT, 54;
Göttingen: Vandenhoeck & Ruprecht, 1959); B.A. Copas and E.L. Carlson, *A
Study of the Prophet Micah* (Grand Rapids: Zondervan, 1950); J. Lindblom, *Micha
literarisch untersucht* (Acta Academiae Aboensis; Åbo: Åbo Akademi, 1929);
B. Renaud, *Structure et attaches littéraires de Michée IV–V* (Cahiers de la *Revue
biblique*, 2; Paris: Gabalda, 1964); I. Willi-Plein, *Vorformen der Schriftexegese
innerhalb des Alten Testament* (BZAW, 123; Berlin: de Gruyter, 1971).
15. The authorship of this prophecy is a bone of contention in modern research.
There are scholars who argue in favour of Micah; others speak of an anonymous
prophetic tradition which crystallized in the books of Micah and Isaiah. In my view
there is no doubt about the Isaianic authorship, which I attempted to prove by literary
analysis; see my article 'History and Eschatology in the Book of Micha' (Hebrew),
Bet Miqra 16 (1963), pp. 48-65, 52-56. Micah's addition to the original prophecy
(v. 4.5) reflects his deviating view about the nations.

future nation, and the political role he assigned to Judah in the present and future alike are all completely different from the conceptions of Isaiah.

As to the image of the future king and people, Isaiah spiritualized the ancient popular tradition as reflected by biblical prose and Psalm literature, in particular the royal Psalms. Micah, on the other hand, drew directly from this tradition when forging his historical and social views. Let us examine this premise in further detail.

According to Isaiah,[16] the spirit of the Lord will rest upon the future king: the spirit of wisdom and understanding (רוח חכמה ובינה), the spirit of council and valour (רוח עצה וגבורה), the spirit of knowledge and the fear of the Lord (רוח דעת ויראת יהוה). These features are, according to tradition, the divine endowment bestowed upon a righteous king. According to the sources the spirit of the king is the spirit of the Lord which rests upon him (cf. for instance 1 Sam. 10.6; 11.6; 10.13, 14; 19.9); a king should be wise and understanding (חכם ונבון; see 2 Sam. 14.17; 1 Kgs 3.9, 12; 5.9, לב חכם ונבון); he is a man of council (that is, planning) and valour (see Isa. 6.5; 9.4; 2 Kgs 18.20). The last feature, valour, is essential for the king's leadership in war (see 1 Kgs 15.23; 16.5, 27; 22.46), while his wisdom and understanding will become evident in his role as righteous judge and ruler, for with righteousness he shall judge the poor (דלים), and decide with equity (במישור) for the meek of the earth (ענוי ארץ). For parallels see Ps. 45.7-8; 72.1-4; Prov. 14.28ff.; 15.8ff.; 25.2ff.; see also 1 Kgs 3.9-12; and Jer. 23.5ff. This image of the righteous king is also commonplace elsewhere in ancient oriental literature (see Wildberger pp. 451-52). In the Bible the divine judge is portrayed in a similar manner (see Ps. 9.10; 68.6; Job 5.15ff.). But what is peculiar to Isaiah's approach is the spiritualization of tradition.

In ancient Hebrew literature the king shall break the enemies of Israel 'with a rod of iron and dash them to pieces like a potter's vessel' (Ps. 2.9). In this manner shall he punish the wicked and the evil, with his rod. But according to Isa. 11.4, 'he shall smite the earth with his *mouth*, and with the breath of his *lips* he shall slay the wicked'.

Again, in ancient Hebrew literature the king is portrayed as a great warrior who girds his sword upon his thighs (Ps. 45.4), rides forth

16. Cf. my paper '"For to us a Child is Born, to us a Son is Given" (Isa. 9.5)', in *M.Z. Segal Festschrift* (Jerusalem: Israel Society for Biblical Research, 1964), pp. 103-26.

victoriously, sharpens his arrows against his enemies (v. 6) and defeats and subjugates nations (Ps. 2.8-11; 72.8-11). But according to Isaiah the features of the future king contain nothing of a warrior. On the contrary, he will be שר שלום, אבי עד, אל גבור, פלא יועץ—Wonderful Counsellor, Mighty God, Everlasting Father, and Prince of Peace (9.6). As a matter of fact, these are the features of the divine king, the human king's divine Father, who bestows them upon him. So he will be the Prince of Peace. Just as he will smite the earth with the rod of his mouth (Isa. 11.4),[17] and slay the wicked with the breath of his lips, so too righteousness, not the sword, will be the girdle of his waist, and faithfulness the girdle of his loins (11.5). This interpretation of ancient ideals is tantamount to a completely new conception of the future king.

Micah, on the other hand, emphasizes in particular the king's traditional features as a warrior.[18] He will enter an anti-Assyrian alliance 'with seven shepherds and eight princes of men' (Mic. 5.3-5), that is, with foreign kings and princes. This is similar to what we know about Ahab, who in 854–53 BCE participated in a regional coalition against Salmaneser III. Moreover, this book contains a series of short declarations, most of which are directly addressed to the nation, namely 2.12-13; 4.8-14; 5.1-5, 6-8, 9-14, the literary *leitmotif* being עתה–ועתה–עתה.

17. In modern research the emendation ערק instead of ארק in 11.4 is widely accepted because of the *parallelismus membrorum*. The above translation is according to the MT.

18. The prophetic utterances we are dealing with are Mic. 2.12-13; 4.1-5, 6-7, 8-9, 10, 11-12, 13-14; 5.1-3, 6-8, 9-14. The authenticity of these passages has been debated since the last century; see the commentaries mentioned in note 14. Most of the scholars would refer at least part of them to an exilic or post-exilic redactor. I broadly discuss the problem in 'History and Eschatology', concluding that there is no valid argument to deny them attribution to Micah. Only the words ובאת עד בבל (4.10) have been added by a later hand, probably by a disciple of Jeremiah.

As to the arrangement of this collection; the two first utterances, 4.1-5, 6-7, are eschatological promises of salvation, while in 4.8-9, 10, 11-12, 13-14 the prophet appeals to the king and people, encouraging them to wage war against the enemy who was besieging Jerusalem. This was probably in 701, when the Assyrians laid siege to Jerusalem. The last declarations, 5.1-3, 4-5, 6-8, 9-14, are again referring to the future, when Israel will raise up against Assyria 'seven shepherds and eight princes of men' (5.5), in order to vanquish her in her own land. This victory will usher in the new era of peace which will see the destruction of all tools of war and idolatry. It seems that he anticipates the fulfilment of these eschatological hopes in the foreseeable future.

In these utterances, Micah sharply criticizes the passivity of the people and their naivety in their fear of the enemy: 'Now why do you cry aloud? Is there no king among you? Have your counsellors perished that pangs have seized you like a woman in travail?' (4.9). But his main concern was to encourage the king and the people to take the military initiative in this war. As a matter of fact, the Assyrian army contained units from many nations, all of which were assembled before the gates of Jerusalem, saying, 'Let her be profaned and let our eyes gaze upon Zion' (4.11). Moreover, they humiliated the king, as it is written 'with a rod they strike upon the meek, the ruler of Israel' (4.14). So his message to the nation was quite different from Isaiah's. Far from preaching passive self-restraint like Isaiah, Micah calls 'Arise and thresh O Daughter of Zion, for I will make your horn iron and your hoop bronze. You shall beat in pieces many peoples, and shall devote to the Lord their booty, their wealth to the Lord of the whole earth' (4.13).

Here Micah repudiates Isaiah's warning to king and people against taking any military initiative, and against any alliances with foreign nations (Isa. 31.1ff.). He prefers active resistance, even together with 'seven shepherds and eight princes of men' (5.4). This interpretation of the theopolitical principle means immediate action.

Micah draws his pictures and images straight from ancient warlike tradition. The people of Israel will not be a poor and small people of shepherds (7.18-25), but a fighting nation, a lion, 'and the remnant of Jacob shall be among the nations, in the midst of the peoples, like a lion among the beasts of the forest, like a young lion among the flocks of sheep which when it goes through, treads down and tears in pieces, and there is none to deliver' (5.7; see also 4.13).

We may, then, sum up the differences of opinion and of political concepts between Isaiah and Micah in the following ways.

1. In Isaiah's view the ideal king rules by the word of God and the spirit of the Lord, which rests upon him. He will be the Prince of Peace (שׂר שׁלום) in the land of Israel. The contrasting image portrayed by Micah is of a warrior king protecting the poor and the widow in his land, and defeating the enemy by the sword.

2. Isaiah's image of the surviving remnant of Israel is that of a peaceful, poor community dwelling restfully in the country, while Micah dreams of a fighting nation who will defeat the enemies

through its valour and courage. They will be a strong nation feared by their enemies.

3. The resulting difference between the two in grappling with the situation of their days is also remarkable: Isaiah calls for steadfastness and resistance to the Assyrian conqueror, believing in the final redemption by the Lord. Micah calls for an immediate military initiative in order to break the siege of the enemy.

In the future, if Assyria should attempt to attack again, Micah predicts a military alliance between the king of Israel and other rulers in order to repulse the enemies and destroy their country (5.4). Again, the vision of peace is common to both prophets, but the peace in the land of Israel as pictured by Micah will be the outcome of Israel's military strength. Only after having vanquished her chief enemy will the Lord destroy her own horses, chariots and strongholds, together with the last vestiges of idolatry which are left in the land (5.9-14). The eschatological peace as described by Isa. 2.1-4 will not include the universal acceptance of monotheism, although all nations will make their pilgrimage to Jerusalem.

We may conclude that the major issue between Isaiah and Micah is the concrete meaning of the theopolitical principle. Isaiah believes in divine intervention for the redemption of the besieged Jerusalem; therefore his main demand on two different historical occasions is calmness and hopeful patient belief on the part of the self-defending city, while Micah declares that divine assistance can be hoped for only if Judah wages an offensive war in order to smash the enemy. Again, Micah's appreciation of human nature deviates from Isaiah's, who optimistically believes in the free acceptance of monotheism by all nations. In Micah's view, this decision will be the outcome of the final destruction of the historical forces of evil. Even in Israel, however, the last vestiges of idolatry will have to be destroyed and eliminated before the occurrence of this great event.

BABYLON THE GREAT AND THE NEW JERUSALEM:
THE VISIONARY VIEW OF POLITICAL REALITY
IN THE REVELATION OF JOHN

Klaus Wengst

Primitive Christian congregations were a tiny minority in the society of the Roman Empire. No state could be formed from them, and the people in them had no opportunity to assume political responsibility. Indeed, the thought of such responsibility was probably far from their minds. Nonetheless these congregations were obviously a political phenomenon and as such were noticed early by the Romans. This can clearly be seen from their designation as *christiani* or *christianoi*. Here we are certainly dealing with an external designation, that is one from the Roman perspective, for the combination of a name with the ending *-iani* is frequently encountered in the Roman period and always indicates the political affiliation of a person. Accordingly, we find as early as the first century measures being undertaken by imperial agencies against these little groups, measures which extended to the extreme of deadly persecution. Primarily because of such experiences, the congregations, for their part, took notice of the politics of the Empire. The occasional description and evaluation of such policies has come down to us in the extant writings, in which the spectrum runs all the way from apologetics in search of a *modus vivendi* to radical rejection.

Why was it that the Empire took notice of these tiny groups and reacted against them? Did they represent—implicitly and perhaps not even consciously—a political claim, a political challenge? If so, in what did this challenge consist? For present purposes I can only pursue these questions on the basis of a very small sample of writing, namely the Apocalypse of the visionary John. This text was probably written at the end of the reign of Domitian, at a time when the author was exiled to the small island of Patmos. He conceives his work as a missive to all the congregations in the province of Asia, which he encourages to stand firm in the midst of their tribulation under and resistance against the Empire, an Empire which appears to him in his acceptance of the visions of the prophet Daniel as the incarnation of the diabolical and bestial.

In this context I shall limit myself to discussion of chs. 17–18, the vision of the whore of Babylon riding upon the beast, and chs. 21–22, the contrasting vision of the new Jerusalem. These passages are especially pertinent to the question posed here, because in them the Empire is characterized according to its various aspects, and also because we find in them a vision of the congregation and of its hope for the future. Furthermore, John himself quite consciously connected the two visions. Before doing anything else, we must clarify his intention in making such a connection. In 17.1 and 21.9 he takes up in practically identical words an element from the vision of the vials in order to introduce the vision which follows in each case: 'And there came one of the seven angels which had the seven vials [in 21.9, we have, additionally, "full of the seven last plagues"] and talked with me, saying unto me, Come hither: I will shew unto thee the judgment of the great whore', or, by contrast, 'the bride, the Lamb's wife'. After a further characterization of the whore in 17.1, we read in 17.3 and also in 21.10: 'So he carried me away in the spirit into the wilderness', or, by contrast, 'to a great and high mountain'. In the first case John sees the whore sitting upon the beast and in the second case the New Jerusalem as the bride descending from heaven. He does not feel compelled to introduce his visions through the mediation of an angel. In 19.11, 17, 19 and 20.1, 4, for example, he does this through a concise *kai eidon*. When in 17.1, 3, and 20.9 he refers to the visions of the vials, which he has already completed, and formulates the introductions in parallel to each other, this can only mean that he is consciously connecting with each other the visions which follow. The New Jerusalem as the bride is the antithesis of the whore of Babylon, and this means that the congregation is conceived as the antithesis to the Roman Empire. But this could be a politically explosive assertion. In the following sections I shall look at, first, which aspects of the Roman Empire are emphasized in chs. 17–18, and, secondly, the characteristic aspects of the antithetical conception.

1. *The Judgment of the Great Whore*

In 17.1 the visionary is promised a vision of the judgment of the great whore, and in 19.2 he looks back upon the completed judgment. In the description of the judgment the reason for it is also given. The description indicates a definite perception of reality which is given visionary expression.

The Symbol of the 'Great Whore' and her Name 'Babylon'
In 17.5 the name of the woman riding on the beast is given: 'Babylon the great, the mother of harlots and abominations of the earth'. In ch. 18 we constantly read of 'Babylon the great' and 'that great city Babylon'; that is to say, the whore symbolizes the city which is called Babylon. This name is introduced in 17.5 as 'a mystery'. In other words, this is a coded name. Only Rome can be meant by it, since at the time of John it was the major metropolis. After 70 CE this designation of Rome could be found in Jewish circles. Rome had destroyed Jerusalem along with the temple, just as Babylon had done before. And just as the old Babylon had been subjected to God's judgment, so also would the new Babylon be subjected. If it is the case that the whore called Babylon symbolizes Rome, then we are dealing with a peculiar duplication, for the 'scarlet coloured beast' upon whom the woman is sitting in 17.3 is, according to the further description, 'full of names of blasphemy, having seven heads and ten horns'—identical with the first beast from the sea in ch. 13, which also symbolizes Rome. Can both things be understood in context with one another? It might be that 'beast' and 'whore' are each intended to express a certain aspect of Roman authority. In the case of the first beast in ch. 13 its all-compelling power is stressed, a power before which all the world goes down on its knees and cries out in amazement: 'Who is like unto the beast? Who is able to make war with him?' (13.4). In other words, this beast represents Rome in its irresistible military might. But then what aspect is expressed symbolically by the metaphor of the whore? As is the case with so many other images, John took the image of the whore from his Bible. In Ezekiel 16 and 23 and also in Isaiah 1 Jerusalem is called a whore. The aspect which is supposed to be expressed by this designation and which also makes the designation possible is that of faithlessness. So we read in Isa. 1.21: 'How is the faithful city become a harlot! It was full of judgment; righteousness

lodged in it; but now murderers'. Faithlessness towards God is manifested in the injustice of the upper classes: 'Thy princes are rebellious, and companions of thieves: every one loveth gifts, and followeth after rewards: they judge not the fatherless, neither doth the cause of the widow come unto them' (Isa. 1.23). Faithlessness towards God, which is the occasion for the image of the whore, is connected with the attainment of economic advantage. In their greediness for money the powerful of this earth trample upon justice with their feet, and thus they make a whore out of God's faithful city.

In Nah. 3.4 the city of Nineveh is called a whore. The entire chapter prophesies the downfall of this Assyrian metropolis. Verse 4 gives the reason for this: 'Because of the multitude of the whoredoms of the well-favoured harlot, the mistress of witchcrafts, that selleth nations through her whoredoms, and families through her witchcrafts'. Clearly the writer is thinking in this case not only of the military expansion of Assyria and its policy of deportation, but also of its economic power and attraction. This is indicated in v. 16: 'Thou hast multiplied thy merchants above the stars of heaven'. A connection between whoredom and commerce arises under the aspect of venality. This connection is found most clearly in Isa. 25.15-18, the passage which is the most important for Revelation 17. Here the focal point is the commercial centre of Tyre. This city is called upon to sing a whore's song: 'Take a harp, go about the city, thou harlot that hast been forgotten; make sweet melody, sing many songs, that thou mayest be remembered' (v. 16). In the following text we read that the city will once again receive the wages of a whore: 'And she shall commit fornication with all the kingdoms of the world upon the face of the earth' (v. 17). Thereafter in v. 18 commercial profit and the wages of a whore are juxtaposed. This means of course that commercial profit is characterized as the wages of a whore and world commerce as a whoredom. In other words, the world system of commerce is a system of prostitution. It makes the metropolises luxurious and fat, but it plunders the countries and the people. In this context we should also indicate Ezek. 28.16, where it is said to the king of Tyre that 'By the multitude of thy merchandise they have filled the midst of thee with violence'. The word used here, *hamas*, most likely means structural power. Commerce as it is undertaken, dictated by the metropolis, produces structures of power in which it is then carried on. This determines the social group which will be benefited thereby;

the metropolis. It will become clear that in designating Rome as the great whore John is taking up and carrying on this tradition.

The aspect of commerce also comes to the fore in the description of the clothing and jewellery of the woman in 17.4: 'And the woman was arrayed in purple and scarlet colour, and decked with gold and precious stones and pearls'. This is surely not the usual description of the appearance of a prostitute. The clothing here consists of luxurious fabrics and the jewellery is the most luxurious that exists. Both are intended to characterize the appearance of the dominant social class of the metropolis, the display of wealth at the imperial court and in the leading houses of Rome. The luxurious articles cited here appear once again in 18.12 when the items borne to Rome are being enumerated. This shows that in the description of the whore as a woman of luxury John really was thinking of Rome as a metropolis of trade. In this connection we should also read the statement that occurs twice in chs. 17 and 18 to the effect that 'the kings of the earth have committed fornication with her' (17.2; 18.3). These references are to Rome and its vassals. The elite classes of the subjected peoples have now been integrated into the power system as its dependants. They have made their arrangements with the metropolis and therefore have been permitted to maintain their own dominance. They take their pleasure with the Roman whore—in 18.9 their luxurious way of life is in parallel to their whoredoms—and they pay for this pleasure through the exploitation of their people.

But this hardly turns them into opponents. John writes in 17.2: 'And the inhabitants of the earth have been made drunk with the wine of her fornication'. The worldwide system of commerce draws everyone into its train. The climate it has created of general venerality and general greed as well as the lust for money and goods thereby produced have addicted everyone. Everybody wants to do business; everybody wants a share of the wealth.

As with the assertion about the whoredom of the kings, so too the assertion about the drunkenness of the nations in 18.3 is once again taken up: 'For all nations have drunk of the wine of the wrath of her fornication'. According to 14.8 Babylon 'made all nations drink of the wine of the wrath of her fornication'. Both things go together. This system, which is clearly prosperous, impresses everyone, and everyone is more than willing to be impressed. The entire world is, as it were, drunk on the religiously ornamented might of the metropolis and, according to the pseudo-realistic evaluation, considers it to be the reality which determines all things. Everybody goes along with it as a partisan and as a prisoner of the system.

The Merchants and their Wares

In 18.3 John cites the merchants along with the kings who co-operate with Rome. In v. 23 he designates them as 'the great men of the earth'. He was probably thinking first and foremost of the Roman knights who worked as powerful businessmen. The juxtaposition of kings and merchants in this sequence, which is then repeated in vv. 9-11, makes it clear that the entire political and military system of power functions in order to secure world trade. John's assertion about the great merchants shows his keen powers of observation: 'And the merchants of the earth are waxed rich through the abundance of her [i.e. Babylon's] delicacies'. The luxury of the parasitic metropolis becomes a 'power' in its own right. Its need for luxury takes on a dynamic of its own which organizes commercial life and directs the channels of trade. Accordingly it seems appropriate to translate the word in the text, *dynamis*, as 'dynamics'. This states precisely what John means here: the great merchants are the ones who go along with this control through the need for luxury. Thus the metropolis attains its life of luxury, and they get their profit, both at the expense of the majority of the populations living in the provinces.

John knows what he is talking about. In 18.12-13 he enumerates all the things that are brought to Rome:

> The merchandise of gold, and silver, and precious stones, and of pearls and fine linen, and purple, and silk, and scarlet, and all thyine wood, and all manner vessels of ivory, and all manner vessels of most precious wood, and of brass, and iron and marble, and cinnamon, and odours, and ointments, and frankincense, and wine, and oil, and fine flour, and wheat, and beasts, and sheep, and horses, and chariots, and slaves—and even souls of men.

Furthermore, in v. 14 he cites fruit. In this enumeration a certain grouping is seen. At the beginning we find the noble minerals gold and silver whose possession was economically important, from which the most valuable coins were minted and which could also be made into jewellery. Thereafter come jewels and pearls, which in their turn are followed by precious fabrics. The subsequently cited lemon wood ('thyine wood') was used for elegant building purposes, and the following objects, mostly from costly materials, were employed for refined interiors. Thereafter we find the necessities for an upper-class lifestyle and for elegant tastes as well as upper-class foodstuffs. At the very end we find cattle, means of transportation, and slaves. These last are indicated at first as 'bodies', and then emphasized as 'souls of men'. Through this juxtaposition John emphasizes the monstrosity of turning even human beings into commercial commodities. In addition to the mostly luxurious commodities we also find in his enumeration the basic foodstuff wheat, but significantly not barley, which was the principal food of ordinary people in the provinces.

John's catalogue is confirmed by other ancient sources, which, however, were written from another perspective and which give a positive judgment of the same reality. Aelius Aristides tells us that the nations around the Mediterranean always supplied the Romans with their products:

> They bring goods from every country and every sea, and provide whatever the seasons grow in all the regions, rivers and lakes as well as everything that the skills of the Greeks and the barbarians produce... It is impossible not to find here [in Rome] any good produced in any country, and that always and in abundance (*Speech on Rome* 11).

The Visionary Anticipation of the Fall

John, then, clearly perceives the 'dynamics of luxury' and also the connection between the economy controlled by it and the political power structures, and he also sees that the price of this system is paid in blood. In 18.9-19 he adopts the genre of the funeral lamentation. In a vision he anticipates the downfall of Rome, and sees the city lying in smoking ruins. Those most closely allied to Rome emit a wail of mourning and lamentation. Here too John is influenced by the Hebrew Bible, his direct model being Ezekiel 26 and 27, the lamentation for Tyre. The three groups of mourners—kings, merchants and shipmasters—are also encountered. The kings, who appear first, stand for the political and military power. Accordingly in their lamentation in v. 10 they call Babylon 'that mighty city'. The great merchants, who appear in second position, stand for world trade, which has accommodated itself to the luxurious need of the metropolis and is secured by political and military might. Accordingly the merchants describe 'that great city' in their lamentation in v. 15 as being supplied with luxurious items and decorated with noble jewellery. The shipmasters, who appear third, stand for the routes of trade, which are likewise politically and militarily secured. Accordingly, in the lamentation in v. 19, 'that great city' is cited as the source of wealth for the ship-owners. They 'were made rich by reason of her [i.e. the city's] cost-liness'. Here we find once again the 'dynamics of luxury'. Production is oriented towards the requirements of the metropolis, and so are trade and cargo space. It is no coincidence that the middle section of the lamentation concerning world commerce is particularly expanded, for this is where the emphasis belongs. The reason for the lamentation of the merchants is given succinctly: 'for no man buyeth their mer-chandise any more' (18.11). Here we have revealed a totally mercan-tile mentality; buying and selling are everything. An entire world is being destroyed here and the merchants complain that nobody now wants to buy their wares! Their weeping and wailing is—like that of the kings and the sailors—utterly hopeless. They stare with fixed gaze upon the smoking ruins of Rome. They, who were fixated upon this metropolis, remain so in its downfall.

The three points given in 18.3—the drunkenness of all in and because of this atmosphere of general venality, the selfish co-opera-tion of the local elite classes with the metropolis, and world trade determined by the desire for luxury—are given as the valid reasons for the previously described downfall of 'great Babylon'. This system bears the seeds of its destruction within itself. After the renewed description of the downfall in 18.21-23b, there follows in vv. 23c-24 yet another reason which corresponds to the one given in v. 3, but which at the same time contains a clarification: 'For thy merchants were the great men of the earth; for by thy sorceries were all nations deceived. And in her was found the blood of prophets, and of saints, and of all that were slain upon the earth'. As in v. 3, we here find the people deceived by superficial brilliance and the merchants now taken as the actual bearers of power. But instead of the kings we now find the blood of the previously mentioned victims, the victims who are produced by this system. In this instance John's vision goes beyond the Christian martyrs to include all the victims of Rome.

John is surely not giving an objective evaluation of the accomplish-ments of Rome, but is rather expressing a radical and complete rejec-tion from the perspective of the lowest and most tangential classes, that is from the perspective of the victims. He reads his Bible and perceives in it the reality of his own time. He transforms his reading into a description of visions which are saturated with actual experience and clear-eyed observation. What positive alternative does he offer to this negative vision of reality as determined by Rome?

2. *The 'New Jerusalem' as a 'Bride'*

The Visionary Transformation of Reality

John's visions contradict experienced reality. At the time of his writing Jerusalem lay in ruins, occupied at best by animals, while the metropolis of Rome radiated splendour and delighted in its pulsating vitality. In his visions precisely the reverse is the case. From the ruins of Rome rises only smoke, testifying to the city's utter destruction. In contrast, Jerusalem is radiant in its incomparable beauty and has inconceivable dimensions: 'And I John saw the holy city, now Jerusalem, coming down from God out of heaven, prepared as a bride adorned for her husband' (21.2). This city is now illuminated by the glory of God (21.11, 23; 22.5). The city itself and its main street consist of pure gold (21.18, 21). Precious stones form the foundations of the wall (21.19-20), and pearls decorate its gates (21.21). A river 'clear as crystal' flows through it (22.1), on the banks of which the tree of life stands as a double boulevard (22.2). The paradisiacal beginning of the Bible has been integrated into the New Jerusalem.

But is not this transformation of reality into visionary images only a flight into a dream world, an impotent gesture? I believe that it is the attempt of a powerless man to attack in writing the triumph of power, a power which strode over corpses and which is continuing to produce further victims. It is the attempt not to leave the last word to this mighty world power, but rather to hold history open for the coming of God. Taking up biblical visions John brings God into the argument. In this way John offers to himself and to those like him the courage to endure in contradiction and in resistance.

John's Distancing of himself from a Perverted Reality

We have seen that John clearly observes and sharply criticizes an economy determined by the need for luxury. But this does not lead him to condemn the articles of luxury themselves or to ban them from his conception of the New Jerusalem. Clearly he, too, appreciates the beauty of gold, precious stones and pearls. In the New Jerusalem they occur—as described in the preceding section—in opulent abundance and unbelievable size. In other words, we find here the same things that the whore had as jewellery and that occur in the first group of the cargoes to Rome. But no one any longer profits from these. They are no longer the private possession of a tiny upper class. The city, its wall and its gates are all made of them. Luxury has now become accessible to all—in the case of the main boulevard quite literally so; in other words, the luxurious has been socialized.

Now it is surely not the case, just as it was not the case for those for whom he was writing, that John was tempted to acquire and to hoard for himself gold, precious stones and pearls. But he does not start with the luxury items when he seeks to put a distance between himself and the existing society as a perverted reality. He commands his readers and hearers explicitly and emphatically to withdraw from the system: 'Come out of her [i.e. Babylon], my people, that ye be not partakers of her sins, and that ye receive not of her plagues' (18.4). He cannot possibly mean here that the congregation should literally depart from the city of Rome. After all, his writing is directed to the congregations in the province of Asia. This can then only mean that they are to distance themselves from the type of life considered normal. What concerns him is a refusal to participate in the dominant system of power and injustice. Such a refusal has as its consequence social isolation that requires to be consciously affirmed. If the existing structures are sinful, participation in them is necessarily complicity with sin. This complicity includes participation in the consequences of sin. This is the only sense in which the judgment of God can be understood, as being caught up by one's own sin, as the rebounding of misdeeds upon their doers.

The question of the refusal to participate becomes concrete for John in the case of a problem which has a long tradition in the history of primitive Christianity and which had been a subject of debate in the congregations, namely the question of the use of 'meat offered in sacrifice unto idols', as both Jews and Christians termed the meat derived from ritual sacrifices in the temples.

In this case we are dealing not with an isolated religious question, but with the general question of social communication and participation, whether it refers to public festivals connected with the temples and therefore also with the gods, or to private or social festivities in the context of ritual sacrifices in the temples. John pleads for uncompromising refusal. The effect that such refusal could have is shown by the end of Pliny's letter to Trajan about the Christians. Surveying the period before his activities against the Christians he speaks of 'almost deserted temples', 'ritual sacrifices discontinued for a long period of time', and of 'sacrificial meat for which hitherto purchasers could only very seldom be found'.

The Nations Seen as God's Own

According to 21.3 John hears a loud voice coming from the throne of God: 'Behold, the tabernacle of God is with men'. With all clarity we now hear of the presence of God among the people, who previously in Revelation were often nothing more than a *massa perditionis*. In this sense the leaves of the tree of life are meant 'for the healing of the nations' (22.2) which had previously been made drunk by the wine of the whore. They walk in the light of the city (21.24a), and the presence of God gives them a sense of direction in their lives. And even the kings, who up until now were only the adherents of the beast and the suitors of the whore, and who actually had long since been cast into the lake of fire and brimstone (20.15), are once again present and transport their glory into the New Jerusalem. No longer do they supply the great metropolis and no longer is there a liaison with the violent might and with the profit for the few. The kings become the partners of all people, and what they bring with them is participated in by all.

'And he [i.e. God] will dwell with them', continues the voice in 21.3, 'and they shall be his peoples, and God himself shall be with them, and be their God'. As is so often the case, John's language here is saturated with biblical tradition. So we read in Zech. 2.14-15: 'Sing and rejoice, O daughter of Zion: for, lo, I come and I will dwell in the midst of them, saith the Lord. And many nations shall be joined to the LORD in that day, and shall be my people: and I will dwell in the midst of thee'. We must also remember Lev. 26.12: 'And I will walk among you and will be your God, and ye shall be my people'. The fact that the last cited passage speaks of the 'people' of Israel, whereas John uses the plural 'peoples', has been understood by Christian exegetes as an antithesis to Jewry in the sense of the cliché of Christian universalism over against Jewish particularism. The plural 'peoples' surely contains an antithesis for John, but it is directed against the claim of Rome that it has integrated all the peoples into its empire. This claim of Rome is reflected in Revelation in 13.7, according to which the beast has been given power 'over all kindreds, and tongues, and nations'. The claim appears a second time when the description of the whore in 17.1 as sitting 'upon many waters' is interpreted in 17.15: 'The waters which thou sawest, where the whore sitteth, are peoples, and multitudes, and nations, and tongues'. The focal point here is the peoples round the Mediterranean, over whom Rome claims dominance. This claim is contested in the vision of the New Jerusalem, according to which all peoples belong to God. John is here probably taking up the motif of the pilgrimage of the peoples to Zion, which was previously mentioned in the passage quoted from Zechariah. This motif designates the peoples as belonging to Israel. The fact that John really does not separate the New Jerusalem from Israel but in fact defines it in terms of Israel becomes very clear in his description of the city wall.

The Wall as a Definition of the New Jerusalem

Even the New Jerusalem has its wall. To be sure, this wall has no essential function because its gates are always open (21.25), but it is impossible for John to imagine a city without a wall. A wall is an essential part of any ancient city; it defines a city. Therefore it is all the more relevant that John describes the wall as having twelve gates with 'names written thereon, which are the names of the twelve tribes of the children of Israel' (21.12). The New Jerusalem is accordingly defined as a restored nation of twelve tribes. Access to the New Jerusalem can only be seen in terms of access to Israel. When according to 21.14 the wall has twelve foundation stones and upon them 'the names of the twelve apostles of the Lamb' are written, this is a further confirmation of the fact, for according to primitive Christian tradition 'the twelve' are the representatives of the nation of the twelve tribes. This connection also explains the height of the wall as being 'an hundred and forty and four cubits' (21.17). This is the square of the number twelve and again underscores that John conceives the New Jerusalem in terms of Israel. The image of the church in ch. 7 is consistent with this; in the first part John lets the number 'an hundred and forty and four thousand', the square of the number twelve multiplied by one thousand, the number of the incalculably great multitude, expressly come from the twelve tribes of Israel which he then individually enumerates (vv. 1-8), and in the second part he speaks of 'a great multitude, which no man could number, of all nations, and kindreds, and people, and tongues' (v. 9). The conception is obviously that from Israel comes the basic stock and the form, and the peoples expand the nation of the twelve tribes into its full dimension. This parallelism of ch. 7 with essential elements of the description of the New Jerusalem makes it clear that John understands the latter as an image of the church. He defines it on the basis of Israel without which the church cannot exist. The conclusions from this insight have unfortunately not been drawn until today.

Consequences of the Presence of God

The New Jerusalem has no temple, which is most unusual for an ancient city. The temple with its priests not only serves the requirements of a religious cult but also assumes the function of a bank, is a focal point in society, and—particularly in the case of the imperial temple—legitimizes political dominance. 'And I saw no temple therein [that is in the city of Jerusalem]: for the Lord God Almighty and the Lamb are the temple of it' (21.22). Here there is no longer any hierarchy and no dominance of people over people. Although at the conclusion of his vision John says of the inhabitants of the New Jerusalem 'And they shall reign for ever and ever' (22.5), this dominance is without any object in the truest sense of the word: it no longer has any objects. Such a manner of speaking can only have meaning in the opposition to political dominance being practised elsewhere, which at the time when John was writing still existed and under which he and his people had to suffer.

The vision of the New Jerusalem is not only a hopeful image for John of the future, but is also intended to give his congregations orientation in the present. Accordingly, he advocates a participatory and a fraternal model of a congregation. Twice he says of the people in the congregations that the messiah, the Lamb—the antithesis of the imperial ruler—has made them 'kings and priests unto God' (1.6; 5.10). Where God is present, no mediator is required and there can be no dominance of people over people. No matter how unprepossessing these congregations may be, they challenge the mighty and brilliant Empire and form a tiny antithetical society. They attempt to practise a reality antithetical to the perverted reality of imperial power. The radical rejection of Rome, which in John's Apocalypse is shown among other things in the visions of the judgment in ch. 18, can surely be explained from the experience of persecution which formed the perspective of those on the lowest level. On the other hand, we can recognize in the outline of the New Jerusalem elements which—from Rome's perspective—turn the congregation into a city within the city, a state within the state. Rome could not tolerate this and persecuted the Christians until it discovered that the church, once it had grown stronger, could be used as an ideological adhesive for the Empire.

The visionary John defined the church as an outgrowth of Israel and in contrast to the imperial Roman power. It is a bitter irony of history that, as I have indicated, the church in the course of its further development abandoned Israel and let itself be defined in terms of Rome. This was particularly bitter for the Jews, who became the main victims of the church once it had become imperial. In my opinion it is a vital matter for the church to overcome its neglect of Israel by remembering its own beginnings and to learn what it could mean today to be defined in terms of Israel. There are some beginnings towards this end. I am thinking primarily of the pertinent utterances of the Second Vatican Council and the decree of the synod 'Towards the Renewal of the Relationship of Christians and Jews' of the Protestant Church in the Rhineland. These beginnings have already had some encouraging results. But in terms of the church in the world at large they have not had a very deep effect and they could easily be cast aside once again. At any rate, we are only at the beginning of a long road. But for the church this road of new perceptions of Israel is, I believe, a road of hope.

INDEXES

INDEX OF REFERENCES

OLD TESTAMENT

INDEX OF AUTHORS

JOURNAL FOR THE STUDY OF THE OLD TESTAMENT

Supplement Series